ConservaLexicon

GLOSSARY

THE LINGO AND DIALECTICS OF CONSERVATIVE WISDOM AND LIBERAL PATHOLOGY

Joe Schaller

A great deal of intelligence can be invested in ignorance when the need for illusion is deep.

Saul Bellow

ISBN-13: 978-1974668076
ISBN-10: 197466807X

CONTENTS

INTRODUCTION

"In a time of universal deceit, telling the truth is a revolutionary act." – **George Orwell**

After decades of foraging bookstores and the internet I have finally found my reference book source for no-holds-barred politically incorrect conservative wisdom, and enlightened myself in the process of creating it.

As a form of dictionary, a lexicon offers the vocabulary of a language, social class, field or a subject. In January of 2015, I put together a PSA list of eighteen defined terms pertaining to the massive welfare state in my region of northwestern New Mexico. Since then I have expanded on my list with publications including *ConservaLexicon III*, a pricier color version suitable for a coffee table with over 700 bits of wisdom. *ConservaLexicon Glossary* has now reached over one thousand insights in what is my fourth edition – more detail, more nuance.

From "Abengoa" to "zombie company", this is more than just an exploration into the lingo and cultural literacy of conservative thought. *ConservaLexicon Glossary* juxtaposes contradictory ideas, and exposes the psychosocial cultural dynamics, the underbelly of liberalism, in the process.

We live in an Orwellian political world of propaganda and indoctrination advanced by a corrupt media-academic-bureaucratic complex. Deception is the method for grasping power and control. Many loyal Republicans are even confused regarding basic conservative principles. In my glossary I present a list of words, terms, expressions, quotes, fallacies, facts, data, and definitions conflicting with the prevailing paradigm of acceptable ideology, language and notions of political correctness, while also providing historical, economic, and scientific perspective and context. *ConservaLexicon* is meant as an essential educational resource for any who seek enlightenment and wish to halt the advance of cultural indoctrination.

Each entry in my Lexicon is a potential study, story or book condensed into a paragraph. I cover a broad swath: political science, social science, behavioral science, natural science, economics, history, language arts, cultural arts, current events, pop culture and self-help. I have retained several references to Gallup and McKinley County, New Mexico from my original publication.

Warning to liberals: The liberal bubble is a warm fuzzy confine of illusion and delusion. As Saul Bellow puts it – "A great deal of intelligence can be invested in ignorance when the need for illusion is deep." The harsh realities outside of the bubble can be devastating to some and to others a slap-in-the-face wake-up call. Prepare to have your bubbles burst.

"Enough with the PCBS!" – **Joe Schaller**

ConservaLexicon

CHAPTER ONE

FREEDOM

Like the sign suggests, if you expect the government to provide you with food, shelter, and health care, Libertyland is not the place for you. If you believe your self-worth is determined by the color of your skin, stay away. Don't anticipate a trophy for finishing last, for credit is given only where credit is due. If you assume there will be conformity of thought, you'll be distressed by the diversity of ideas. If your delicate sensibilities are easily offended by words or you consider yourself a victim of some imagined social injustice and await special treatment and safe zones, you'll receive little sympathy in Libertyland. Your content of character will determine how people judge you and if you are shunned it's likely because you have disrespected the rights of others or your character is lacking moral integrity. Those who have not learned the skills of survival in a free society may at first find life difficult off the Federal plantation. In the land of liberties there is no reward for the vices of bullying, laziness, dependency, ignorance, or envy. Where freedom rings there is no bigotry of low expectation for minorities – everyone is expected to pull their own weight. Success is attained only by hard work, patience, temperance, wisdom, and courage. Individualism, self-sufficiency, productivity, and independence are celebrated qualities of character. Big boy pants are the apparel and Libertyland is looking for a few good men and women to fill them.

Quotes

"The more laws and restrictions there are, the poorer people become. The more rules and regulations, the more thieves and robbers." –   **Lao Tzu,** ancient Chinese philosopher

"The secret to happiness is freedom... And the secret to freedom is courage." – **Thucydides**

"We hold these truths to be self-evident: that all men are created equal; that they are endowed by their Creator with certain unalienable rights; that among these are life, liberty, and the pursuit of happiness." – **Thomas Jefferson**

"Those who can give up essential liberty to obtain a little temporary safety deserve neither liberty nor safety." – **Benjamin Franklin**

"Firearms stand next in importance to the Constitution itself. They are the American people's liberty teeth and keystone under independence." – **George Washington**

"Nothing is more difficult, and therefore more precious, than to be able to decide." – **Napoleon Bonaparte**

"Capitalism needs neither propaganda nor apostles. Its achievements speak for themselves. Capitalism delivers the goods." – **Ludwig von Mises**

"People sleep peaceably in their beds at night only because rough men stand ready to do violence on their behalf." – **George Orwell**

"Civilization is the process of setting man free from men." – **Ayn Rand**

"Economic freedom is ... an indispensable means toward the achievement of political freedom." – **Milton Friedman**

"Underlying most arguments against the free market is a lack of belief in freedom itself." – **Milton Friedman**

"I'm in favor of legalizing drugs. According to my values system if people want to kill themselves, they have every right to do so. Most of the harm that comes from drugs is because they are illegal." – **Milton Friedman**

"I hope we have once again reminded people that man is not free unless government is limited. There's a clear cause and effect here that is as neat and predictable as a law of physics: as government expands, liberty contracts. – **Ronald Reagan**

"Poverty is the deprivation of opportunity. . . No famine has ever taken place in the history of the world in a functioning democracy." – **Amartya Sen**

"Capitalism is always evaluated against dreams. Utopia is a dream. It doesn't exist." – **Rush Limbaugh**

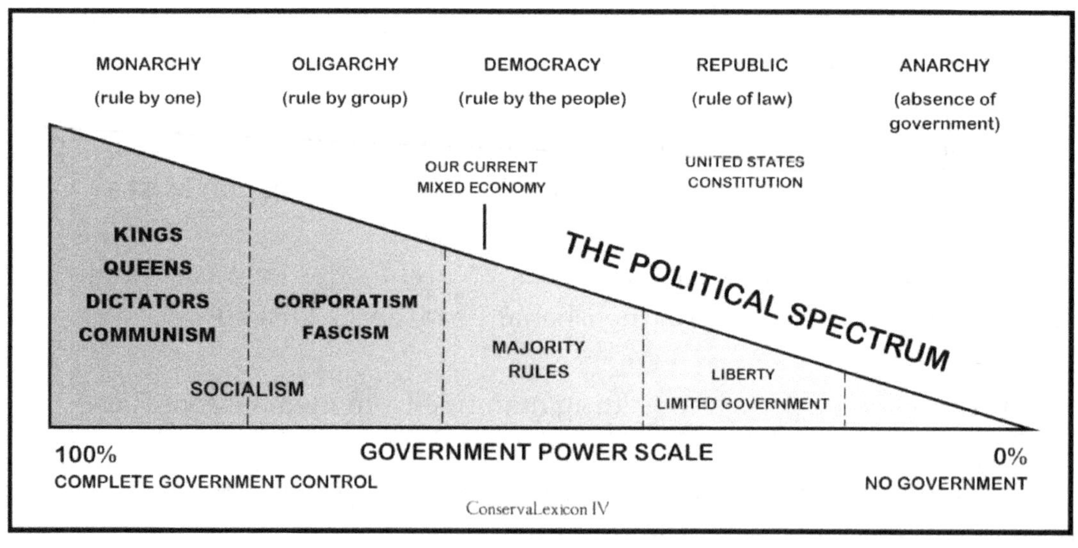

AMERICAN EXCEPTIONALISM: "While most nations evolved from tribal clans and royalty the US was born, and born of ideas: that all men are created equal, that they have been given by God certain rights that can be taken from them by no man, and that those rights combine to create a thing called freedom." – Peggy Noonan…. The American spirit was essentially anarchistic – the antithesis of collectivism-statism-socialism – an exceptional spirit which has bedeviled radicals around the world to this day.

AMERICAN REDOUBT MOVEMENT: A conservative political migration initiative created by novelist James Wesley Rawles of The Survival Blog. The movement encourages citizens to pull up stakes and move to a more open and free location, a safe haven similar to Galt's Gulch – to vote with their feet. This movement has targeted a multistate area in the Intermountain West of Idaho, Montana, Wyoming, Eastern Oregon, and Eastern Washington as a relocation zone - **Conservapedia.**

ANARCHISM: Essentially, no government. Society is based on voluntary cooperation and free association of individuals and groups. Capitalism is related to anarchism in that voluntary exchange with no physical force is the method. A free market cannot exist until force has been barred though, and that means objective law, backed up by government.

AUSTERITY: Generally, refers to the measures taken by governments to reduce expenditures in an attempt to shrink their growing budget deficits. The short term pain of public sector layoffs is offset by long term economic gain in the private sector. Sweden abandoned their soft-socialist experiment in 1992 with austerity measures and struggled a few years before their economy took off. Canada, New Zealand, Ireland, Netherlands and the U.K. have all experienced successful austerity measures. There are no success stories based on tax hikes or bigger government.

BETTER LIFE INDEX: An OECD scale comparing countries performances in terms of 11 dimensions of well-being. Rather than focusing on the socioeconomic gap between the top ten percent and bottom ten percent a comparison of countries bottom well-being is most relevant. Mexico has a relatively small gap yet a horrible index rating. The US has a relatively large gap yet an excellent rating, our bottom ten percent scoring equal to Italy's top ten percent.

BILL OF RIGHTS: The first ten amendments to the Constitution were written by James Madison in response to calls from several states for greater constitutional protection for individual liberties. The Bill of Rights lists specific prohibitions on governmental power. See *appendix.*

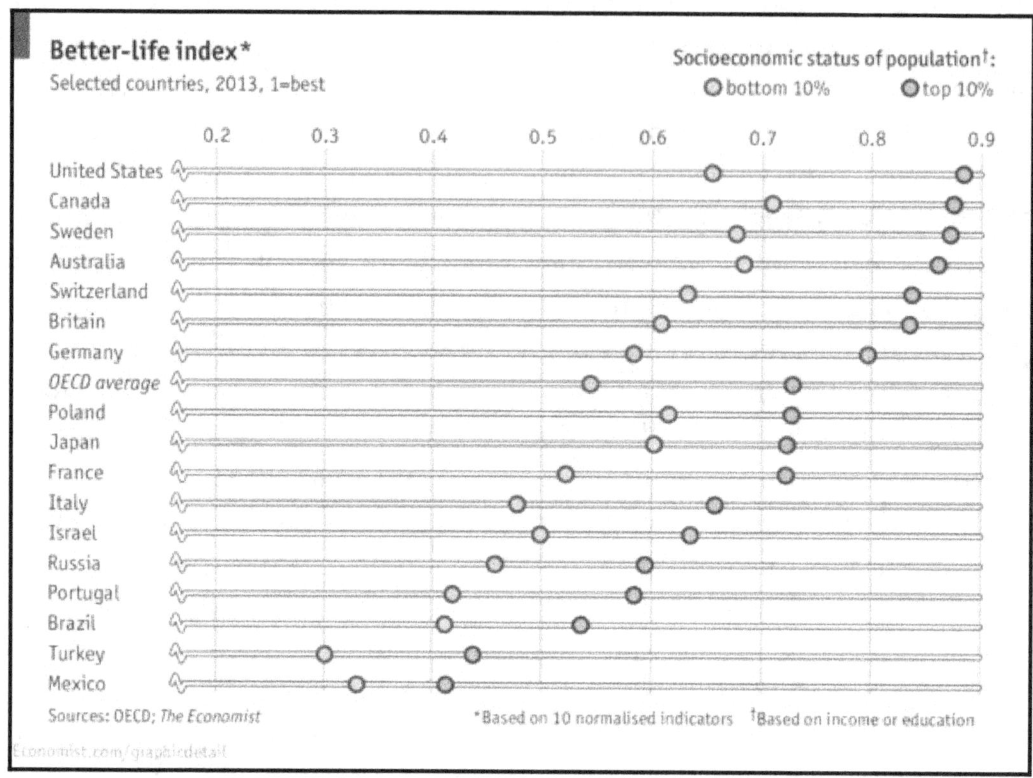

BLACKS, ECONOMIC RISE: The poverty rate among black families fell from 87 percent in 1940 to 47 percent in 1960, during an era of virtually no major civil rights legislation or anti-poverty programs. It dropped 17 percent in the 1960s and one percent in the 1970s. In various skilled trades, the incomes of blacks relative to whites more than doubled between 1936 and 1959. The rise of blacks in professional and other high-level occupations was greater in the five years preceding the Civil Rights Act of 1964 than in the five years afterwards. – **Thomas Sowell, economist.**

BRACERO PROGRAM: a.k.a. Mexican Farm Labor Program of 1942 to 1964 which granted temporary work visas to economic oriented migrants. The number of illegal immigrants was reduced by 90% during that time.

BREXIT: The "British exit" or UK withdrawal from the European Union, rejecting the bureaucratic constraints of expanded government in favor of their own independence, autonomy, and freedom. It was a massive blow to the oppressive forces of globalism and socialism.

CAPITALISM, FREE MARKET: Voluntary exchange. It is a social system based on the recognition of individual rights, including property rights, in which all property is privately owned. It demands the best of every man, and rewards him accordingly. In a free market men trade their goods or services by mutual consent to mutual advantage, according to their own independent judgment. Free market success depends on providing quality products and exceptional service, all at a competitive price. Entities that rip off their customers usually wither and die. In a capitalist society all human relationships are voluntary. In contrast to bureaucratic collectivism, capitalism rewards ingenuity, productivity and success – not so for ineptitude, idleness and failure.

CAPITALISM, CLEAN: Along with short lifespans the world before the industrial age of capitalism was one of unsanitary stench and disease highlighted by horse manure, unwashed sweaty bodies, kerosene, outhouses, sewage, dust, mud, and pest infestation. Smoke from open fires choked cities, forests were stripped of trees and most of the crops went to feed working animals. Fossil fuels and capitalism changed all of that, improving environmental conditions and lengthening lifespans.

CAPITALISM, REAL: Free enterprise capitalism creates wealth and makes the world a better place. Crony capitalism consolidates wealth in the hands of cronies both in industry and in government. Real capitalism offers a way to a better life for the poor and middle class. Government dominated crony capitalism keeps people in economic castes and limits social mobility.

CAPITALISM/SOCIALISM DICHOTOMY: Capitalism is voluntary exchange in a free market. Socialism uses force and coercion for redistribution of wealth. Capitalists understand economics, socialists understand squandering. As Winston Churchill put it, "The inherent vice of capitalism is the unequal sharing of blessings; the inherent virtue of socialism is the equal sharing of misery."

CATO INSTITUTE: One of the most influential Libertarian organizations in the US, Cato has a mission "to broaden the parameters of public policy debate to allow consideration of the traditional American principles of limited government, individual liberty, free markets, and peace."

CIVIL LIBERTIES vs CIVIL RIGHTS: "Civil liberties" concern basic rights and freedoms that are guaranteed – either explicitly identified in the Bill of Rights and the Constitution, or interpreted through the years by courts and lawmakers. "Civil rights" revolves around the basic right to be free from unequal treatment based on certain protected characteristics (race, gender, disability, etc.) in settings such as employment and housing. – **findlaw.com**

CIVIL RIGHTS AMENDMENTS: Congressional Reconstruction included the 13th, 14th, and 15th amendments to the Constitution from 1865 to 1870 which extended formal and legal protections to former slaves. President Andrew Johnson and the Democrat Party were unified in their opposition. All three passed only because of universal Republican support.

CLASSICAL LIBERALISM: You might say it is the opposite of modern liberalism and equivalent to fiscal conservatism. With its extremely limited government through the 19th century America became the model liberal nation with principles of laissez faire capitalism, free trade, private property rights, due process, constitutionalism, and individual liberties. In America, in the early 20th century the term liberal was co-opted by the socialist party when they became unpopular, similar to how many modern liberals have taken to labeling themselves progressives – a consistent pattern of deception, their trademark.

COASE THEOREM: The concept that economic efficiency is achieved best by full allocation of, and completely free trade in, property rights. What really matters is that everything is owned by someone, and that, initially, who owns what doesn't matter. The Coase theorem also asserts that when property rights are involved, parties naturally gravitate toward the most efficient of mutually beneficial outcome.

CONSERVATISM: Individual freedom, personal responsibility, Judeo-Christian values, free market capitalism, fiscal responsibility, constitutionally limited government, content of character.

CONSERVATISM, FISCAL and SOCIAL: Whereas liberals tend to be liberal across the board, both fiscally and socially, conservatism has two components which sometimes creates GOP division. Fiscal conservatism principles are of limited government and liberty, both individual and economic. It is an economic philosophy of prudence in government spending and debt. The Tea Party and Libertarians promote principles of fiscal conservativism.

Social conservatism is focused on *In God We Trust* and *E Pluribus Unum* principles of American nationalism and exceptionalism with values of a God-based religious vigor in the society, the melting-pot ideal, and traditional Judeo-Christian or family values. It is exemplified by the Christian right.

CONSUMPTION: The starting point of real prosperity. "Consumption, not production, is the ultimate end and object of all industry and commerce." – **Adam Smith.**

COOLIDGE, CALVIN: Silent Cal, the great refrainer and restrainer, presided over the Roaring Twenties. His method; If you have to do, do less. Coolidge vetoed entitlements, subsidies, pensions, and blocked militant labor unions. His results; Low unemployment, lower taxes, higher wages, fewer strikes, new technology, and during the time of the rise of progressivism he actually shrunk the federal budget. By doing "nothing", America's economy boomed. Just think, if Coolidge had not declined to run for a second term, the Great Depression might have been a minor recession.

COOPERATIVES and CHARITIES: A cooperative is a firm owned, controlled and operated by a group of users for their own benefit. Each member contributes equity capital, and shares in control of the firm on the basis of one-member, one-vote principle. – **BusinessDictionary.com**

A non-profit charity can receive tax-deductible donations from community members and foundations, and is limited in the amount of business activity it conducts unrelated to its charitable purpose.

CROWDFUNDING: The use of small amounts of capital from a large number of individuals to finance a new business venture. It allows startup companies to raise money without giving up control to venture capital investors. It offers investors the opportunity to earn an equity position in the venture.

DECADE OF GREED OR GENEROSITY, the 1980s: During the era of prosperity the Left considered that wanting to keep your own money is "greed" and so labeled the "decade of greed". The facts show that charitable giving, both individual and corporate, skyrocketed, the affluent paid more in taxes than ever before, and more people volunteered their time for churches and civic groups.

DEMOGRAPHIC WORLD TRENDS: *Aging populations in China and Japan threaten their economies. *Life expectancy for Russian males is 64, primarily due to high levels of alcohol consumption and smoking. *While Russia is near the bottom for technical innovation, Japan, Taiwan, South Korea and Israel are at the top. *A lack of education is the primary challenge for India. – **Nicholas Eberstadt, AEI**... Western Europe's aging population is being offset by a rise in Middle East immigration – a double-edged sword.

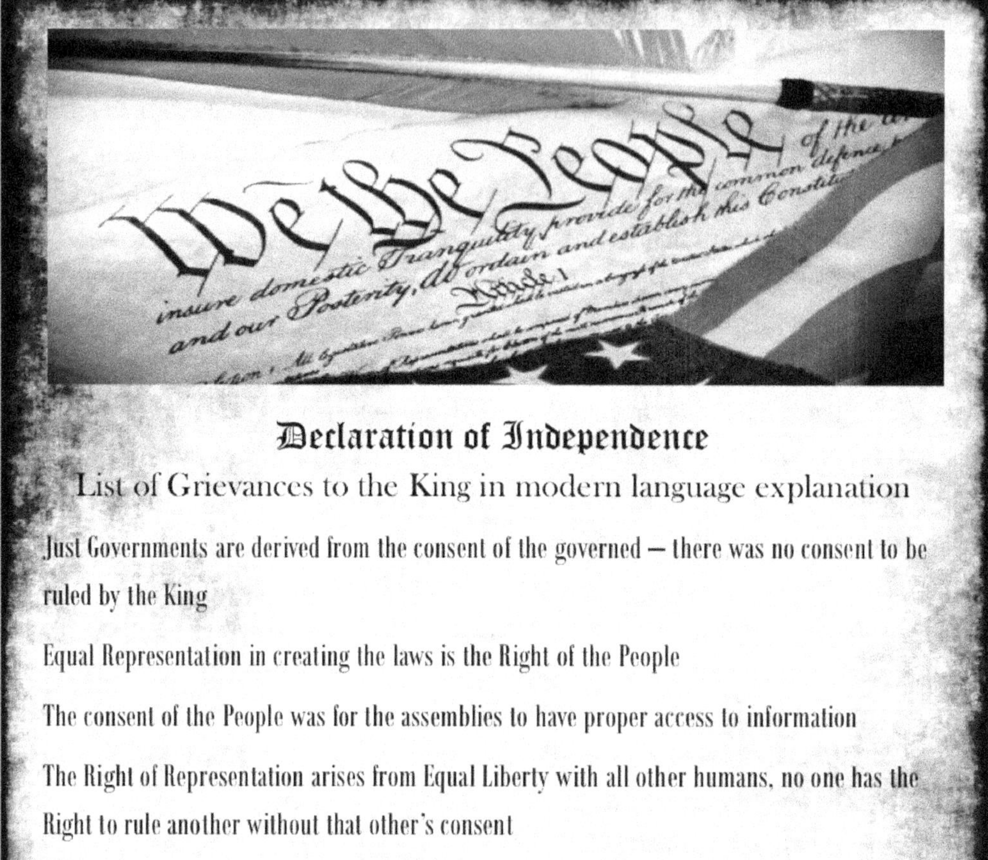

Declaration of Independence

List of Grievances to the King in modern language explanation

Just Governments are derived from the consent of the governed — there was no consent to be ruled by the King

Equal Representation in creating the laws is the Right of the People

The consent of the People was for the assemblies to have proper access to information

The Right of Representation arises from Equal Liberty with all other humans, no one has the Right to rule another without that other's consent

Government should make unused land available to the people by homestead or auction

Without a judiciary to punish criminials and to seek redress from an injurer, Life, Liberty and Property are insecure

Just Government must have a Separation of Powers with Checks and Balances

The Legislature must approve Executive Appointments or they are illegitimate

Government derives its just powers from the consent of the governed

To ensure the security of Rights and Liberties, all citizens must be subject to the Judiciary

The purpose of Government is to protect Life, Liberty and Happiness

DOCTRINE OF NATURAL LAW: The Founders basis for the Declaration of Independence; Natural Law justifies the moral basis of law and is a check on man-made law that is not just. To be a Natural Law, a rule, regulation, or

law must be consistent, "natural" in accord with the norms of voluntary behavior, and just. In other words, it must be both right (endowed by God) and legal (man-made), and it must serve the public good rather than the interests of any faction. It would block laws resulting from identity politics.
– **Sam Holliday**

DON'T TREAD ON ME: Used with the coiled rattlesnake on the Gadsden Flag, "don't tread on me" reflects the basic principle of individual liberty, to live your own life without external interference. The rattlesnake will warn other creatures that are infringing on its territory and will respond appropriately.

EARNED SUCCESS: Productive effort is linked to life satisfaction. Free enterprise empowers people to earn success and thereby achieve happiness. Money is merely a measure, not a source, of earned success.

Economic Freedom and the Income Earned by the Poorest 10%

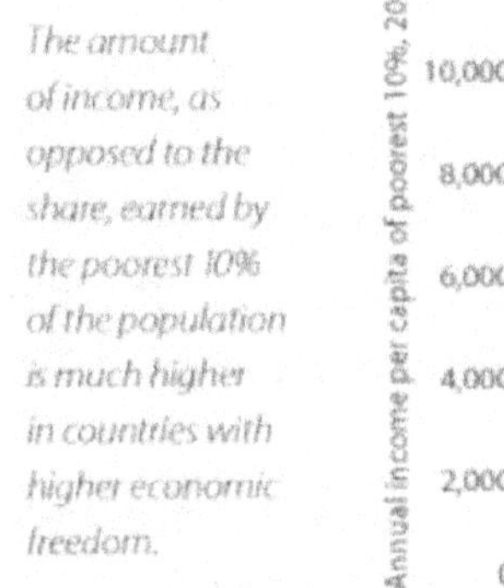

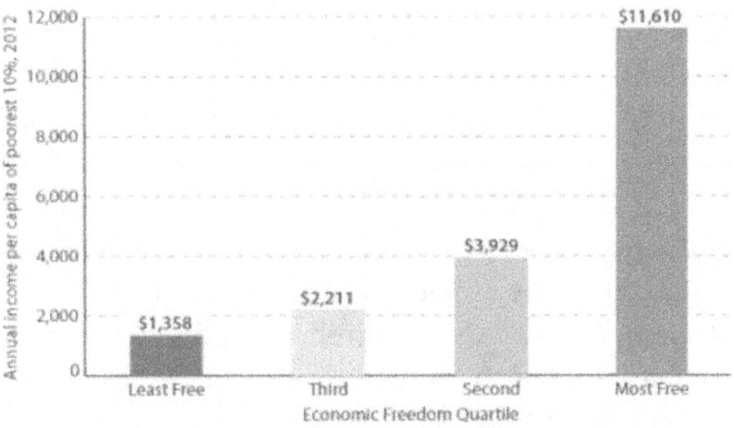

ECONOMIC FREEDOM INDEX: Economic freedom is the fundamental right of every human to control his or her own labor and property. According to the index, the cornerstones of economic freedom are personal choice, voluntary exchange, freedom to compete, and security of privately owned property. Various economic freedom indices, such as Heritage Foundation and Fraser Institute, objectively rank countries, states and regions. Top EFI ratings are typically Singapore, Hong Kong, New Zealand, Australia, Switzerland. Bottom EFI ratings include North Korea, Venezuela, Cuba, Iran, Argentina, and California. Under Barack Obama America matched its lowest global ranking ever in 2016 at #11 on the Index for Economic Freedom, its seventh decline in eight years.

ECONOMIC FREEDOM ZONES: Rand Paul's plan to conduct an experiment with considerably lower taxes and regulation in economically endangered areas.

ECONOMIC MOBILITY: Contrary to social barrier theories most working Americans who were initially in the bottom twenty percent of income-earners, rise out of it. More of them end up in the top twenty percent than remain in the bottom. People who were initially in the bottom twenty percent in income have had the highest rate of increase in their incomes, while those who were initially in the top twenty have had the lowest. The greatest barriers prove to be the welfare state as well as the emotional trauma to children raised in broken homes.

FACTORY EXPLOITATION MYTH: The Industrial Age revolution of the 19th century began an expansion of our life spans from 40 to 80. For many attempting to escape the hardships of the farm, factories brought wages, employment, inexpensive goods and improved standards of living to a rapidly growing population. The rapid population increase was due to an improvement in economic and social conditions. A greater regularity in supply led to a decrease in mortality as well. There was also an increase in the social and economic independence of women, a decrease in child labor, growth of cooperative societies and growth in literacy.

FEDERALISM, DUAL: Also referred to as divided sovereignty, is a political arrangement in which power is divided between the federal and state governments in clearly defined terms, with state governments exercising those powers accorded to them without interference from the federal government. In order to avoid the "bully state" the Founding Fathers limited federal power by granting state's rights, essentially allowing them to compete with one another. The evolution of federalism has been one of diminished state's rights.

FRIEDMAN, MILTON: He contradicted the prevailing Keynesian economic views of his time. As one of the staunch defenders of free market capitalism, Friedman's 1962 work, *Capitalism and Freedom,* was arguably the most important economic book of the 1960s. He may have also been America's most famous and influential libertarian.

FOUNDING FATHERS: The men who pledged their lives, fortunes, and sacred honor for the cause of liberty and independence. The key players who structured the democratic government of the American Republic were George Washington, Thomas Jefferson, John Adams, James Madison, Alexander Hamilton, James Monroe, John Jay and Benjamin Franklin.

FREEDOM: The absence of necessity, coercion, or constraint in choice or action. What is the basic principle that differentiates freedom from slavery? It is the principle of voluntary action versus force. Capitalism exemplifies the freedom to succeed, as well as the freedom to fail and start over again.

FREEDOM INDEX: "A Congressional Scorecard Based on the US Constitution" rates congressmen based on their adherence to constitutional principles of limited government, fiscal responsibility, national sovereignty, and a traditional foreign policy of avoiding foreign entanglements. – **The New American magazine**

FREEDOM IN THE WORLD: A yearly survey and report by Freedom House that measures the degree of civil liberties and political rights in each state and territory around the world.

FREE MARKET: "In a free economy, where no man or group of men can use physical coercion against anyone, economic power can be achieved only by voluntary means: by the voluntary choice and agreement of all those who participate in the process of production and trade. In a free market, all prices, wages, and profits are determined—not by the arbitrary whim of the rich or of the poor, not by anyone's 'greed' or by anyone's need—but by the law of supply and demand." – **Ayn Rand**… Free markets turn scarcity into abundance.

FREE MARKET ENVIRONMENTALISM: An approach to environmental problems focusing on improving environmental quality using property rights, markets and tort law. In practice, capitalist economies have enjoyed steady improvement in environmental quality, while totalitarian governments have been the worst desecrators of the planet.

FREE TRADE vs PROTECTIONISM: Nearly all economists agree that freer trade improves productive efficiency and offers consumers better choices, and in the long run these gains are much larger than any effects on employment. Protectionism protects domestic industries and their workers by providing subsidies for their production and imposing tariffs on competing foreign products. The real effect of protectionism is to increase monopolies under the premise of a 'trickle down' benefit.

GENEROSITY INDEX: Despite now being the party of the super-rich, the Democrat Party are still tightwads. Several studies reveal republicans give thirty percent to fifty percent more to charities than democrats. Similarly, in European countries they love to provide government safety nets for the poor yet give far less as individuals than Americans.

GLOBALIZATION: In contrast to collectivist globalism, globalization refers to the worldwide phenomenon of increased technological, economic, and cultural interconnectedness between nations. It is essentially capitalism on a global, rather than a national, scale. In a globalized economy, economic activity is unrestricted by time zones or national boundaries. There is an international exchange of labor forces, ideas, knowledge, products, and services. Opponents of globalization characterize the phenomenon as a form of Western expansionism and cultural imperialism, claiming that it will merely increase the opportunities for wealthier nations (and their multinational corporations) to take advantage of poorer ones. The reality is one of increased wages, prosperity, reduced poverty and improved living conditions for all.

GLOBAL SLAVERY INDEX: Provides a map, country by country, of the estimated prevalence of modern slavery, together with information about the steps each government has taken to respond to this issue. They estimate nearly 46 million people are in some form of modern slavery in 167 countries. Fifty-eight percent are in five countries: India, China, Pakistan, Bangladesh and Uzbekistan.

HAPPINESS ECONOMICS: Freedom breeds satisfaction. World Values Survey studies reveal economic as well as individual freedom has been found to exert an independent impact on life satisfaction over and above the impact on per-capita income levels and other indicators of material well-being. Economic freedom exerts a strong and persistent impact on both individual life control and life satisfaction.

HERITAGE FOUNDATION: One of the most influential conservative organizations in the US. Heritage publishes the yearly growth of federal spending, revenue, debt and deficits, entitlement programs, political theory books, and the Annual Index of Economic Freedom.

HOMESCHOOLING: The failure of government schooling, particularly with the rise of liberal indoctrination, led to the rise of the homeschooling grassroots movement in the 1980s with students now numbering over two million, and parents enjoying a basic freedom of choice.

HUMAN FREEDOM INDEX: Presents the state of human freedom in the world based on a broad measure that encompasses personal, civil, and economic freedom. – **Cato Institute**

HUMAN RIGHTS and PROPERTY RIGHTS: "There is no such dichotomy as 'human rights' versus 'property rights.' No human rights can exist without property rights. Since material goods are produced by the mind and effort of individual men, and are needed to sustain their lives, if the producer does not own the result of his effort, he does not own his life. To deny property rights means to turn men into property owned by the state. Whoever claims the 'right' to 'redistribute' the wealth produced by others is claiming the 'right' to treat human beings as chattel." – **Ayn Rand**

INCOME INEQUALITY: In contrast to the forced equality of socialism, income inequality provides the incentive for creative people to gamble on new ideas, promotes personal freedom, and rewards hard work, talent and achievement. What once seemed like impossible luxuries become available to almost everyone.

INDEX of CULTURE & OPPORTUNITY: Takes stock of the cultural ecosystem that is needed to sustain freedom and opportunity. Through charts that track cultural and economic changes, and expert commentary that explains the trends, the Index reports on important indicators in American society and analyzes what they mean for our future. – **Heritage Foundation**

INDIAN TERMINATION POLICY: After several federal acts and programs since the Dawes Act of 1887 failed to assimilate Native tribes into American society, Congress began the "termination era" in 1953 aimed at terminating federal obligations to tribes. Reservation land would be sold off and the money divided among tribal members. It was seen by many in terms of freedom and opportunity, with comparisons to the Emancipation Proclamation. Alas, the dependency on federal guardianship runs deep on the reservations and the security offered as wards of the state was preferred over freedom. With so much resistance the policy was abandoned in the 1960s and the Bureau of Indian Affairs remains the legal guardians of almost all tribes.

INDICATORS, CULTURE: * Marriage Rate * Divorce Rate * Total Fertility Rate * Single-parent Households * Teen Drug Use * Abstinence Among High Schoolers * Abortion Rate * Religious Attendance * Volunteering * Violent Crime Rate * – **Heritage Foundation**

INDICATORS, GENERAL OPPORTUNITY: * Reading Proficiency * Charter School Enrollment * Private School Choice Participation * High School Graduation Rate * Student Loan Debt * Employment-Population Ratio * Unemployment Rate * Job Openings Rate * Job Hires Rate * Money Taxed Away by Federal Government * Start-up Job Share * Major Federal Regulations * Economic Freedom * - **Heritage Foundation**

INDICATORS, POVERTY & DEPENDENCE: * Labor Force Participation Rate * Unwed Birth Rate * Self-sufficiency * Total Welfare Spending * Subsidized Housing Participation * Food Stamp Participation * TANF Participation * TANF Work Participation Rate * - **Heritage Foundation**

INDIVIDUAL, The: The individual is premier and has inherent rights by virtue of his existence. Those rights are given by God, and are natural rights that cannot be granted or withheld by government. This core concept of the Declaration of Independence, the Bill of Rights, the Constitution, and liberty itself is an affirmation of treating each person as an individual and not as a member of a group. You can see its implications for private property, which is the foundation of free markets.

INDIVIDUALISM: In contrast to collectivism it "regards man—every man—as an independent, sovereign entity who possesses an inalienable right to his own life, a right derived from his nature as a rational being. Individualism holds that a civilized society, or any form of association, cooperation or peaceful coexistence among men, can be achieved only on the basis of the recognition of individual rights—and that a group, as such, has no rights other than the individual rights of its members." – **Ayn Rand**

INDIVIDUALIST: … is a man who says: "I will not run anyone's life—nor let anyone run mine. I will not rule nor be ruled. I will not be a master nor a slave. I will not sacrifice myself to anyone—nor sacrifice anyone to myself." – **Ayn Rand**

INSOURCING: We hear a lot about US firms outsourcing jobs overseas ("stealing US jobs") but we don't hear much about the jobs that are insourced by foreign companies even though those insourced jobs totaled more than 6.4 million Americans in 2014 and represent 5.2 percent of all private sector US jobs, a significant and positive impact on our economy. – **Mark J Perry, AEI**

LAFFER CURVE: At some point if you make tax rates higher you bring in less revenue to the government. The curve starts at zero percent taxes and ends at 100%, both resulting in zero revenue. The hump in the curve between the two indicates maximum taxation before revenue decline begins. If the goal is to soak the citizens for the greatest amount of money, evidence reveals that anything over 33% results in decreased revenue.

LAISSEZ-FAIRE: Opposing governmental interference in economic affairs beyond what is minimally necessary.

LIBERTARIAN PARADOX of individual freedoms in a welfare state: Open borders and drug legalization are both impossible in a welfare state in which personal irresponsibility is rewarded.

LIMITED GOVERNMENT: The primary intent of our Founding Fathers and the U.S. Constitution was to limit the powers of the federal government.

LIVING WAGE: A euphemism for raising minimum wage as a welfare handout. Real world "living" wage is what you make after a short probationary period and have proven yourself as a dedicated worker with such value to the company that you create negotiation leverage.

MAGNA CARTA: The "Great Charter" of English liberties over 800 years ago, provided the foundation for individual rights in Anglo-American legal systems and a symbol in the battle against oppression. Whenever liberty seemed in danger, men spoke of the charter as their defense.

MILITIA: All citizens are the militia. The Second Amendment reads, "A well regulated Militia, being necessary to the security of a free State, the right of the people to keep and bear Arms, shall not be infringed." The primary purpose was to protect the citizens against a tyrannical government.

MIXED ECONOMY: The economic reality of the middle ground, a purgatory, between the free markets of capitalism and the planned economies of socialism. Most modern economies feature a synthesis of two or more economic systems.

NATIONALISM: A political ideology of self-governance and sovereignty over a homeland territory. Nationalism holds that a nation should govern itself, free from unwanted outside interference, and seeks to preserve the nation's culture. It values national identity, self-determination, solidarity, and patriotism.

NON-AGGRESSION: A libertarian principle often mistaken for pacifism. Non-aggression is an ethical stance that initiation of physical force or fraud against persons or property is illegitimate. In contrast to pacifism, non-aggression does not preclude violent self-defense. Defensively securing liberty is also a libertarian principle.

NO VICTIM, NO CRIME: Habeas Corpus [Latin, you have the body.] - the Court must show the actual victim or evidence of the crime. The idea that a criminal act requires some harm to be done is overly simplistic though. Non-harm means that one may threaten or imperil people at will so long as the threat remains unrealized, while the libertarian non-aggression principle forbids this. A credible threat of aggression is the same thing as the actual aggression. If you threaten someone by way of a hostile action you are creating a victim. It is clear that 'no victim means no crime' is an inadequate standard for use of defensive force.

OBJECTIVISM, AYN RAND: Advocates rational selfishness, which means the values required for human survival. It is the concept of man as a heroic being, with his own happiness as the moral purpose of his life, with productive achievement as his noblest activity, and reason, rather than faith, as his only absolute. Individual rights and laissez-faire capitalism are at its core. Objectivism is a libertarian philosophy however not all libertarian thinking is compatible with Objectivism.

NUCLEAR FAMILY (traditional): A family unit that includes two married parents of opposite genders and their biological or adopted children living in the same residence. It is historically the foundation of society.

OPPORTUNITY: The reason women, gays, minorities, and oppressed from around the world are willing to spend thousands of dollars and put up with years of paperwork migrating to the United States.

PALESTINIAN STATE PROPOSALS: 1937: Proposed by the Peel Commission – rejected by the Arabs. 1947: Proposed by the U.N. – rejected by the Arabs. 1967: Israel offered land for peace – rejected by the Arabs via the Khartoum Resolution. 2000: Offered by Israeli PM Ehud Barak – rejected by Yasser Arafat. 2008: Offered by Israeli PN Ehud Olmert – rejected by Mahmoud Abbas.

PARTICIPATION RATE: A measure of the active portion of an economy's labor force. It refers to the number of people who are either employed or are actively looking for work. The number of people who are no longer actively searching for work (out of labor force) would not be included in the participation rate. The unemployment rate must always be taken in context with the participation rate since if everybody stopped searching for work in favor of welfare handouts the unemployment rate would be zero.

PATRIOTISM: Maintaining the values and principles of America's Founding Father Patriots who stood up to the tyranny of an oppressive government. Those principles emphasized limited government, individual freedoms, personal responsibility, free market capitalism and their revolutionary extremist conviction that all men are created equal.

PERSONAL RESPONSIBILITY: In a capitalist society the price you pay for individual freedom is personal responsibility. Transients from welfare states often have difficulties adapting to the responsibilities of a free society.

POLITICAL DONORS PARTY: Of the top 40 organizations making political contributions 24 give almost exclusively to the Democratic Party while only four give exclusively to the GOP. Some 20 labor unions give almost exclusively to democrats yet on the generosity index for charitable giving are far down the list. Corporate giants such as Walmart, Alcoa and Koch Industries are the most generous organizations in the world for donations to charity.

PREDATORY PRICING: An industrial age myth of big business eliminating competition by offering goods at exceptionally low prices in order to gain a monopoly and then restrict output and raise prices. The problem with this model is it's impossible to find an actual example. In practice, monopolistic industries continued high output with lower prices.

INDUSTRY NET PROFIT MARGINS AND TAX RATES COMPARISON

U.S. TAX RATES

Average federal, state & local taxes as a portion of GDP, per household 25%
Gasoline taxes at $2.00/gallon 25%
Average individual income tax 9.5%
Average state sales tax 7%

INDUSTRY NET PROFIT MARGINS

Public perception for average company 34%
Media and Entertainment 28%
Apple 22%
Accounting 20%
Legal services 15%
Brewers 14%
Big Oil 6%
Health insurance companies 4%
Restaurants 4%
Auto dealers 3%
Walmart 3%
Grocery stores 2.5%
Cattle ranching and farming 2%

PROPORTIONAL TAX or FLAT TAX: The same percentage of tax is levied from all taxpayers, regardless of their income.

PROSPERITY CITIES: Coined by Erick Brimen, indicating small places that create the "environment for success" in order to rescue others from the tragedy of centrally planned economies. Brimen argues that if successful countries such as Greece and Venezuela can be turned into basket cases, we must find a new approach. Like free trade zones, empowerment zones, and charter cities, a prosperity city is a small place where government leaves people mostly free to pursue their own interests. Hong Kong, Dubai, and Shenzhen are examples.

REAGANOMICS: Ronald Reagan's policies called for widespread tax cuts, decreased social spending, increased military spending, and the deregulation of domestic markets. Principles of supply-side economics were applied to stimulate economic growth.

REPUBLIC: Representative government ruled by law (US Constitution). The American system is not a democracy, it is a constitutional republic. A democracy, if you attach meaning to terms, is a system of unlimited majority rule, a form of collectivism, which denies individual rights.

REPUBLICANS – Ron Lipsman:

RINO: Republican In Name Only. They really do not believe that progressivism and big government are bad for America – it's just that the Democrats are screwing it up and Republicans should be entrusted with the task of implementing the progressive agenda because they will do it more efficiently and cost effectively than liberal Democrats.

CRUEL's: Confused Republicans who are Unable to Exercise Leadership. These are conservative politicians whose hearts and minds may be in the right place, but they are unable to 1. articulate their beliefs 2. explain the connection between progressivism and the ill that beset the nation 3. describe clearly how conservative policies will enhance liberty and economic prosperity, and 4. deflect the vicious slanders that the Democrats hurl at them.

CCC's: Committed Conservative Constitutionalists. These are politicians who have a clear understanding of what the progressives have wrought and how the country has changed. They can envision and describe the bleak future that awaits us if we don't have a major course correction. Furthermore, such people also have a clear idea of what must be done to return the country to its founding ethos, reinstitute the ideals of free market capitalism, constitutional and limited governance, and American exceptionalism and thereby restore the republic. Moreover, they can explain these ideas clearly and simply.

RIGHTS: "It's not an endlessly expanding list of rights – the "right" to education, the "right" to health care, the "right" to food and housing. That's not freedom, that's dependency. Those aren't rights, those are the rations of slavery – hay and a barn for human cattle." – **Alexis de Tocqueville**, historian.

"A 'right' is a moral principle defining and sanctioning a man's freedom of action in a social context. There is only one fundamental right (all the others are its consequences or corollaries): a man's right to his own life." – **Ayn Rand**

ROBBER BARON MYTH: PC historians have portrayed entrepreneurs of the late 19th century Industrial Age as greedy, exploitative capitalists. However, rather than running rampant over common folk before being reined in through antitrust legislation, industrialists achieved their dominance thru cutting costs and pleasing customers. In a genuine free market, producers cannot compel customers to purchase their products, or prevent others from competing. True monopolists must rely on government privilege. The US government is the most monopolistic institution that has ever existed. – *The Politically Incorrect Guide to Capitalism*

SCHOOL VOUCHERS: Market competition among private schools leads to increased student achievement and decreased education costs. In regions of low performing public schools, vouchers provide "opportunity scholarships" for parents to pick the private schools of their choice to enroll their children. Labor unions and bureaucrats will have nothing of it.

STATUE OF LIBERTY: The symbol of liberty and individual freedom, the antithesis of progressivism. The tablet represents the Declaration of Independence with its radical notion of the times that "all men are created equal". The "give me your tired" poem inside the lower level was a later add-on however the statue does not celebrate immigration, it salutes the achievement of the settlers who founded the colonies and, in time, won independence from their mother country.

SUPPLY AND DEMAND, LAW OF: Common sense economics. The law of supply and demand defines the effect that the availability of a particular product and the desire (or demand) for that product has on price. Generally, if there is a low supply and a high demand, the price will be high. In contrast, the greater the supply and the lower the demand, the lower the price will be.

SUPPLY SIDE ECONOMICS: "Build it and they will come". Argues that economic growth can be most effectively created by lowering barriers for people to produce (supply) goods and services as well as invest in capital. This is done with tax cuts and deregulation.

SURVIVALIST RETREAT: A retreat is a commonly used term for a place of refuge for those in the Survivalist movement. They are intended to be self-sufficient and are generally located in lightly populated rural areas with small town or conservative values. Most survivalist retreats are organized by extended families, but some "group retreats" or "covenant communities" are formed along the lines of an Intentional Community. – **Conservapedia.**

SWEATSHOPS: From the Industrial Age to modern day Third World countries, man has escaped the grueling conditions, isolation and squalor of agricultural life in the fields to work in factories in what some consider to be "poor conditions". Sweatshops can be awful places to work, but they are often less awful than other jobs sweatshop workers could take and they offer better pay, indoor conditions, social contact and city life. When people argue against them, the question we should ask is; "Compared to what?".

TAX CUTS INCREASE REVENUE: Under Coolidge, Kennedy, Reagan, Gingrich and Bush, lowering federal taxes resulted in increased tax revenues. It is an economics IQ test.

TAXED ENOUGH ALREADY: Tax the rich? Already done it. America's taxes are the most progressive in the world. That means our top 10 percent pay a much higher share of the tax burden than the upper classes in other countries do. That's not all, in 2017 we still had the highest corporate tax rate in the world.

THANKSGIVING, THE FIRST: The Pilgrims of Plymouth Colony originally tried to set up a socialist-type existence where everybody got an equal share of everything that was produced. They discovered that the laggards and the lazy just fed off everybody else and they all nearly starved as a result. They turned to capitalism, and that was the basis for the first Thanksgiving. They had the courage to abandon the original socialism and move toward something else, and it worked so well they had enough bounty to share with the natives. That's right, it wasn't about the Indians sharing, it was the other way around, and that was the thanks.

THINK TANKS: The term denotes a group of people who are paid to do nothing but read, discuss, think, and write, usually to address and redress a matter of vital importance to humanity. Think tanks argue, advocate and lobby for policy changes at local, state, and federal levels. – **thebestschools.org**. . . The Heritage Foundation and American Enterprise Institute are two of the most influential conservative think tanks. The Cato

Institute and Ludwig von Mises Institute are two of the most influential Libertarian tanks.

TRADER PRINCIPLE: Attaining value from other people through mutually beneficial trade rather than force, fraud, or parasitism. The principle of trade is the principle of justice.

TRICKLE-DOWN THEORY: A straw man fallacy. It cannot be found in even the most voluminous and learned histories of economic theories.

TWO COWS ANALOGY:

Socialism; You have two cows. The government takes one and gives it to your neighbor.

Communism: You have two cows. The government seizes both and gives you some milk.

Capitalism; You have two cows. You sell one and buy a bull.

Environmentalism; You have two cows. The government bans you from milking or killing them.

Political Correctness; You are associated with (the concept of "ownership" is a symbol of the phallocentric, warmongering, intolerant past) two differently-aged (but no less valuable to society) bovines of non-specified gender.

Liberalism; You have two cows, your neighbor has none. You feel guilty, so you pass legislation to help him get a cow. You wear a ribbon to show you care.

Libertarianism and objectivism: You have one cow. You don't care how many cows your neighbors have.

URBANDICTIONARY.COM: Founded in 1999 as a parody. If you seek no-holds-barred slang and phrases with a politically incorrect bent, this is an excellent crowdsource of definitions.

VENTURE CAPITAL: Think *Shark Tank*; the funding of new and risky enterprises to create wealth for many. The downside for entrepreneurs is that venture capitalists usually get a say in company decisions, in addition to a portion of the equity.

WORLD INDEX OF MORAL FREEDOM: Measures; "how free from state-imposed moral constraints are human beings depending on their countries of residence"? Indicator categories are religious, bioethical, drugs, sexuality, and gender & family. – **Foundation for the Advancement of Liberty**, a libertarian think tank based in Madrid, Spain.

YANKEE INGENUITY: Is a stereotype of inventiveness, technical solutions to practical problems, know-how, self-reliance and individual enterprise associated with the Yankees who originated in New England and developed much of the industrial revolution in the United States after 1800.

ConservaLexicon

CHAPTER TWO

CONTROL

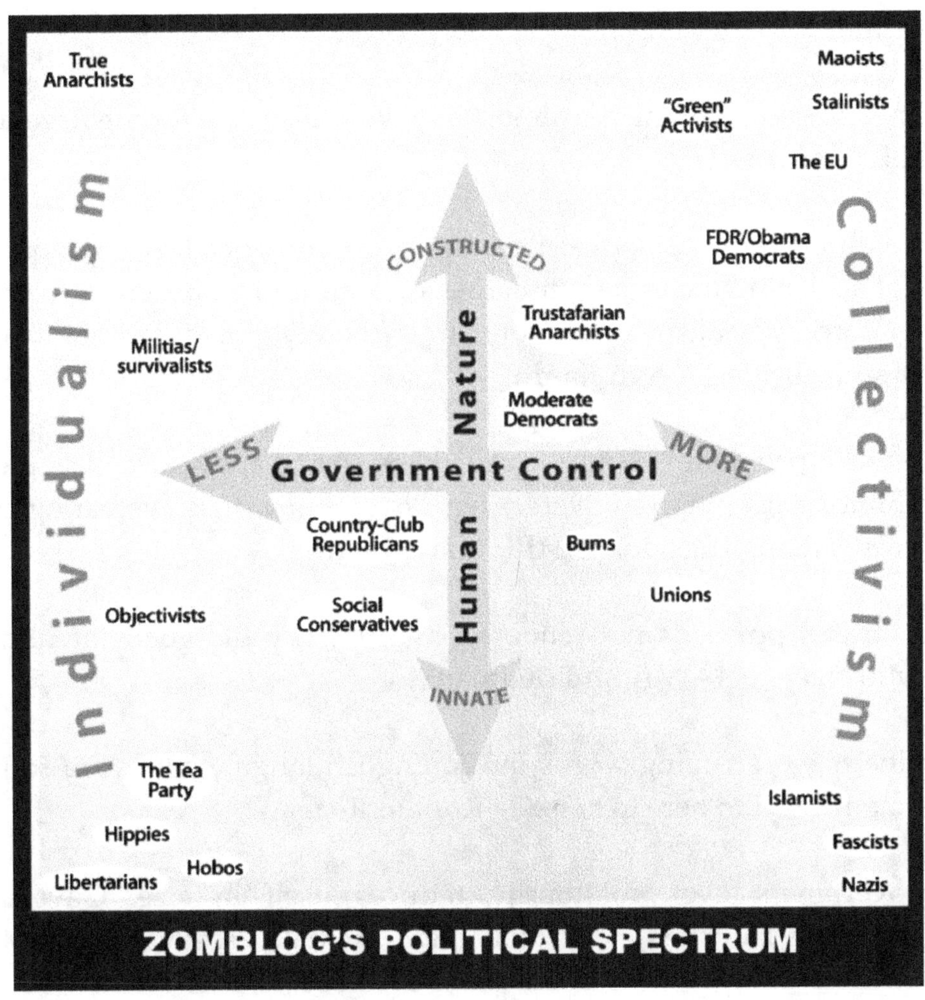

Quotes

"Everyone wants to live at the expense of the state. They forget that the state wants to live at the expense of everyone." – **Frederic Bastiat**

"When the people fear the government there is tyranny, when the government fears the people there is liberty." – **John Basil Barnhill**

"Socialism is a philosophy of failure, the creed of ignorance and the gospel of envy. It's inherent virtue is the equal sharing of misery." – **Winston Churchill**

"The urge to save humanity is almost always a false face for the urge to rule it." – **H.L. Mencken**

"There is no difference between communism and socialism, except in the means of achieving the same ultimate end: communism proposes to enslave men by force, socialism – by vote. It is merely the difference between murder and suicide." – **Ayn Rand**

"The case for prohibiting drugs is exactly as strong and as weak as the case for prohibiting people from overeating. We all know that overeating causes more deaths than drugs do." – **Milton Friedman**

"Concentrated power is not rendered harmless by the good intentions of those who create it." – **Milton Friedman**

"The nine most terrifying words in the English language are, I'm from the government and I'm here to help." – **Ronald Reagan**

"No government ever voluntarily reduces itself in size. Government programs, once launched, never disappear. Actually, a government bureau is the nearest thing to eternal life we'll ever see on this earth!" – **Ronald Reagan**

"In this present crisis, government is not the solution to our problem; government is the problem." – **Ronald Reagan**

"If you want an example of the failure of socialism, don't go to Russia, come to America and go to the Indian reservations." – **James G Watt**

"Socialists cry 'Power to the people', and raise the clenched fist as they say it. We all know what they really mean – power <u>over</u> people, power <u>to the State</u>." – **Margaret Thatcher**

"The problem with socialism is that you eventually run out of other people's money." – **Margaret Thatcher**

"Anyone who studies the history of ideas should notice how much more often people on the political left, more so than others, denigrate and demonize those who disagree with them – instead of answering their arguments." – **Thomas Sowell**

"I have never understood why it is 'greed' to want to keep the money you have earned but not greed to take somebody else's money." – **Thomas Sowell**

"It is not power that corrupts but fear. Fear of losing power corrupts those who wield it and fear of the scourge of power corrupts those who are subject to it." – **Aung San Suu Kyi**

"But we have to pass the bill so you can find out what is in it, away from the fog of the controversy." – **Nancy Pelosi**

"When buying and selling are controlled by legislation, the first things bought and sold are legislators." – **P J O'Rourke**

ABORTION and PATRIARCHY: Abortion allows men to dictate how a woman views her body. With abortion, men get to keep using women as sexual objects. Consent becomes irrelevant because the woman has given away her consent and rights when she supports or gets an abortion. Through abortion, patriarchy has convinced women of the lie that they now have control over their bodies and their sexual activities.

AGENDA 21 - UNCED 1992: "Smart-growth" policies to the extreme - a globalist New World Order of a controlled and planned world society attained behind the veil of environmental justice. Agenda 21 is "a comprehensive plan of action to be taken globally, nationally and locally by organizations of the United Nations Systems, Governments, and Major Groups in every area in which human impacts on the environment." The Commission of Sustainable Development was also created in 1992 to ensure effective follow-up of UNCED, to monitor and report on implementation of the agreements. Thankfully Agenda 21 is non-binding, and therefore poses little threat in and of itself.

ALTRUISM: The foundation of collectivism and statism. It is the selfless concern for the well-being of others, that man has no right to exist for his own sake and that self-sacrifice is his highest moral duty, virtue and value.

BAILOUTS: Government bailouts are an element of crony socialism or corporatism. They are anti-capitalist. Zombie companies are propped up at the expense of successful companies and small business. Bailouts are a feature of "lemon socialism".

BLACK MARKET: As one of the many consequences of government central planning and intervention in the free market, black market "under the table" transactions allow the participants to illegally avoid price controls and taxes – an underground version of the free market.

BOONDOGGLE: A project, typically government, that is considered a useless waste of both time and money, yet is often continued due to extraneous policy or political motivations. It can be allowed to continue for what seems unusually long periods, as long as funds are available. Also known as zombie projects.

BOOTLEGGERS and BAPTISTS: "Durable social regulation evolves when it is demanded by both of two distinctly different groups. 'Baptists' point to the moral high ground and give vital and vocal endorsement of laudable public benefits promised by a desired regulation. Baptists flourish when their moral message forms a visible foundation for political action. 'Bootleggers' are much less visible but no less vital. Bootleggers, who expect to profit from the very regulatory restrictions desired by Baptists, grease the political machinery with some of their expected proceeds. They are simply in it for the money." – **Bruce Yandle**

BOOTLEGGERS & BAPTISTS, MODERN: Environmentalist "Baptists" want to shut down carbon emitters for moral reasons, preferring central government command-and-control regulation which requires larger bureaucracies to design and enforce the rules. The environmental "bootleggers" are the opportunistic industrialists that love command-and-control regulations that raise rivals' costs and limit the entry of new competition. They welcome taxpayer subsidies and government-guaranteed loans for their green projects and "clean" technologies, while taking a seat at the regulators table.

BULLY STATE: The nanny state dressed up in stewardship clothing, threatening people rather than nudging. It is state sponsored shaming, coercion and propaganda. It is often associated with the authoritarian (rather than economic) component of fascism.

BUREAUCRACY: A system of government in which most of the important decisions are made by state officials rather than by elected representatives.

BUREAUCRAT: Forces you to obey his decisions, whether you agree with him or not – and the more advanced the stage of a country's collectivism, the wider and more discretionary the powers wielded by him. If he makes a mistake, you suffer the consequences; if he fails, he passes the loss on to you, in the form of heavier taxes. A bureaucrat's success depends on his political pull.

CENTRAL PLANNING: A collectivist/socialist principle. Central and urban planning are the guidance of the economy by direct government control over a large portion of economic activity, as contrasted with allowing markets to serve this purpose. Central planning always fails because it is not about efficiency, it is about the desire to control others - also, the planning elites don't have a clue regarding basic economic realities.

CITIZEN ADVISORY BOARD: Uses power and influence in shaping policies of local government. Ideally their responsibilities include studying critical issues, taking public testimony and performing independent research. The process should be non-biased, avoiding group-think, and challenging prevailing paradigms. Sadly, many advisory boards act as propaganda machines engaged in passing on biased information used to promote political causes such as green activism.

CLASS CONFLICT: Frequently referred to as class warfare, class envy, or class struggle, it is the antagonism which exists in society due to competing socioeconomic interests between rich and poor. The view that the class struggle provides the lever for radical social change is central to socialism.

CLASS ENVY: Coveting thy neighbor's goods is an emotion based on a subjective perception of other people's wealth regardless of how it was earned. It is the justification for collectivist redistribution of wealth by force with the historical unintended consequence of the equality of impoverishment. Class envy is the foundation of Marxism. Discussions of income inequality aren't about prosperity but about petty spite. Why should you care how much money I make, so long as you are happy?

CLASSLESS SOCIETY: Karl Marx's ultimate condition of social organization, expected to occur when true communism is achieved. The historical reality is, as Winston Churchill put it, "the equal sharing of misery".

CLINTON URANIUM SCANDAL: Tens of millions of dollars from uranium investors flowed into the Clinton Foundation. Then Bill Clinton received a $500,000 speaking fee from a Russian bank tied to the Kremlin before Secretary of State Hillary Clinton helped decide whether to approve the sale to the Russian government of a company that held one-fifth of America's uranium capacity.

COLLECTIVE BARGAINING: Negotiations by representatives of a group of employees, often a labor union, pertaining to conditions of employment, such as wages and working conditions. Employees may bargain collectively without any interference from outsider labor unions.

COLLECTIVE NARCISSISM: The coercive faith of progressivism has the character of an endemic narcissism. It is an arrogant faith led, and largely populated, by a relentlessly aggressive, power-obsessed political class dedicated to imposing a social justice on the world. Collective narcissism (related to ethnocentrism) asserts that one can have an excessively high opinion of a group, and that group can function as a narcissistic entity. In the broadest terms, this narcissistic entity is America's left-wing political establishment and the purveyor of an authoritarian collectivist faith. It is a faith largely populated by those in the high-visibility, look-at-me intellectual professions of politics, the arts, teaching, journalism, and various political foundations. - **Bruce A Riggs,** *Leftism: A Radical Faith*

COLLECTIVISM: "Collectivism is the subjugation of the individual to a group – whether to a race, class or state does not matter. Man must be chained to collective action and collective thought for the sake of what is called 'the common good'." – **Ayn Rand**... Statism has always been the political corollary of collectivism.

COLLEGE, FREE EDUCATION: A progressive goal which constitutes crony capitalism at its finest – i.e., public funding of a private sector industry operated by loyal disciples of left-wing ideology turning out the mutually desired product; an expanded pool of graduates schooled in the progressive belief system - free liberal indoctrination masquerading as free education. – **Joseph A Frascino, MD**

COMMUNISM: Socialism to the extreme. Under fascism or progressivism, enterprises are state directed. Under communism or socialism they are state-owned. "Communism proposes to enslave men by force, socialism enslaves by vote. It is merely the difference between murder and suicide." – **Ayn Rand**

CONCEIT OF THE ANOINTED: In Thomas Sowell's, *"The Vision of the Anointed"*, he portrays the central planner ruling elites – the anointed – of socialism. Hundreds of government agencies and millions of federal employees search for regulatory ways to protect us and make things "fair". These "experts" know better than the rest of us on how to run our lives. Their conceit is so strong that they insist on maintaining control even when they fail time and time again.

CONTROL FREAK: In the field of behavioral sciences there is a differentiation between Obsessive Compulsive Disorder and Obsessive Compulsive Personality Disorder. Those with OCD will be very rigid about running their own lives. Those with OCPD have a need to run other people's lives. The former might be neat freaks or hoarders and cause problems and inconvenience for family members or acquaintances however the latter are "control" freaks and they cause problems for everyone. They are uncomfortable without rules and established procedures, and are very uncomfortable if everyone else does not follow THEIR rules. They naturally gravitate toward government service, academia and media.

CORPORATE WELFARE, CRONY CORPORATISM and FASCISM: The contrast to free market capitalism. Corporatism is defined as a partnership between government and established firms characterized by regulatory government agencies that cartelize industries like a gang or syndicate, at the expense of small business. Corporatism is one of the defining economic characteristics of fascism and progressivism, both requiring big powerful government and heavy-handed rulers. It is our current US system, a mixed economy. Crony corporatism arises from the need of socialist governments to control the state. This requires businesses to operate closely with the government to achieve the greatest success.

CORRUPTION: The misuse of public power by elected politicians or appointed civil servants for private gain. The key word is public. Private sector corruption begins only when it interfaces with the public sector

---

CORPORATISM: One of the defining characteristics of economic fascism. Big corporations screw the working man by government-enforced price fixing, all the while advertising the scheme as "good for the working man". Corporatism is a partnership between government and established firms characterized by regulatory agencies that cartelize industries.

---

however it is the government which holds the upper hand of power.

CRITICAL THEORY: From the Frankfurt School of Cultural Marxism, Critical Theory is the destructive criticism of all the main elements of Western culture including Christianity, capitalism, authority, the family, patriarchy, hierarchy, morality, tradition, sexual restraint, loyalty, patriotism, nationalism, heredity, ethnocentrism, convention and conservatism. Under the impact of Critical Theory many of the sixties generation, the most privileged in history, convinced themselves that they were living in an intolerable hell.

CRONY CAPITALISM: An oxymoron. Government favoritism is the antithesis of capitalism. The fact that money is involved doesn't make it capitalism. The proper term is "crony corporatism" or just "cronyism".

CRONYISM: The appointment of friends and associates to positions of authority, without proper regard to their qualifications. On the larger scale of big business, cronyism is often used interchangeably with "corporate welfare" and "corporatism" – government picking the winners and losers. Contrary to the freedoms of capitalism, cronyism utilizes coercion which breeds exploitation and corruption.

CRONYISM, CULTURAL: What's true for the economy is true for the culture, as well. While cronyism is most recognizable when it generates economic windfalls for the favored few, it also operates in other realms. For decades, the Left has been seeking special advantages from government in its effort to reshape the character of American society – think abortion and same-sex marriage lobbies. So, if you're against the government arbitrarily picking winners and losers in the economy, you need to be against it doing the same in the culture. If Solyndra and the Export-Import Bank are a problem, so too is government funding for Planned Parenthood and government discrimination against Catholic Charities. – **Ryan T Anderson, The Heritage Foundation**

CROWDISM: Is what happens when individuals, deciding to act in their own interests, band together to make any rule other than "the individual does what the individual wants" taboo. Crowdism often occurs in politics and activism. Crowdists are radical individualists who are in a group only to use guilt to compel others to yield to them, want the advantages of society without the obligations, and depend on "useful idiots" to advance their agenda. – **Brett Stevens**

CYNICISM: "A cynic believes that men are innately depraved and therefore, that the most practical method of dealing with men is to count on their stupidity, appeal to their knavery, and keep them in constant terror. In private life, this belief creates a criminal; in politics, it creates a statist. But, contrary to the cynic's belief, crime and statism do not pay." – **Ayn Rand**

D.C. ELITE: Call it Camelot, Panem of *The Hunger Games*, The Swamp, or even Mordor, but according to Forbes' 2017 rankings, five of the 10 wealthiest counties in the US are located in the Washington, D.C. metro area.

DEATH PANEL: A panel of bureaucrats whose task it is to examine everyone needing medical attention and decide who gets denied healthcare.

DEEP STATE: "State within a state". A body of people, typically influential members of entrenched government institutions - career bureaucrats - believed to be involved in the secret manipulation or control of government policy. The term has gained widespread popularity during the Trump administration's assault from internal state forces. The deep state is the logical consequence of runaway expansion and scope of government powers.

DEMOCRACY: A government ruled by the majority (mob rule). Democracy is a form of collectivism – it readily sacrifices individual rights to majority wishes.

DIALECTICS: In Marxist pseudo-thought refers to the process by which contradictions are resolved via corrosive debate. A dialect is just a regional subset of a language; dialectics is an intellectual shell game that provides leftism with an aura of philosophic seriousness. – **Joseph S Salemi, poet**

DODD-FRANK: In order to punish investment banks and promote Democrat and big-bank interests, two corrupt Democrats 1) Spawned 400 crippling regulations on banks and their capacity to lend 2) Favored big banks in coastal cities over smaller banks in the heartland 3) Enshrined bailouts into permanent law 4) Harmed bank lending among smaller banks, hampering startups which need bank capital 5) Established the largely unaccountable Consumer Financial Protection Bureau.

DOUBLE-DIPPING: Public servants "retire" after twenty years of service, immediately collecting lavish pensions, and then take on full time public employment with a similar job elsewhere. The incentive is to retire early. Cash-starved governments end up squandering funds and then slash services to pay for pensions.

ECONOMIC DISPARITY IN GALLUP NM: McKinley County NM and Navajo Nation receive $billions in federal monies yet has the number two national ranking for poverty while Gallup was recently ranked number one for millionaires per capita in the country. Obtaining government contracts is the key to success in Gallup along with anti-capitalist policies on the Navajo Nation funneling most sales dollars off the reservation.

EGALITARIANISM, Ayn Rand: An anti-concept used to mean the equality of personal attributes and virtues, regardless of natural endowment or individual choice, performance and character. Since nature does not endow all men with equal beauty or intelligence, and the faculty of volition leads men to make different choices, the egalitarians propose to abolish the "unfairness" of nature and volition, and to establish universal equality in fact – in defiance of facts. Since personal attributes or virtues cannot be "redistributed", they seek to deprive men of their consequences – or the rewards and benefits created by personal attributes and virtues.

To understand the meaning and motives of egalitarianism, suppose a doctor is called to help a man with a broken leg and, instead of setting it, proceeds to break the legs of ten other men, explaining that this would make the patient feel better. The doctor then advocates the passage of a law compelling everyone to walk on crutches – in order to make the cripples feel better and equalize the "unfairness" of nature.

EUROPEAN HEALTH CARE: Despite tremendous economic expense European socialized medical care is on the brink of collapse. The US boasts 15% longer cancer survival rates and the best cardiac care in the world thanks to our advanced technology. People from around the world come here for surgeries they can't obtain due to waiting lists. The most efficient European health care systems rely more on a system of private insurance, such as Switzerland.

EXPROPRIATION: The implementation of Marxist ideas of abolishing private ownership on the means of production and "socializing" private property. Expropriation occurs when a government agency takes private property for a purpose deemed to be in the "public interest". In the US the government has the right to take property through "eminent domain". While there is compensation, the expropriation occurs without the property owner's consent.

EUROPEAN HOUSING: We often hear the praises of life in Europe under their soft socialism however when we examine a family's most prized possession, the home, their average square footage is about 1,000 square feet. The average in the US is 2,300.

FAIRNESS: Those who hold political power are authorized to pick winners and losers in the economy, at the expense of the consuming public, the taxpayers, and others who may be adversely impacted but who are ignored in the discussion.

FASCISM: The phenomenon of government picking winners and losers in the, ahem, free market. The essence of fascism is elites imposing order, using crisis as pretext, and cult of personality as the vehicle. The economic plan for both fascism and progressivism is corporatism. The only difference is the face it puts on for the public. Whereas progressivism puts on a populist pro-worker face, fascism puts on a patriotic nationalist face. Both require big powerful government and heavy-handed rulers. Citizens retain the responsibilities of owning property, without freedom to act and without any of the advantages of ownership. The US has evolved into a fascist system - a mixed economy to be sure, but essentially a "closet" fascist system called progressivism. The authoritarian side of fascism is the use of governmental power to suppress rights of individuals.

See appendix for *John T Flynn's Eight Marks of Fascist Policy.*

FASCISM, ECONOMIC: Many prefer to focus on the authoritarian component of fascism, however it is primarily an economic system. Fascism and progressivism give government control of the economy, while leaving ownership in private hands. That way politicians get to call the shots but, when their bright ideas lead to disaster, they can always blame those who own businesses in the private sector. Under socialism, government ownership of the means of production means that politicians also own the consequences of their policies, and must face responsibility when those consequences are disastrous.

FASCISM, THE LIBERAL PHILOSOPHY: "Fascism is private ownership, private enterprise, but total government control and regulation. Well, isn't this the liberal philosophy?" – **Ronald Reagan**

FEDERAL DUPLICATION AND REDUNDANCY: In 2012 the Government Accountability Office identified 1,500 different programs that are wasteful, duplicative, or inefficient totaling $400 billion in annual spending. Since then Washington's response has been to ignore a majority of the austerity recommendations and increase budget spending by $500 billion to create an annual burden of $12,500 for every man, woman and child in America as well as leaving a debt of $60,000 for each one of our children and grandchildren.

FEDERAL RESERVE BOARD: "The Fed" is our central bank wielding enormous control over the nation's purse strings. They can alter the amount of money (money supply) and the cost of money (interest rates).

FIREFIGHTERS COUNTRY CLUB: A lesson in labor union corruption. By NFPA standards, the Gallup NM firefighters union has finagled their way into five fire stations in a town requiring one or two, 49 firefighters when 25 to 35 would suffice, and a fire department budget of $4.3 million when well under $3 million would be appropriate. All that in one of the most impoverished regions in the nation.

FORCED EQUALITY: In contrast to equal opportunity and income inequality, the forced equality of socialism means less opportunity to pursue what makes you individually great.

GANDHI: In the West, Mahatma Gandhi is much admired, however like most socialists he was a moral thinker at heart and not much of an economist. He admitted he would rather see Indians poor under his system than rich in another. Socialism proved to be an economic and political disaster for the emerging republic of India – one which took nearly fifty years to recover.

GLOBAL COMMONS: Global resource domains in which common-pool resources are found, such as the oceans, atmosphere, outer space and

Antarctic. The global appeal for the 'common good' is a convenient way to advance a globalist agenda of regulation by central planners. And what better way for global control than by international regulation of our atmosphere triggered by an invented climate change crisis which is nearly impossible to prove or disprove, and all financed by the $1.5 trillion climate crisis industry.

GLOBALISM: In contrast to capitalist globalization, globalism is the liberal authoritarian notion of central planning taken to the global extreme. We should not think of ourselves as "American citizens" but as "global citizens". Failed expansion of collectivist central government power in the Soviet Union, European Union and United Nations has not stopped liberals in their never-ending neurotic quest for control of others.

GREAT DEPRESSION: One of the favorite arguments of modern liberals is that the Great Depression was somehow caused by an "unfettered" free market in the 1920s. It was rather the excessive government entanglements instigated by the Wilson, Hoover and Roosevelt Administrations, rather than any inherent instability in the private economy, that created, and later prolonged, the Depression.

GREEN JOBS FALLACY: A subgenre of the "government spending brings prosperity" fallacy. After Spain's massive wind and solar projects, they discovered that despite massive taxpayer subsidies, green energy programs destroyed two jobs for every "green job" created. The unavoidable higher energy prices hurt those of lower incomes the worst. This is consistently the consequence of taking money out of the market and redirecting it by state fiat in order to do something in which there is no natural market for.

GREEN/BLUE LAWS: Blue laws are designed to restrict Sunday activities for religious reasons. They have now expanded to nanny state green laws, such as the banning of plastic grocery bags, as the Neo-Puritanical environmental religion shames us into submission.

> **GUN CONTROL:** Russia has one tenth the number of firearms per capita as the US. Their murder rate is three times greater. The only question that needs to be asked is, what happened to the Russian culture that made them so dysfunctional and violent.

GUN CONTROL FAILURE: Facts reveal that gun control exacerbates violent crime: 1. D.C.'s gun ban worsened Washington's homicide rate. 2. Gun bans in Australia and Britain didn't work. 3. The vast majority of mass shootings occur in gun-free zones. 4. There is a clear correlation between higher firearm ownership and reducing police killings. 5. There is a correlation between fewer mass public shootings and higher gun ownership. 6. As the number of guns per person has increased, gun violence has declined. 7. The number of defensive gun uses are higher than the number of criminal firearm uses.

HOPLOPHOBIA: Unlike bogus phobias such as homophobia and Islamophobia, hoplophobia, the morbid irrational fear of guns, is a real, clinically recognizable, and common *complex specific phobia.*

INQUISITION: An official investigation, especially one of a political or religious nature, characterized by lack of regard for individual rights, prejudice on the part of the examiners, and recklessly cruel punishments. Unofficial inquisitions include politically correct witch-hunts and the bullying of identity politics.

INTENTIONAL COMMUNITY or COMMUNE: A planned residential community designed from the start to have a high degree of social cohesion and teamwork. The members typically hold a common social, political, religious or spiritual vision, and often follow an alternative lifestyle. They typically share responsibilities and resources.

INTERVENTIONISM, economic: "Every government interference in the economy consists of giving an unearned benefit, extorted by force, to some men who are deemed victims, at the expense of others. By what criterion of justice is a consensus-government to be guided? By the size of the victim's gang." – **Ayn Rand**

JAWBONING or MORAL SUASION: An unofficial technique of public and private discussions and arm-twisting using one's position of authority, which may work by the implicit threat of future government regulation. The power of the presidency has been used to jawbone businesses and labor.

KEYNESIAN ECONOMICS: The rather pea-brained notion that government can spend its way into economic prosperity. History has repeatedly proven that this is nonsense, including FDR's New Deal.

LABOR UNION GANGS: Another form of collectivism gone awry. Not satisfied with collective bargaining, labor unions often use gang tactics of threats and coercion to get what they want. Don't we teach our children to stand up to bullies and avoid criminal gangs?

LABOR UNION HISTORY: The artificially high wages forced on the economy by compulsory unionism imposed economic hardships on other groups—

particularly on non-union workers and on unskilled labor, which was being squeezed gradually out of the market. Widespread unemployment is partly a result of organized labor's privileges and of allied measures, such as minimum wage laws.

LABOR UNIONISM CONSEQUENCES, FORCED: Right to Work states have 1.3 percent lower unemployment and forced-unionism states have three percent higher wages however the key stats in this issue are 1. The 22 percent higher cost of living in those democrat forced-unionism states and 2. The large migration of population and businesses to Republican RTW states.

Top 25 Political Contributors, 1989–2014

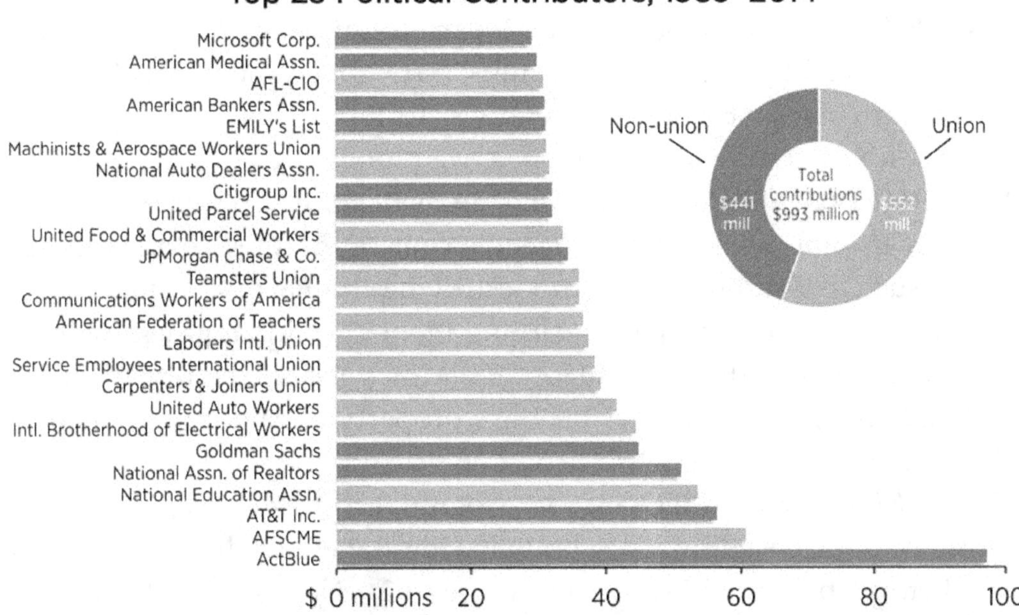

Source: OpenSecrets.org, Center for Responsive Politics, "Heavy Hitters: Top All-Time Donors, 1989–2014." Produced by Veronique de Rugy and Rizqi Rachmat, Mercatus Center at George Mason University, February 28, 2014.

LABOR UNIONS, PUBLIC SECTOR: There is an authoritarian vs market driven ideological difference between public and private unions. Unlike private industry, public unions aren't bargaining against capitalists for a fair cut of the cooperative surplus. They're bargaining against everybody who pays taxes or benefits from government spending. Interest groups fight to grab a bigger share of government revenue. In the private sector, consumers have the right to opt out. With public sector overreach, taxpayers end up forced to bear the cost.

LIBERAL ACADEMIC/MEDIA COMPLEX: A manifestation of class solidarity. Those who commandeer to themselves the production of ideas and dissemination of information develop distinctive interests and perspectives, which lead to what the Marxists used to call "class consciousness". The power of this complex has an ability to push the rest of us in directions dangerous to the national welfare.

LIBERAL AGENDA: "... gratifies various types of pathological dependency; augments primitive feelings of envy and inferiority; reinforces paranoid perceptions of victimization; implements manic delusions of grandeur; exploits government authority for power, domination and revenge; and satisfies infantile claims to entitlement, indulgence and compensation." – **Lyle Rossiter Jr, M.D.,** *The Liberal Mind*

LIBERALISM: 1. Self-righteous elitism 2. Unaccountability 3. Covetousness 4. Collective thought 5. Control of others thru government regulation and political correctness 6. Good intentions trump actual consequences 7. Neurotic escape from reality to satisfy a need for control.

LIBERAL MENTAL DISORDERS: There is an astonishing 76% more therapists per capita in Blue States. **NewsMachete.com** offers these explanations: 1. Phobias, such as fears that they are destroying the Earth 2. Guilt, for being white or male or having a job or earning money 3. Unhappiness with their bodies or sexuality, due to schizophrenia or gender identity disorder 4. Greed and envy, towards other people's property 5. Anger towards people of different genders or races

LIBERAL NEUROSES TRIFECTA: 1. Cognitive Dissonance; the mental discomfort experienced by a person who simultaneously holds two or more contradictory beliefs, ideals and values. 2. Narcissistic Rage; when grandiose self-worth, vanity and entitlement are challenged (narcissistic injury), either explosive or passive-aggressive rage may ensue. 3. Psychological Projection; projecting one's personal malevolence unto a perceived enemy, achieving a release from guilt and shame, and a recommitment to virtue signaling and slandering of non-liberal realists. – **Chateau Heartiste**

LIMOUSINE AND LATTE LIBERALS: Pejoratives used to illustrate hypocrisy of the liberal elite. They would take away our freedoms yet consider themselves exempt from mass transit, high mpg vehicles, gun control and public schools for their children. Broadly similar to the English "champagne socialist", the French "gauche caviar", the German "salonkommunist" and the Italian "radical chic".

LOBBYING: Any attempt by individuals or private interest groups to influence business and government leaders to create legislation or channel an activity that will help a particular organization. Lobbyists for "foreign principals" are required to register with the US government.

MARXISM: The collectivist liberal ideology of force and coercion behind the curtain of political correctness while manipulating the strings of its authoritarian offspring; socialism, communism, statism, fascism and progressivism.

MARXISM, BARNYARD: The view that all wealth is theft, that there is no essential difference between making money in the marketplace and robbing a bank. All your sorrows are the fault of a designated one percent, such as the Jews. It is rhetoric designed to divide.

MEDICAID-MEDICARE unintended consequences: Prior to Medicaid, low-income individuals had 4.3 doctor visits a year, high-income individuals had 5.1 – the poor were doing quite well in securing health care. Reduced cost or pro bono services provided by doctors showed a dramatic decline with the introduction of Medicaid though, and the stimulation of demand from Medicaid-Medicare played a huge role in raising health care costs overall. Natural market systems were undermined that would have lowered costs and increased consumption of medical services.

MINIMUM WAGE LAWS, unintended consequences: 1. Increased unemployment among teenagers, racial minorities and unskilled labor 2. Price inflation 3. Small business suffers to the benefit of big business. Economist **Thomas Sowell** puts it this way, "The real minimum wage is always zero, regardless of the laws, and that is the wage that many workers receive in the wake of the creation or escalation of a government-mandated minimum wage, because they lose their jobs or fail to find jobs when they enter the labor force."

MONOPOLY: The exclusive possession or control of the supply or trade in a commodity or service. Every coercive monopoly was created by government intervention into the economy: by special privileges, such as franchises or subsidies, which closed the entry of competitors into a given field, by legislative action. The most monopolistic institution that has ever existed is the US government. That may be why federal worker salary and benefits average well over $120,000, double the private-sector average of just over $60,000, according to the Bureau of Economic Analysis.

MOONBATTERY: "The roots of liberalism — and its associated madness — can be clearly identified by understanding how children develop from infancy to adulthood and how distorted development produces the irrational beliefs of the liberal mind. When the modern liberal mind whines about imaginary victims, rages against imaginary villains and seeks above all else to run the lives of persons competent to run their own lives, the neurosis of the liberal mind becomes painfully obvious." - **Lyle Rossiter, The Liberal Mind: The Psychological Causes of Political Madness**. . . Basically, liberalism is a willful failure to mature beyond adolescence that can have catastrophic consequences for society.

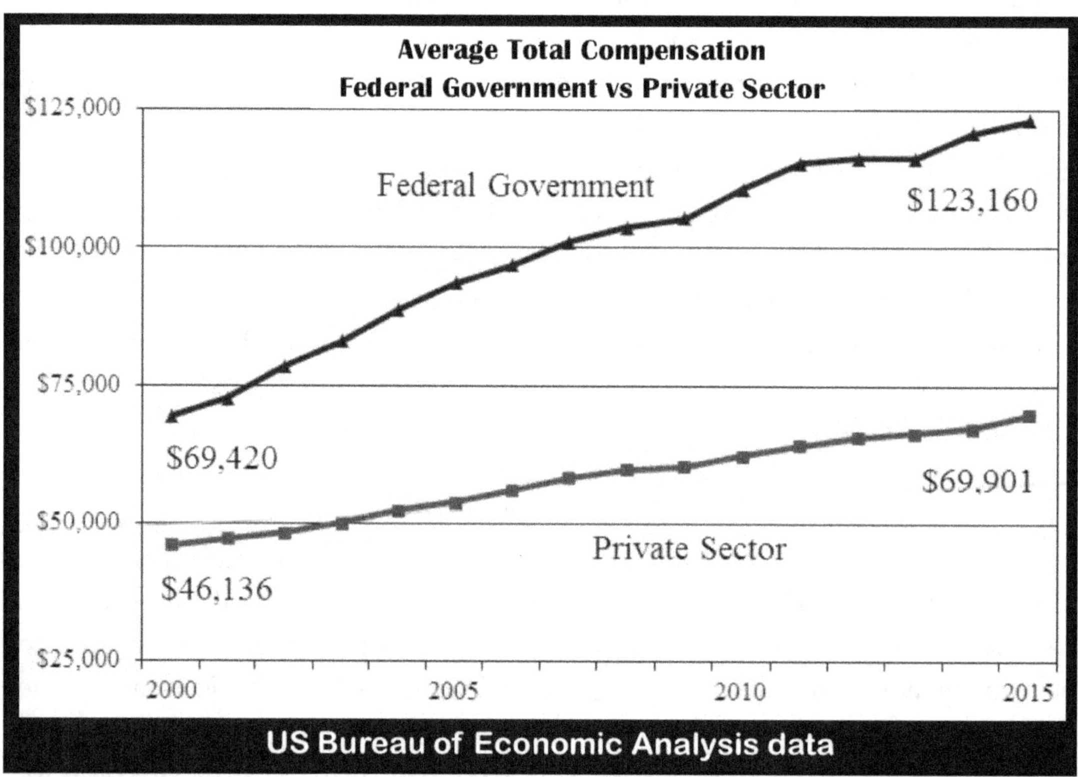

MULTILATERALISM: The process of organizing relations between groups of three or more states. After WWII multilateralism was first projected as humanitarian and prudent, yet actually became the foundation of a new globalist scenario with the ultimate goal of suppression of U.S. nationalism and sovereignty.

NARCISSISTIC PERSONALITY DISORDER: NPD is a mental disorder in which people have an inflated sense of their own importance, a deep need for admiration and a lack of empathy for others. But behind this mask of ultra-confidence lies a fragile self-esteem that's vulnerable to the slightest criticism. Both Presidents Obama and Trump are considered in psychiatric circles to display NPD. Many dictators and criminals such as Adolf Hitler, Joseph Stalin and Saddam Hussein had or have NPD.

NATIONALIZATION: The process of a government taking control of a company or industry, which generally occurs without compensation for the loss of the net worth of the seized assets and potential income. Nationalization is more common in developing countries. Privatization, which is the transfer of government-run operations into the private business, occurs more frequently in developed countries. – **Investopedia**

NAZI: For all those misinformed and indoctrinated liberals and millennials out there who believe Hitler was a right-winger, let's be clear, Nazi stands for National SOCIALIST German Workers Party. Under the fascist-Nazi axis, the government officials held the economic, legal and political power of life or death over the citizens.

NANNY STATE: a.k.a. busybody politics. Politicians, bureaucrats and citizen boards know more about how to live your life, manage your health, and raise your kids than you do. Mandatory recycling? No thanks.

NEOCONSERVATIVE or NEOCON: Essentially an interventionist foreign policy.

NEO-MCCARTHYISM: Unlike its predecessor, the new age witch-hunts are coming from self-professed liberals and their media outlets, which betray a fundamental democratic principle – protecting, even encouraging, free speech in the form of minority opinions. This is having a predictably chilling effect as young scholars and journalists are worrying whether they should be cautious in what they write and say publicly for the sake of their careers.

NEW DEAL FAILURE: FDR's New Deal was the largest real-world test of the Keynesian spending myth in recent history. FDR's Treasury Secretary put it this way, "We have tried spending money. We are spending more than we have ever spent before and it does not work. We have just as much unemployment as when we started and an enormous debt to boot."

NIMBY: Not In My Back Yard. Typically exposes the hypocrisy of latte liberals - "I'm all for low-come housing, half-way houses, homeless shelters, abortion clinics, wind turbines, cannabis dispensaries etc., but.........". The NIMBY concept may also be applied to people who advocate some proposal (e.g., tax increases, immigration or energy conservation) but oppose implementing it in a way that might affect their lives or require any sacrifice on their part.

OIKOPHOBIA: The liberal elite find America and our Constitution revolting. Whereas xenophobia is fear of the alien, oikophobia is fear of the familiar and is at the heart of progressive statist anti-American sentiment. It is the disposition in any conflict to side with "them" against "us", and the felt need to denigrate the customs, culture and institutions that are identifiably "ours". Oikophobia is further fostered by politically correct Cultural Marxism. Call it snobbery or adolescent arrested development, in America the elitist "oiks" envision themselves as an intellectual aristocracy and defenders of enlightened universalism.

ONE PERCENT, The: The target of collectivists is the successful wealthy elite which make up a small percentage of society. Socialist Adolf Hitler's one percent was the Jews. Bernie Sanders' perceived one percent that he would like to jail is Wall Street which he scapegoats for the government-created sub-prime mortgage crisis and 2008 economic collapse.

ONE PERCENT, The real: Compensation for federal civilian workers averaged $120,000 in 2014, which was 78 percent higher than the private sector average of $67,000 (Cato Institute). The non-defense, non-postal service part of the federal government comprises about 1.37 percent of the total US workforce. The pay disparity creates a perverse incentive to work for the government, attracting good talent away from the private sector.

OVERHEAD SMASH: "'The overhead smash' is my phrase for the tendency of regulations to add to overhead — the fixed costs of doing business — which smashes smaller competitors while protecting the big guys. In the food safety realm, small farms are begging to be exempted from these rules that only big farms can afford." - **Timothy P Carney**

PARIS CLIMATE AGREEMENT BENEFITS: Using the Model for the Assessment of Greenhouse Gas Induced Climate Change developed by researchers at the National Center for Atmospheric Research, even if all CO_2 emissions in the US were effectively eliminated, there would less than two-tenths of a degree Celsius reduction in global temperatures. In fact, the entire industrialized world could cut carbon emissions down to zero, and the climate impact would still be less than four-tenths of a degree Celsius in terms of averted warming by the year 2100. – **Heritage Foundation**

PARIS CLIMATE AGREEMENT CONSEQUENCES: Impacts on the American economy one could expect by 2035; an annual average shortfall of nearly 400,000 jobs; a total income loss of more than $20,000 for a family of four; an aggregate GDP loss of over $2.5 trillion; and increases in household electricity expenditures between 13 percent and 20 percent. – **Heritage Foundation**

POLITICAL RELIGION: Government ideologies attain power equivalent to those of a state religion, with which they often exhibit significant similarities in both theory and practice. These include fascism, socialism, environmentalism and Islamic fundamentalism.

PORK BARREL: Political patronage, which is the use of state resources to reward individuals for their political support. Pork barrel is government as a source of handouts that redistribute money from hard-working people to those who avoid work.

PRE-EXISTING CONDITIONS PARADOX: "Providing health care for people with preexisting conditions is the equivalent of selling somebody a homeowner's policy for a hundred dollars while the fire is burning their house down. It just doesn't happen, yet in health care we're doing it. And it screws up all of the actuarials. . . You just can't do it because you're not talking insurance on preexisting conditions; you're talking welfare." – **Rush Limbaugh**.... The paradox is that you must force everyone to buy health insurance: Otherwise, people would wait until they got sick and buy policies knowing that the insurance companies could not turn them down or charge them extra.

PROFESSOR VALUES: Similar to Hollywood and media values, professors' common value system typically includes liberal beliefs, social justice activism, censorship, historical revisionism, anti-patriotism, anti-Americanism, anti-Christian, and anti-capitalism.

PROGRESSIVE TAXES: Takes a larger percentage of income from high income groups than from low income groups and is based on the concept of ability to pay. The US has the most progressive income tax in the world.

PROGRESSIVISM: Who would ever be opposed to progress? However, progressivism is politically correct for socialism, collectivism, economic fascism and statism. It is an ideology that favors the use of government action - the police power of the State - to promote socioeconomic values.

When you hear "progressive" think of continuous and insidious expansion of government.

PRO-LABOR LEGISLATION: The Davis-Bacon Act of 1931 required all federally funded construction pay to be at "locally prevailing wages". This effectively allowed federal contracts to be awarded to the more experienced white unions. The Family and Medical Leave Act of 1993 brought about lower salaries, particularly of young married women.

PROTECTIONISM: It's a scientifically and mathematically provable fact that all tariffs, at any time and in any country, will harm economic growth, eliminate net jobs, destroy prosperity, and lower the standard of living of the protectionist country because tariffs are guaranteed by the ironclad laws of economics to generate costs to consumers that outweigh the benefits to producers. – **Mark J Perry, AEI**

PUBLIC CHOICE THEORY: The study of political behavior. Public choice economics assumes that government figures are merely human. They should be expected to look out for themselves rather than to act as saintly public stewards.

PUBLIC INTEREST: "Since there is no such entity as 'the public' and since the public is merely a number of individuals, any claimed or implied conflict of 'the public interest' with private interests means that the interests of some men are to be sacrificed to the interests and wishes of others." – **Ayn Rand**

PUBLIC SECTOR CRONY UNIONISM: Literally a conspiracy between politicians, bureaucrats, and labor unions to create and sustain a fourth branch of government specifically designed to increase the cost, size, and power of government. Now that unions have laid much of the private sector to waste the share of unions members are increasingly coming from the public sector. We in effect get government employees using government funds to campaign for the expansion of government.

PUBLIC/CIVIL SERVANTS: Nice work if you can get it. Public servants are employees of the state protected from the ravages of the commercial world by contracts written by other civil servants and featuring minimal working hours, maximum holidays and generous pensions all at the expense of taxpayers who actually produce things in the private sector. In theory, the government serves as servants of taxpayers, rather than authoritarian masters.

PUBLIC WORKS: Diverts capital from the private sector for wasteful massive government spending projects, with the unintended consequence of inhibiting healthy job creation. As the economy recovered during the Great Depression, FDR's New Deal spending programs on public works created a double-dip depression.

RATIONING HEALTH CARE: Rationing denotes allocating essential resources in situations of scarcity, usually in an absolute limitation in supply, or when high production costs or excessive demand for consumption limits supply. In a free market rationing seldom occurs. It is when government intervenes that demand increases, costs skyrocket, supplies become limited, quality of service declines, and rationing occurs, as evidenced by our Medicaid, Medicare, VA and Indian Health Services. "Death panels" are another term for health care rationing.

REGRESSIVE TAX: A tax that takes a larger percentage from low-income people than from high-income people. A regressive tax is generally a tax that is applied uniformly. This means that it hits lower-income individuals harder. Examples are gas tax, cigarette tax, environmental surcharge and solar power incentives.

REGULATION vs PROTECTION: Regulation denotes a "law, rule, or other order prescribed by authority, especially to regulate conduct." Protection is defined as "the act of protecting or the state of being protected; preservation from injury or harm." Regulation is coercive, perhaps punitive; protection is warm and fuzzy. "Environmental protections" is merely politically correct for "environmental regulations". Most regulations only protect the powers and control of government to limit our freedoms.

REGULATORY CAPTURE: "Industrial farms and major food processors hire the best lobbyists and thus get a seat at the table when the FDA writes the rules. Thus, the biggest players in the regulated industry have "captured" the agency that regulates them." – **Timothy P Carney**

RELIGION OF SOCIALISM: Brings back religion from heaven to earth - the utopian paradise. Socialism looks beyond to another and a higher social life in this world through whose ultimate possibilities the socialist finds his ideal, his religion. The problem is, morality is defined as "whatever advances the cause". It is a morality play without the morals. The French Revolution, Italian fascism, Nazi Germany and the Soviet Union are all examples of socialist religions.

RENT CONTROL: Setting a government cap on apartment rental rates has the unintended consequence of housing shortages. Rent control laws stymie a city's long-term growth because few developers want to build apartments that can be rented only at below-market prices. Controls also encourage landlords to reduce their maintenance costs so quality suffers and "slumlords" are created. Landlords are also less likely to rent to "disadvantaged" groups.

RESERVATION SOCIALISM: Private property on tribal land is not recognized nor can one buy or sell land, resulting in substandard housing. Capitalism is considered threatening and businesses are reluctant to bring investments onto reservations resulting in most monies spent elsewhere. The myth of communalism is accepted and successful entrepreneurs are ostracized as sell-outs. Those who have jobs usually work for the public sector. Those who don't have jobs subsist on welfare handouts that provide basic food. Sovereignty is claimed however in reality power and authority comes from an authoritarian federal government led by the Bureau of Indian Affairs and distinguished by a long history of corruption and no independent court system. There is also a free health care system and free access to education.

> **REUSABLE GROCERY BAGS:** Sticky, smelly, filthy, cloth bag carriers of bacteria and viruses which waste more energy and resources than thin polybags. They are made with plastic in China and shipped thousands of miles overseas. Nanny state control freaks love them.

REVOLVING DOOR: The movement of high level employees from public sector jobs to private sector jobs, and vice versa. Many legislators and regulators become consultants for the industries they once regulated and some private industry heads receive government appointments that relate to their former private posts. Opponents point to the many, many opportunities for conflicts of interest. - **Investopedia**

SHADOW GOVERNMENT: Sometimes conspiracies really exist. An insurgency of sorts, a shadow govt, secret govt, invisible govt cryptocracy where actual political power resides not with elected representatives but with private individuals in contact with bureaucrats behind the scenes.

SHARIA LAW HUMAN RIGHTS: As is practiced in many Muslim countries today, Islamic Sharia law is clearly incompatible with the Universal Declaration of Human Rights. Islamic intellectuals envision Islam as simply a penal code, and an Islamic state, a penal colony, which enforces the "pure" Islam. "Instead of Islam being a moral vision given to humanity, it becomes constructed into the antithesis of the West. In the world constructed by these groups, there is no Islam; there is only opposition to the West." – **Khaled Abou El Fadl, US Islamic reformer.**

SMART-GROWTH: Development and conservation strategies intended to protect our health and environment, however the efforts—often described as "New Urbanism," "sustainable development," or "open land preservation"—have long been resisted by some members of the community due to their negative impact on economic growth, competitiveness, and the nation's standard of living. Communities implementing smart-growth policies have significantly higher home prices, which precludes moderate-income households from homeownership. In turn, these high home prices have forced buyers to take on excessive levels of mortgage debt, which contributed to the default and foreclosure problems that led to the recession. – **Heritage Foundation**.... Taken to the extreme, smart-growth is Agenda 21.

SOCIAL CONTRACT FALLACY: A common argument among advocates of a larger role of government in our lives is the idea of the "social contract". The idea is that as a "society", we are all obliged to help our "fellow man", and therefore the State, supposedly representing society, has authority over the individual. A contract implies a mutually agreed upon arrangement yet the State lays claim to certain authorities over myself and individuals by force and threat of force, not thru a mutual agreement on our part.

SOCIALISM: The politically incorrect synonym for collectivist "social justice" and contemporary "progressivism", as well as today's Democratic Party system of choice. The essential characteristic of socialism is the denial of individual property rights. Instead of prosperity, socialism has brought economic paralysis and/or collapse to every country that tried it.

SOCIALISM AS MODERN-DAY SLAVERY: Communism enslaves men by force, socialism by vote. Freedom of speech, freedom of the press, democracy, freedom of religion and freedom of association cannot exist in the absence of a free market economy. If a man cannot keep the fruits of his labor, if the government has full control over his economic activity – that man is nothing but a slave. Every increase of government's economic power comes at the expense of individual liberty with less freedom of choice left to the individual.

SOCIALISM'S COMMON CHARACTERISTICS: Everybody has a different definition of socialism, however there are common characteristics; love of big government, nationalization of industry, massive taxation, and redistribution of wealth.

SOCIALIST FAMINES: Our belief that famine is caused by drought is wrong. Rather, famines come about when political systems fail to encourage agriculture and distribution successfully. And those political failures have a pattern: they occur in centralized, authoritarian systems. Free market economies do not produce famines. – **Amartya Sen, economist**

SOCIALIST LABORATORY: What is the longest running socialist experiment? Modern socialism began in America, on Indian reservations. They had as a goal to keep the native population in poverty, impotent and dependent on government. For some reason, textbooks do not offer a page or two on the corruption, the bureaucratization, and the multigenerational poverty created by tribal-run socialism.

SOCIALIST POLLUTION: Socialist countries have experienced the most widespread pollution on Earth. Where property is communally or governmentally owned and treated as a free resource, those resources inevitably become over-and-misused with little regard for future consequences – a "tragedy of the commons". The failure of legal institutions to enforce property rights was at one time a problem in the US, not the free enterprise system.

SOCIAL JUSTICE: The distribution or redistribution of wealth, opportunities or privileges in a society. Social justice is a euphemism for an economic mugging by political force. It is punitive not restorative. . . "While democracy seeks equality in liberty, socialism seeks equality in restraint and servitude." – **Tocqueville**.

SOCIETAL COLLAPSE: The fall or disintegration of human societies including abrupt societal failures such as the Mayan Civilization as well as gradual declines like the fall of the Western Roman Empire and Soviet Union. Government central planning overreach and disintegration of cultural mores (fundamental moral values) are typical catalysts.

SPAIN'S GREEN DISASTER: In 2000 Spain began their subsidized renewable energy programs. Their electricity prices increased by 92% from 2005 to 2011 driving low income Spaniards into energy poverty. An estimated 2.2 jobs were destroyed for each green job created. Each green job cost taxpayers $770,000. Only one of ten of the green jobs were permanent. Spain's unemployment rate peaked at 26% in 2013, up from 7.9% in 2007. Spain's CO2 emissions still increased by 35% from 1994 to 2011.

STATE SOVEREIGNTY vs CENTRAL AUTHORITY: The Founding Fathers created a 'union' of States only for the benefit of mutual protection against foreign threats, but no one was willing to grant a new central authority (federal) taxing and war-making power without restrictions; nor for regulation of commerce. State sovereignty was to be jealously protected. The Founding Fathers must be rolling over in their graves.

STATISM: "The political expression of altruism is collectivism or statism, which holds that man's life and work belong to the state—to society, to the group, the gang, the race, the nation—and that the state may dispose of him in any way it pleases for the sake of whatever it deems to be its own tribal, collective good." – **Ayn Rand**

STATOLATRY: The worship of the State analogous to idolatry. "He who says the state is God, deifies arms and prisons. The worship of the state is the worship of force. There is no more dangerous menace to civilization than a government of incompetent, corrupt, or vile men. The worst evils which mankind ever had to endure were inflicted by bad governments." – **Ludwig von Mises**

STIMULUS PACKAGE 2009: The trillion-dollar ARRA American Recovery and Reinvestment Act had horrific results; a declining work force, extremely weak GDP growth, increased child poverty, a continued-weakening housing market, and a "green economy" that wasted $billions in green energy and electric car boondoggles and fraud - all that while creating massive debt. "Shovel-ready" became a cruel hoax. Well-to-do public sector unions, wealthy Obama supporters, and Democrat donors were recipients of large benefits. In the end, the stimulus package turned out to be a massive partisan wealth transfer.

SUB-PRIME MORTGAGE CRISIS: The housing bubble bust coinciding with the 2008 economic collapse initiated by Presidents Carter and Clinton's Community Reinvestment Act which encouraged irresponsible mortgage loans to those who could not afford them; all done in the name of "fairness" and "equal opportunity". The economic collapse had far less to do with Wall Street banking than government regulation.

SUBSIDY: Money that is paid usually by a government to keep the price of a product or service low or to help a business or organization to continue to function. Subsidies are components of corporate welfare, crony corporatism and progressive statism.

SWEDEN SOCIALISM EXPERIMENT: Sweden was built on capitalism however from 1970 until 1989, taxes rose exorbitantly, killing private initiative, while entitlements became excessive. As a consequence, Sweden endured two decades of low growth. In 1991-93, the country suffered a severe crash in real estate and banking that reduced GDP by six percent. Public spending had surged to 71.7 percent of GDP in 1993, and the budget deficit reached eleven percent of GDP. Austerity measures and a non-socialist government returned Sweden to prosperity.

TENURE: The status of holding one's position on a permanent basis without periodic contract renewals. It is a teacher's dream that allows them to conduct their classes however they so desire without worry of being fired. The private sector's average tenure is half that of public service.

TITLE IX: The 1972 law that prevents gender-based discrimination for student athletes. Finally, women had the equal opportunity to compete for sports on a level playing field with the men – you would have thought. What actually happened was women did not have to compete with the men but were given special treatment to compete apart from men since women are not equal to men athletically. Unintended consequences included physical education classes cut to fund women's sports which do not create revenue. Many men's low revenue sports were dropped as well.

TOTALITARIAN RELIGIOSITY: Totalitarianism represents the twentieth-century version of traditional religiosity; it is in many ways the secular equivalent of the religious life.... This "totalitarian religiosity" continues as a secular, politico-centric faith, disdainful of theistic beliefs and contemptuous of those who subscribe to them. It is a faith that, in its historical manifestations, has birthed the murderous tyrannies of the extended twentieth century -- tyrannies that have marched under left-wing banners of Marxism, Communism, and National Socialism, or, more generally and descriptively, Coercive Collectivism. - **Bruce A Riggs, Leftism: A Radical Faith**

TRIBALISM: The product of collectivism. If men are unable to reason, and they accept the notion that the individual is helpless, they will seek to join some group—any group—which claims the ability to lead them and to provide some sort of knowledge acquired by some sort of unspecified means.

TYRANNY: "Tyranny is any political system that does not recognize individual rights (which necessarily include property rights). The overthrow of a political system by force is justified only when it is directed against tyranny: it is an act of self-defense against those who rule by force. For example, the American Revolution." – **Ayn Rand**

UNITED NATIONS: "Psychologically, the U.N. has contributed a great deal to the gray swamp of demoralization which is swallowing the Western world. But communists and brutal dictators have gained a moral sanction, a stamp of civilized respectability from the Western world—they have gained the West's assistance in deceiving their victims—they have gained the status and prestige of equal partners, thus establishing the notion that the difference between human rights and mass slaughter is merely a difference of political opinion." – **Ayn Rand**

> **UTOPIA:** An imagined place in which everything is perfect or an impractical scheme for social improvement. It is the paradise envisioned by early 19th century socialists – their heaven on earth.

VALUE-ADDED TAX: Simply put, a sales tax. It is based on a taxpayer's consumption of goods rather than his income.

VAWA: Violence Against Women Act, 1994: **Penny Nance, CEO of Concerned Women for America**, had this to say about VAWA in 2013; "Women are 62 times more likely to be assaulted by live-in boyfriends than by their husbands. If liberal feminists behind VAWA really cared about the well-being of women, then they would be America's biggest proponents of marriage between a man and a woman…. The sad truth is they don't seem to have made enough of a difference to justify the $400 million annual cost to taxpayers…. One DOJ official stated that they have no evidence to date that VAWA has led to a decrease in the overall violence against women."

WILSON'S 'WAR SOCIALISM': Woodrow Wilson embraced authoritarian fascism, what he called "war socialism"; elites imposing order, using crisis as pretext, and cult of personality as the vehicle. World War I was the crisis needed to impose a despotic order on America. His Sedition Act forbade virtually all criticism of the government.

"The enduring notion that experts could plan the economy from Washington was largely born in Wilson's 'war socialism'." – **Jonah Goldberg**

ZOMBIE COMPANY a.k.a. LEMON SOCIALISM: A situation which is in an economy where failing companies continue to operate with government support but cannot stand on their own, needing bailouts in order to operate, effectively putting them on never-ending life support. The common wisdom is that state-run zombie companies drain the vitality from their private counterparts thus stifling many economies such as the UK, Japan, South Korea and China.

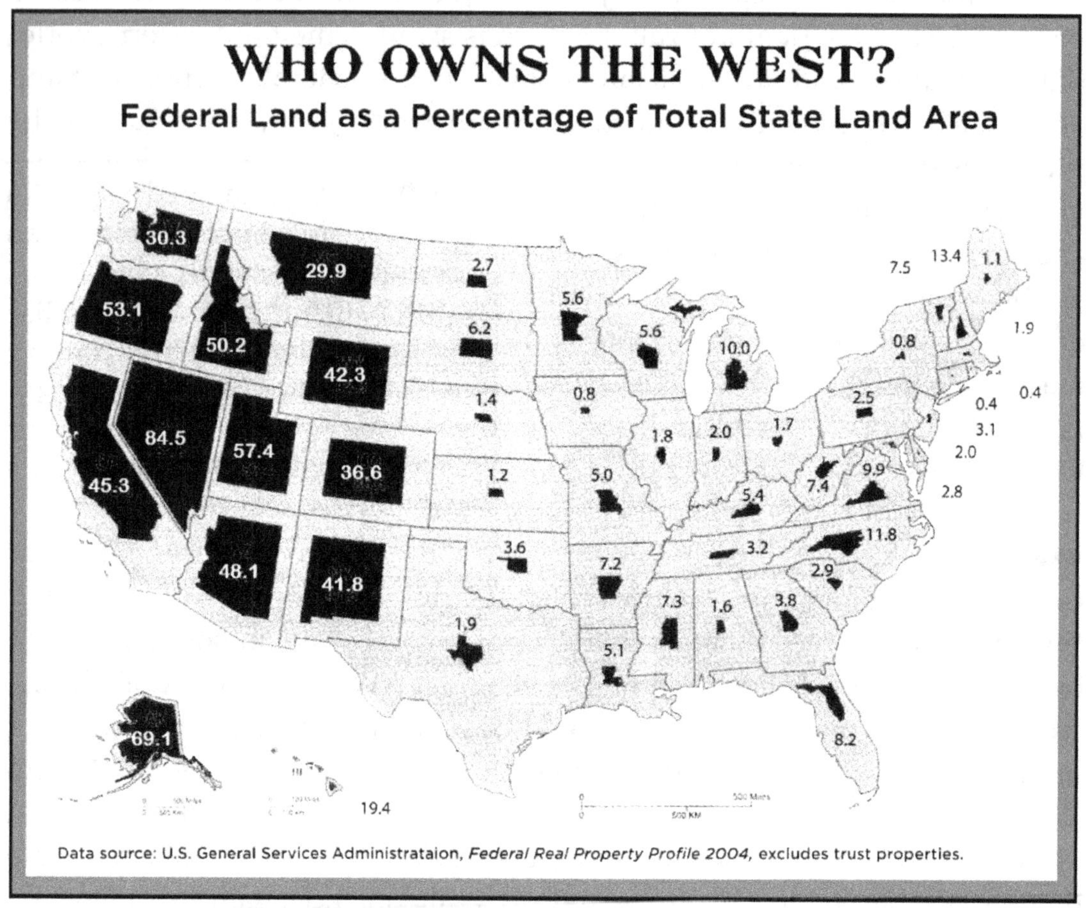

ConservaLexicon

CHAPTER THREE

RESPONSIBILITY

Improper Payments from High-Error Federal Programs

	$ billions	improper payment rate
Medicare Fee-for-Service	$43.3	12.1%
Medicaid	$29.1	9.8%
Earned Income Tax Credit	$15.6	23.8%
Medicare Advantage (Part C)	$14.1	9.5%
Retirement, Survivors, and Disability Insurance (RSDI)	$5.0	0.6%
Supplemental Security Income (SSI)	$4.8	8.4%
Unemployment Insurance (UI)	$3.5	10.7%
Supplemental Nutrition Assistance Program (SNAP)	$2.6	3.7%
Medicare Prescription Drug Benefit (Part D)	$2.2	3.6%
National School Lunch Program (NSLP)	$1.8	15.7%
Rental Housing Assistance Programs	$1.3	4.0%
Federal Direct (Education) Loan Program	$1.3	1.3%
School Breakfast	$0.9	23.0%
Pell Grants	$0.6	1.9%
Children's Health Insurance Program (CHIP)	$0.6	6.8%
Crop Insurance Program	$0.3	2.2%

MERCATUS CENTER
George Mason University

Data note: High-error programs are those programs that reported roughly $750 million or more in improper payments in a given year.
Source: OMB via paymentaccuracy.gov, "High-Error Programs," accessed May 25, 2016.
Produced by Veronique de Rugy and Jason Fichtner, May 2016.

Quotes

Insights on unintended consequences of government handouts back in 1766; "I am for doing good to the poor, but I differ in opinion of the means. I think the best way of doing good to the poor, is not making them easy in poverty, but leading or driving them out of it. In my youth I traveled much, and I observed in different countries, that the more public provisions were made for the poor, the less they provided for the themselves, and of course became poorer. And, on the contrary, the less was done for them, the more they did for themselves, and became richer." – **Benjamin Franklin**

"That government is best which governs the least, because its people discipline themselves." – **Thomas Jefferson**

"Originality and the feeling of one's own dignity are achieved only through work and struggle." – **Fyodor Dostoevsky**

"Most people do not really want freedom, because freedom involves responsibility, and most people are frightened of responsibility." – **Sigmund Freud**

"All growth depends on activity. There is no development physically or intellectually without effort, and effort means work." – **Calvin Coolidge**

"People love chopping wood. In this activity one immediately sees results." – **Albert Einstein**

"Continued dependence on relief induces a spiritual and moral disintegration fundamentally destructive to the national fiber. To dole out relief in this way is to administer a narcotic, a subtle destroyer of the human spirit." – **Franklin Roosevelt**, in the midst of the Great Depression

"Remember that a government big enough to give you everything you want is also big enough to take away everything you have." – **Barry Goldwater**

"You cannot simultaneously have free immigration and a welfare state". – **Milton Friedman**

"People have got the entitlements too much in mind, without the obligations. There's no such thing as entitlement, unless someone has first met an obligation." – **Margaret Thatcher**

"Shovel-ready wasn't as shovel-ready as we expected." – **Barack Obama**

"The black family survived centuries of slavery and generations of Jim Crow, but it has disintegrated in the wake of the liberals' expansion of the welfare state." – **Thomas Sowell**

"The welfare state has always been judged by its good intentions, rather than its bad results." – **Thomas Sowell**

"A hero is someone who understands the responsibility that comes with his freedom." – **Bob Dylan**

"Liberalism is a philosophy of sniveling brats... The second item in the liberal creed, after self-righteousness, is unaccountability." – **P J O'Rourke**

"If you are taught bitterness and anger than you will believe you are a victim. You will feel aggrieved and the twin brother of aggrievement is entitlement. So now you think you are owed something and you don't have to work for it, and now you're on a really bad road to nowhere because there are people who will play to that sense of victimhood, aggrievement and entitlement, and you still won't have a job. – **Condi Rice**

"Family has always been the first line of defense against the state. Our connection with ancestors, and our concern for progeny, forms a story in which the state is not the main character." – **Jeff Deist, president of the Mises Institute**

"The recipe for enlightenment is nine parts elbow grease to one part navel-gazing." – **Joe Schaller**

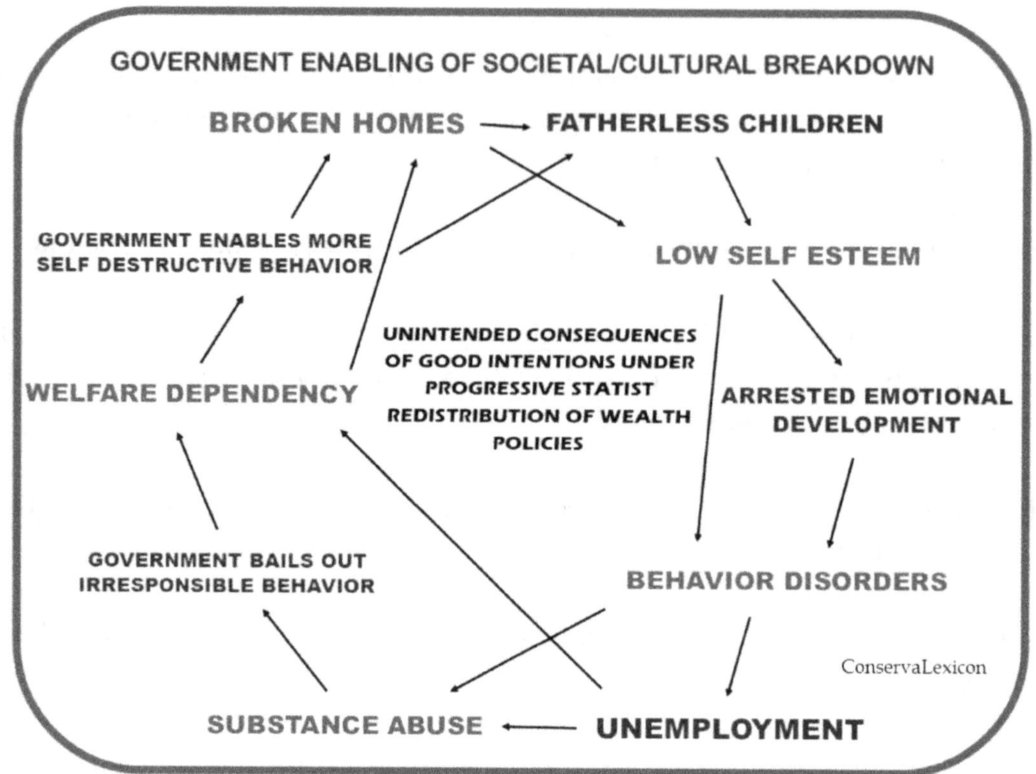

ABSTINENCE: No sexual contact of any kind – 100% effective in preventing pregnancy and STIs. Abstinence may encourage people to build relationships in other ways – there are ways to be intimate with someone that don't involve sexual activity.

ADDICTION BRAIN-DISEASE FALLACY: If addiction is truly a disease, then in some ways it is out of our control and forecloses choices, however a disease is a medical condition that develops outside of our control; it is, then, not a matter of choice. In the absence of choice, the addicted person is essentially relieved of responsibility. The brain-disease model obscures the dimension of choice in addiction, the capacity to respond to incentives, as well as the essential fact people use drugs for reasons.

AFFORDABLE HOUSING FALLACY: Many believe that government intervention is necessary to ensure "affordable" housing, however Thomas Sowell believes government is the problem, not the solution, and destroys the notion with evidence: 1) People paid smaller percentages of their income for housing before the era of government intervention; 2) housing prices rose sharply when more pervasive government regulation began; 3) housing prices in areas with more government intervention rose more rapidly than in areas with less; and 4) growing population and income did not result in far higher housing prices where builders were allowed to construct more housing. – *Economic Facts and Fallacies*

ALCOHOLISM SPONTANEOUS REMISSION or NATURAL RECOVERY: Every illness has a spontaneous remission rate. For the common cold it is 100 percent. The NIAAA and Harvard University report 75 to 80 percent of people recovering from alcohol dependency do so without seeking any kind of help including specialty alcohol rehab programs and AA.

BENEFIT SOCIETIES: Prior to the introduction of socialist safety nets, societal security was provided by extended families, churches, local community and fraternal benefit societies. Benefit societies and fraternal orders were organizations or voluntary associations which provided mutual aid and insurance for members experiencing difficulties. Government safety nets have proven to contribute to the breakdown of society by rewarding irresponsible behavior.

BIRTHRIGHT: A right or privilege to which a person is entitled by birth. For thousands of years around the world, a child had a birthright to be raised by their biological mother and father, thus preserving the foundation of society, the nuclear family. This all came to an end with the rise of welfare state safety nets which enabled the breakdown of the family resulting in sixty percent of children in the US raised in broken homes.

BLEEDING HEART or DO-GOODER: A person who is considered excessively sympathetic toward those who claim to be underprivileged or exploited. Do-gooder methods do not always create the positive outcomes intended. The transfer of money from one group of people to another is usually the outcome.

BROKEN HOME TRAUMA: Research of 8,000 children between age five and 16 by the UK Dept. of Health in 2004 found that broken home children were five times more likely to suffer mental troubles. The findings showed that two parents are much better than one and that children's family backgrounds are as important – if not more so – then whether their home is poor, workless, has bad health, or has no one without any educational qualifications.

CHILD-REARING: Fulfillment of a child's birthright to be raised by their biological mother and father. Once considered to be one of the most challenging as well as rewarding duties, it is now regarded by liberals and pseudo-feminists as demeaning to a mother.

CLOWARD-PIVEN STRATEGY: In 1966 a couple of political activist professors outlined a strategy for overloading the welfare system to "create a crisis". Their goal was a new national system of "a guaranteed annual income and thus an end to poverty". LBJ's War on Poverty was a good start to the process and it appears that President Obama continued the progressive efforts for a destruction of wealth and collapse of our economic system.

CODEPENDENCY: The idea of being overly involved in another person's life-- having a constant preoccupation with the other person's behavior and feeling unnecessarily guilty when not taking care of the other person's needs. Government codependency feeds the welfare addict's needs while feeding their own addictive need to spend.

COLLEGE IMPOTENCE: Former US secretary of education Bill Bennett determined that only 150 of the nation's 3500 universities are worth the cost and provide an adequate return on investment. "We have about 21 million people in higher education, and about half the people who start four-year colleges don't finish. Those who do finish, who graduated in 2011 – half were either unemployed or radically underemployed or in debt."

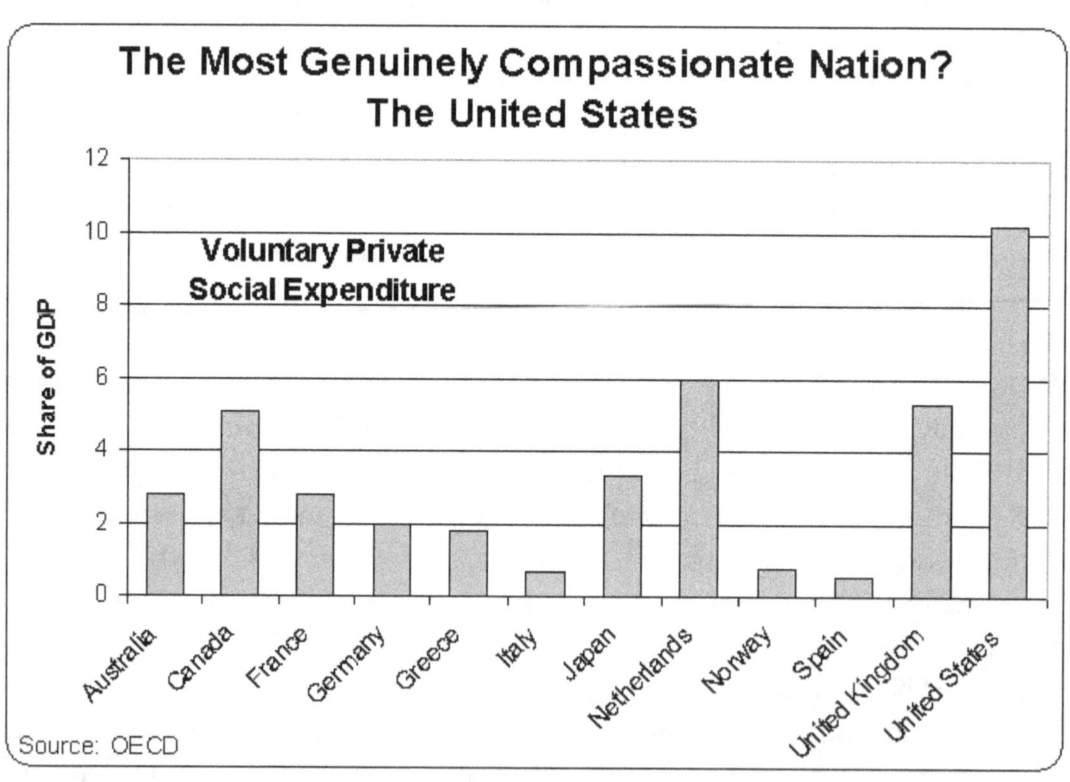

COLLEGE REVENUE THEORY OF COSTS: The idea that colleges and universities exploit all sources of revenue made available to them, and bump up spending to match whatever funds they can raise – if colleges can spend more they will spend more. As a consequence, universities devote less than half of their core spending to actual instruction, with the remainder devoured by research and administration expenses. Unlimited student loans act as a spending enabler.

COMPASSIONATE AMERICA: If you look at rates of "voluntary private social expenditure" among nations, it turns out Americans are easily the most generous people in the developed world. We are so generous that our voluntary giving amounts to 10.2 percent of gross domestic product. The only other nations that even crack 5 percent of GDP are the Netherlands, Canada, and the UK. Most of the supposedly compassionate welfare states have dismal levels of charitable giving. Voluntary social expenditure in major European nations such as France, Germany, Italy, and Spain averages less than 2 percent of GDP. – **Cato.org**

CORPORATE WELFARE QUEEN: Welfare queen refers to people who are accused of collecting excessive welfare payments through fraud or manipulation. This also applies to massive corporate subsidies, tax breaks and bailouts of Fortune 100 companies to the tune of hundreds of billions of dollars annually. It is also known as cronyism, corporatism, progressivism and economic fascism.

DEBT and DEFICIT: Debt is money owed, deficit is net money taken in (if negative). The $20 trillion federal debt is a lifetime running tally while deficit is an amount calculated over a certain period of time. Government deficits siphon funds out of the private sector into pork barrel projects, thus lowering private investments. Relative to GDP the US has the 39th largest debt in the world.

DEMOCRAT PLANTATION MENTALITY: Unquestioning allegiance to so-called progressive policies. Liberal elite masters give economic dependents government handouts in exchange for political support but, at the same time, take away their freedom, independence and self-esteem. Those minorities who stray off the plantation by embracing achievement, education, living well and setting a good example for their children are ironically "selling out" and labeled "uncle toms" and "apples".

DEVIANT BEHAVIOR: Political correctness has blurred the lines of conformity to acceptable norms and values. What once were vices and immoral are now tolerable habits. Those who disapprove by judging content of character are labeled intolerant and judgmental.

ECONOMIC DEATH SPIRAL: Government burdens remain but too many of the providers - employers in the private sector - shrink or depart. Why add jobs in a state that asks each productive worker to carry not just his or her own weight but also the weight of one other person or more? What happens when employers tire of the burdens and leave? Detroit, Puerto Rico, Greece and the former Soviet Union is what.

EMPOWERMENT: A panacea pushed by social workers and governmental agencies onto underachievers. More often than not, empowerment crosses the thin line into enabling.

ENABLING: Removing the natural consequences of someone's behavior, thus perpetuating or exacerbating a problem. Liberalism is an ideology of enabling the victim, creating a victim class and the furtherance of victimhood.

ENABLER: One that enables another to persist in self-destructive behavior by making it possible to avoid the consequences of such behavior.

ENTITLEMENTS vs HANDOUTS: People receiving entitlements (Social Security, Medicare, Veterans Affairs) have contributed to the entitlement programs, whereas people receiving handouts (welfare, food stamps, free housing etc.) have not contributed a fair share, and in fact are taking the monies from the people that are contributing a fair share.

ENTITLEMENT, CULTURE OF: Suggests that many people now have highly unreasonable expectations about what they are entitled to.

ENTITLEMENT, SENSE OF: If someone has a sense of entitlement, the person believes he deserves certain privileges – and they're arrogant about it.

ENTITLEMENT TENDENCIES: Rather than earning success, a narcissistic mentality of entitlement may lead to the bad habits of pursuing shortcuts to power, material success and enlightenment, leading to bullying, moral licensing, breaking the rules, freeloading, cheating, duplicity, laziness, blind faith, stealing, gambling and drug abuse.

FATHERLESS CHILDREN: America's number one cause of societal breakdown, often caused by government perverse incentives. Children and adults raised in broken homes exhibit highly elevated occurrences of domestic abuse, school drop-outs and underachievement, promiscuity, teen pregnancy and abortion, gang participation, criminal activity, depression, suicide, unemployment, poverty, domestic violence, divorce, substance abuse, personality disorders, relationship problems, identity crises, bullying, anxiety disorders and eating disorders.

FEEDME RATIO: Forbes magazine's survey determined the number of clients drawing from the government (welfare recipients, generously paid government employees and people collecting government pensions) compared to those chipping in by working outside the government and paying taxes. When the ratio goes above 1.0 the departure of jobs can lead to an economic death spiral. Of the six states with a Feedme Ratio over 1.0, including California and New York, New Mexico is far in the lead at 1.43 (143 people in the wagon for every 100 pulling it).

FEEWINGS: "The irrational emotions of a catastrophizing millennial." – **urban dictionary**…. "Poor widdo snowfwake cwybully must have had his widdle feewings hurt".

FISH METAPHOR: Give a man a fish and you feed him for a day; teach a man to fish and feed him for life, and for some, sit in a boat all day and drink beer.

FLOPHOUSE, GALLUP'S GLORIFIED: A flophouse is a cheap hotel, rooming house or just a place to crash for the night. Gallup NM's NCI alcohol rehab facility has served that purpose with free room and board for up to 60 days while providing a social experience as well for those escaping the socio-economic squalor and boredom of the Navajo reservation. I would even classify NCI as well as some other charitable establishments in Gallup as enablers of self-destructive lifestyles.

FREELOADER: A person who takes advantage of other people's generosity without giving anything in return.

Highly Elevated Consequences of Fatherless Children
*domestic abuse as children
*domestic violence as adults
*high school drop-outs and underachievement
*teen pregnancy and abortion
*sexual promiscuity
*relationship problems
*criminal activity
*gang participation
*substance abuse
*personality disorders
*depression
*suicide
*unemployment
*poverty
*divorce

FREE RANGE PARENTING: The goal is to raise children to cope successfully with life and attain happiness thru autonomy, freedom and responsibility, with a reasonable acceptance of realistic personal risks.

GOVERNMENT, the Co-Dependent Enabler - Jeff Rutherford:

Excessive Care-taking: Government feels responsible for others' actions, feelings, choices and well-being.

Low self-esteem: Government needs to be needed. Government blames itself for *anything* that goes wrong.

Denial: Government denies that helping others can cause destructive behaviors like overspending.

Fear of anger: Government is afraid to make any of their beneficiaries angry.

Health problems: The stress of Government Codependency can ruin the health of our nation.

Addictive behavior: Government has developed a runaway addiction to other peoples' money.

GREATEST GENERATION: In contrast to the special snowflake syndrome of pajama boy millennials, those born just before or during the Great Depression knew all about scarcity, unemployment, privation, Depression, poverty, rationing, Prohibition and war – with all its horror, heightened emotions, bravery, and moral choices. Their individual experiences in those elemental events shaped their outlook on life forever after - life or death battle, the struggle to survive in an age of scarcity, and a need to be tough.

GREAT SOCIETY: In 1964 LBJ gave his "Great Society" speech, which included a massive system of government programs, with a focus on the "War on Poverty". Over $22 trillion and 80 welfare programs later, while material poverty has declined, Americans are not better off when it comes to self-sufficiency. The societal protectors against poverty, such as work and marriage, have eroded leading to a cultural decline and dysfunctional children.

GUN FREE ZONES: The enablers and places of choice for mass killers. Since at least 1950, all but two public mass shootings in America and Europe – and there have been plenty in Europe - have taken place where general citizens are banned from carrying guns.

HAND-UP: As opposed to a handout, the most compassionate thing you can do is to help someone use their God-given abilities to work and take care of their own needs. Charities often keep individuals in a position of dependency. A hand-up lifts them up and gives them a healthy sense of dignity.

HATE CRIME HOAXES: Victimhood can be profitable, so it's not surprising that charlatans and opportunists seek to take advantage of others empathy. In this age of political correctness there has been an epidemic of hate crime hoaxes since 2011 behind the cover of a complicit media. White males are almost exclusively the targets. As we have become one of the most tolerant, peaceful societies in history, the Left is reduced to chasing imaginary microaggressions and turning to hoaxes to convince the public that bigotry is still alive and well.

HELICOPTER PARENTS: A key element in the wussification of America, these parents are identified by their tendency to hover close to their child, ready to come to the rescue at the first sign of difficulty or disappointment, even in these times when crime rates continue to drop. They treat their college-age children to the same full-service parenting they have implemented since birth: they pay bills and do laundry; they arrange for utilities to be turned on and off. It is not uncommon for helicopter parents to contact professors about their child's exams or insist that a test be re-graded.

HOMELESS vs VAGRANT: Economy-driven homeless find themselves in dire need of help because of illness or loss of job. Lifestyle/addiction-driven vagrants choose to meet their needs by scamming people in the name of charity. In Gallup NM what many call homeless are merely vagrants who have temporarily left their reservation homes.

HUD LOW INCOME HOUSING: The US Dept of Housing and Urban Development policies of perverse incentives have been largely responsible for the step by step breakdown of black and American Indian families since the 1960s War on Poverty.

INDEX of DEPENDENCE on GOVERNMENT: Measures the growth in spending on dependence-creating programs that supplant the role of civil society. The five Index components are: 1. Housing 2. Health Care & Welfare 3. Retirement 4. Higher Education 5. Rural & Agricultural Services. – **Heritage Foundation**

LEARNED HELPLESSNESS: The opposite of earned success. It is the result of rewards and punishments not tied to merit; people simply give up and stop trying to succeed.

LIFE OF JULIA: Barack Obama's plan for cradle-to-grave dependency told in a story of how a woman can live her entire life by leaning on government intervention and other people's money rather than her own initiative or hard work.

LIVING WAGE: A philosophical claim that employers are morally obligated to pay employees enough to afford ambiguously defined "necessities". While the failed price controls of housing, food and gasoline have become a dead end, price controls on wages remain popular. A low wage is unacceptable but the price control consequence of zero wages is apparently just fine.

MEANS-TESTED BENEFIT: A payment available to people who can demonstrate that their income and capital (their 'means') are below specified limits.

MEDICAID BABIES: Twenty-four of the nation's 50 states in 2015 had at least half of their births paid for by Medicaid, according to the Kaiser Family Foundation. New Mexico led all states with 72 percent.

MILLENNIALS: Born from 1982 to 2004. Traits include a collectivist sense of community, sense of entitlement, narcissism and wussification.

MORAL LICENSING: A cognitive distortion in which people internally justify things they do that are wrong.

MUTUAL AID SOCIETIES: Also known as fraternalism, refers to social organizations that gathered dues and paid benefits to members facing hardship. In the early 20th century mutual aid did not carry the same stigma as government aid or private charities, since it was based on reciprocity. Particularly popular among the poor, blacks, and working class, by the 1920s one out of every three males was a member of a mutual aid society.

NATURE vs NURTURE: "It's biological. I was born this way." The "genetic link" argument by criminals, pedophiles, drug addicts, homosexuals, ADHD and other deviant behaviors is a fallacy. Genes are not deterministic. Blaming one's dysfunctional behavior on genetics is a victimization cop-out.

OVER-PARENTING SYMPTOMS: When children aren't given the space to struggle through things on their own, they don't learn to problem-solve very well. They don't learn to be confident in their own abilities, and it can affect their self-esteem. The other problem with never having to struggle is that you never experience failure and can develop an overwhelming fear of failure and of disappointing others. Both the low self-confidence and the fear of failure can lead to depression or anxiety.

PAJAMA BOY: Obamacare's insufferable twenty-something poster man-child exemplifying the special snowflake syndrome and wussification of

America. He is the little brother of "Life of Julia" and the picture of perpetual adolescence.

PANHANDLER, GLORIFIED: A politician seeking state and federal funding for local projects and programs.

PARENTAL CHOICE: Typically refers to educational choice. Free market educational choice programs empower parents to choose the education which best meets their child's needs. When parents can vote with their feet, schools are held directly accountable to them, therefore the schools must offer the type and quality of instruction and programming that parents value. – **Cato Institute**

PATHOLOGICAL ALTRUISM: "Behavior in which attempts to promote the welfare of another, or others, results instead in harm that an external observer would conclude was reasonably foreseeable." – **Barbara Oakley, systems engineer** …. It is a pervasive problem affecting public policy when intentions to help people all too often hurt them. Example; While Social Security goes bankrupt, it discourages citizens from saving.

PERSONAL RESPONSIBILITY: is the price you pay for freedom. It is "the willingness to both accept the importance of standards that society establishes for individual behavior and to make strenuous personal efforts to live by those standards. The demise of personal responsibility occurs when individuals blame their family, their peers, their economic circumstances, or their society for their own failure to meet standards. The three areas of personal decision-making in which the nation's youth and young adults most need to learn and practice personal responsibility are education, sexual behavior and marriage, and work." – **Ron Haskins**…. For the left, liberty is defined as the ability to avoid responsibility.

PERVERSE INCENTIVE: An unintended and undesirable result which is contrary to the interests of the incentive makers. Examples are welfare dependency leading to family breakdown leading to dysfunctional lives. Almost every one of the 80 federal welfare programs incentivize recipients not to get married. On a grander scale the Community Reinvestment Act (CRA) was a perverse incentive which brought about the 2008 subprime mortgage crisis and economic collapse.

POVERTY AVOIDANCE: Brookings Institution's three simple rules for avoiding poverty, applying to all races and ethnic groups. 1. Graduating from high school. 2. Waiting to get married until after 21 and do not have children till after being married. 3. Having a full-time job.

PRIVILEGE vs RIGHTS: A privilege is a special entitlement granted to a restricted group or person, and can be revoked. By contrast a right is irrevocable and inherently held by all human beings. It is self-evident and universal under the laws of nature. Ultimately, a right is the ability to decide for oneself; to make a choice. Whereas a right is something that can be done because it originates commonly within all individuals, a privilege is something that cannot be done without permission. Marxist programs of redistribution of wealth are privileges, not rights. The freedom of speech, religion, press, and to peaceably assemble are not privileges. No person need ask for permission to exercise these rights, nor does any government have the right to deny them. Governments do not grant rights, but rather are meant to protect these rights. – **A J Oatsvall,** Voices of Liberty.

PRODUCTIVENESS: As one of the primary contributors to mental health, productiveness is a virtue which is the recognition of the fact that productive work is the process by which man's mind sustains his life, the process that sets man free of the necessity to adjust himself to his background, as all animals do, and gives him the power to adjust his background to himself.

PRWORA: The Personal Responsibility and Work Opportunity Reconciliation Act of 1996 required a workfare component as a reassertion of America's work ethic. Welfare rolls plummeted 60%, employment among low income surged and poverty rates for single mothers hit historic lows.

RECIPROCITY RULE: People are obligated to repay favors, gifts, and invitations in the future. The sense of future obligation associated with reciprocity makes it possible to build continuing relationships and exchanges. Mutual aid and fraternal benefit societies are based on reciprocity.

REAL WAGE: As opposed to the ambiguous "living wage", real wage measures what that pay will purchase. If a worker's pay increases 10% but prices increase 20% he is not better off. The fundamental issue is not wage rates, but productivity. When production increases, prices fall.

RESERVATION BORDERTOWN SOCIOECONOMIC REFUGEES: The economically and socially impoverished flee the oppression and squalor of reservation socialism seeking freedom and temporary refuge in border towns such as Gallup NM, creating a community paradox of economic gain versus transient social disorder.

RIGHTS vs SLAVERY: "It's not an endlessly expanding list of rights – the "right" to education, the "right" to health care, the "right to food and housing". That's not freedom, that's dependency. Those aren't rights, those are the rations of slavery – hay and a barn for human cattle." – **Alexis de Tocqueville, historian.**

SAFETY NETS: The intent of state provided social safety nets is to prevent individuals from falling into poverty. These include a myriad of welfare programs, unemployment benefits and universal health care. The unintended reality is the safety net becomes a web which creates a perverse incentive to be unproductive and poor. Communism provides the ultimate safety net as witnessed by the successes of Cuba, Venezuela and the former Soviet Union. Subsidies and bail-outs also provide perverse incentives as corporate safety nets.

SELF-ESTEEM MOVEMENT: The rage of the 80s. In that decade self-esteem became a hot topic for motivational speakers and a book genre as well. It is also blamed for its influence on American schools and families. In the name of building self-esteem, teacher, parents and television showered children with unconditional praise. Kids were sheltered from any criticism or adverse consequences. The mollycoddling has yielded a Millennial generation full of emotionally fragile young adults - the snowflakes.

SINGLE-PARENT HOUSEHOLDS: Married couples with children average $80,000 per year income while single moms make $24,000, yet children from low-income two-parent families outperform students from high-income, single-parents. That's not all, the proportion of single-parent households in a community predicts its rate of violent crime and burglary, but the community's poverty level does not.

SINGLE-PAYER HEALTH CARE: Government-run health care systems. In the US the Indian Health Service and Veterans Health Administration are single-payer examples. The disastrous problems of these federal health systems cannot be blamed on "greedy" insurance companies or the private sector, yet despite the failures, the left wishes to double-down on this approach.

SLOW SUICIDE: A prolonged period of self-abuse, harmful behavior, which may result in suicide completion. – **Segen's Medical Dictionary**

SNOWFLAKE SYNDROME: The belief that one is a "unique and special snowflake". Symptoms include inflated self-importance and an unfailing sense of entitlement. Those with exposure to excessive coddling in childhood are at especially high risk.

SOCIAL CONSERVATISM: Refers to conservative values on non-fiscal matters, such as the promotion of traditional marriage, opposition to abortion, opposition to sexual promiscuity, and promotion of Christian values. The views of social conservatives and Christian conservatives often overlap. – **Conservapedia**

SOCIAL SECURITY PONZI SCHEME: Social Security and Medicare have been a means for seniors to redistribute tens of trillions of dollars to themselves from those younger, because they are partial Ponzi schemes. After Social Security's creation, those in or near retirement got benefits far exceeding their costs. Those benefits in excess of their taxes paid inherently forced future Americans to pick up the tab for the difference. Each SS expansion meant those retired and near retirement paid more for only a few years, increasing the unfunded benefits whose burdens had to be borne by later generations. Thus, each expansion started another Ponzi cycle benefiting older Americans at others' expense.

SPECIAL NEEDS DISTRICTS: Apparently, that's what Gallup and McKinley County NM are. 'Special' is politically correct for 'disabled', which became PC for 'handicapped', which became PC for 'retarded'. A special needs person has either learning difficulties, a physical disability, or emotional and behavioral difficulties. Whether an accurate label or not, it is demeaning and should provide incentive to any community to break the chains of government dependency.

TOO BIG TO FAIL: TBTF theory asserts that certain corporations, and particularly financial institutions, are so large and so interconnected that their failure would be disastrous to the greater economic system, and that they therefore must be supported by government when they face potential failure. The fallacy is that any large group, such as coal miners or public servants, can selectively be considered TBTF.

TOUGH LOVE: Promotion of a person's welfare by enforcing certain constraints on them, or requiring them to take responsibility for their actions. Politically, tough love is any policy designed to encourage self-help by restricting state benefits. Also, tough love may be authoritative parenting for development of preferred character traits.

TRADITIONAL MARRIAGE: A time-honored system of securing children's birthrights to their biological parents thus preserving the foundation of society, the nuclear family.

TRUSTAFARIAN: A young spoiled trust fund hippie attracted to countercultural trends, especially anarchism, and subscribing to an unemployed shiftless life of hedonism.

UNCLE TOM or APPLE: Uncle Tom is a term used by black people to try to convince other black people that working, education, living well, and setting a good example for their children is "selling out". An "apple" is an American Indian who is red on the outside and white on the inside.

UNINTENDED CONSEQUENCES, LAW OF: Murphy's Law of government intervention - perverse unexpected effects of government legislation and regulation of free market capitalism. Example; the American Disabilities Act resulted in declines in disabled employment.

VICTIM MENTALITY: Regarding oneself as a victim of the negative actions of others, even in the absence of clear evidence. Passive-aggressive characteristics are commonly displayed. Behavior is of a self-defeating, almost masochistic quality. Also known as a persecution complex.

WAR ON POVERTY LEGACY of FAILURE: The poverty rate among black families fell from 87% in 1940 to 47% in 1960. Then came LBJ's 1964 War on Poverty and the rate dropped only one percent in the 1970s. Violent crime, teen pregnancy and venereal disease skyrocketed. Sixteen trillion dollars later to this day the poverty rate has not dropped. "The black family, which had survived centuries of slavery and discrimination, began rapidly disintegrating in the liberal welfare state that subsidized unwed pregnancy and changed welfare from an emergency rescue to a way of life." – **Thomas Sowell**

WELFARE, MODERN: Welfare is financial or social support given to people in need. Prior to massive government involvement, charities, benevolent associations, friendship societies, and fraternities have historically been successful in providing relief to the needy. The modern definition of welfare, also referred to as the welfare state, is the public administration and bureaucratization of charity. This means that welfare is no longer a voluntary and altruistic action of private citizens, but the governmental extortion of one group of people for the benefit of another. Since welfare provides aid or support to people in need, modern "welfare" is a contradiction because other people with needs are coerced to appropriate and redistribute their resources! The welfare state impairs welfare in the name of welfare. – **Baruti Libre Kafele**

WELFARE PROGRAMS: In 2011 the federal government funded 126 separate and often overlapping anti-poverty programs.

WELFARE REFORM: Establishes a workfare component. Able-bodied adults who receive cash, food, housing and medical assistance should be required to work or prepare for work as a condition of receiving those benefits from the government. The 1996 PRWORA was a highly successful welfare reform program.

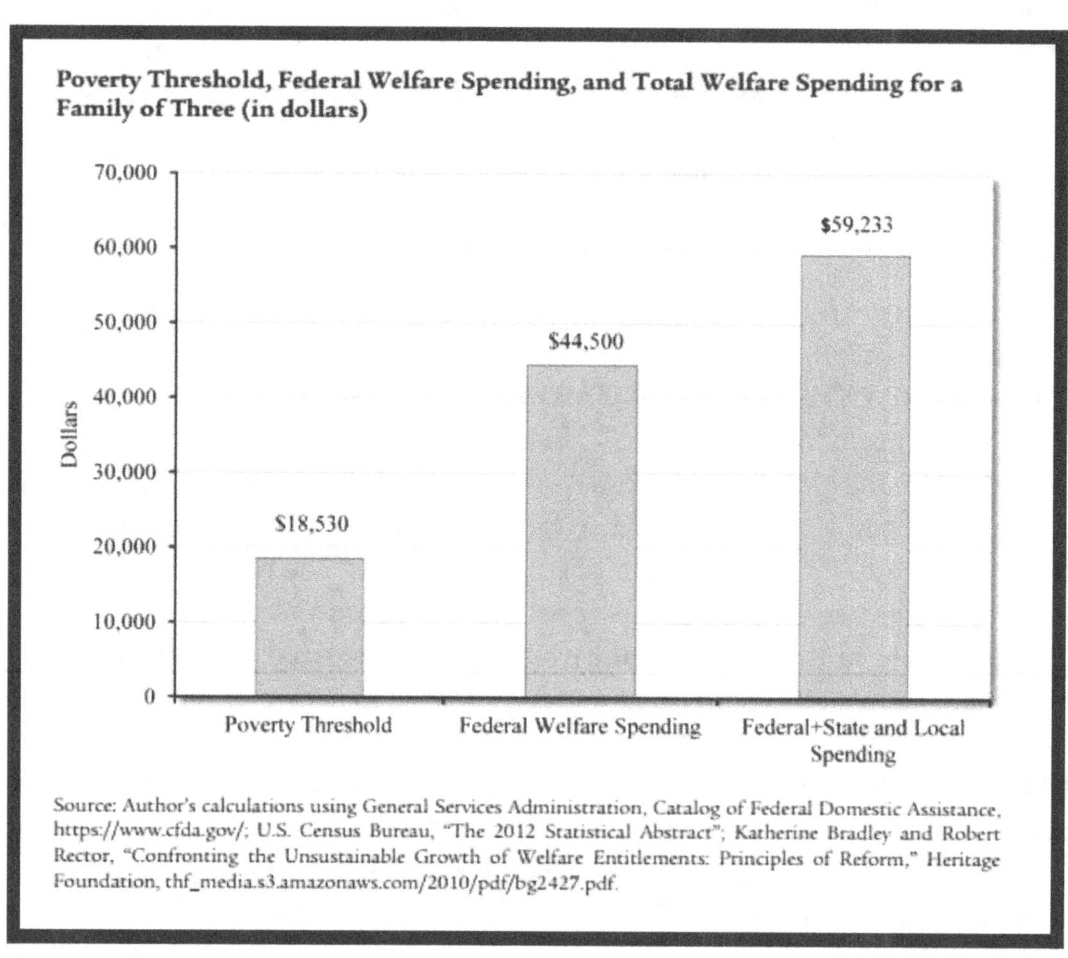

Source: Author's calculations using General Services Administration, Catalog of Federal Domestic Assistance, https://www.cfda.gov/; U.S. Census Bureau, "The 2012 Statistical Abstract"; Katherine Bradley and Robert Rector, "Confronting the Unsustainable Growth of Welfare Entitlements: Principles of Reform," Heritage Foundation, thf_media.s3.amazonaws.com/2010/pdf/bg2427.pdf.

WELFARE SLAVERY: Welfare handouts, erroneously referred to as entitlements, make people dependent. As the opposite of independence, dependence is a form of slavery. The insidious degradation of society by welfare dependency was observed by Ben Franklin in the 18th century. Economist Thomas Sowell puts it this way, "Helping those who have been struck by unforeseeable misfortunes is fundamentally different from making dependency a way of life."

WELFARE SPENDING, HOUSEHOLD: Federal data from 2011 reveals welfare spending alone totals $15,000 for every poor man, woman and child in this country. That amounts to $45,000 for a poor family of three. Combined with state and local spending, government spends $62,000 for a poor family of three. **– Cato Institute**

WELFARE STATE: A concept of government in which the state attempts to play a key role in the protection and promotion of the economic and social well-being of its citizens by providing free services and money. It is a mechanism for the redistribution of wealth taken from productive members of society. Historically conspicuous by an abundance of unintended negative consequences.

WELFARE STATE UNEMPLOYMENT: McKinley County NM has one of the highest welfare dependency rates in the nation and also an extremely low labor force participation rate, yet both the private and public sector are begging for numerous job openings to be filled, many of them requiring minimal skills and qualifications. An example is Gallup's school bus barn with normally ten to twenty job openings. As long as food stamps, EBT cards, disability, extended unemployment benefits and various other welfare handouts are jeopardized by employment, where is the incentive to seek employment or even get an education?

WORK ETHIC: A habit of working as a moral good.

WORKFARE: Requires able-bodied adults to work or train in order to receive welfare.

WORK-LESS LIFE: Neither working nor looking for it. It is the fastest growing contingent among prime working age American men. 2016 had the worst work rate since 1939, worse than even France and Greece.

WUSSIFICATION: To wussify is to make weak and ineffectual. Wussification is the systematic sissifying of men or women, afraid to speak up, afraid to take charge, trending to an increasingly wimpy society. Political correctness is the leading edge of the wussification of America. If members of every possible subgroup in American society are too delicate to survive being joked about, then we have become a nation of wusses, afraid of our own shadows. Related to this is the trend of helicopter parenting replacing traditional free range parenting despite crime rates continuing to decline. The dramatic rise in broken homes is another source.

DECEPTION

POLITICAL CORRECTNESS
* Fascism pretending to be manners
* America's newest form of intolerance
* Willful ignorance
* Intellectual terrorism
* A self-appointed group of vigilantes imposing their views on others
* A steadfast refusal to face the truth
* School yard bullying and shaming
* Linguistic tyranny
* A modern day witch hunt
* Cultural Marxism
ConservaLexicon

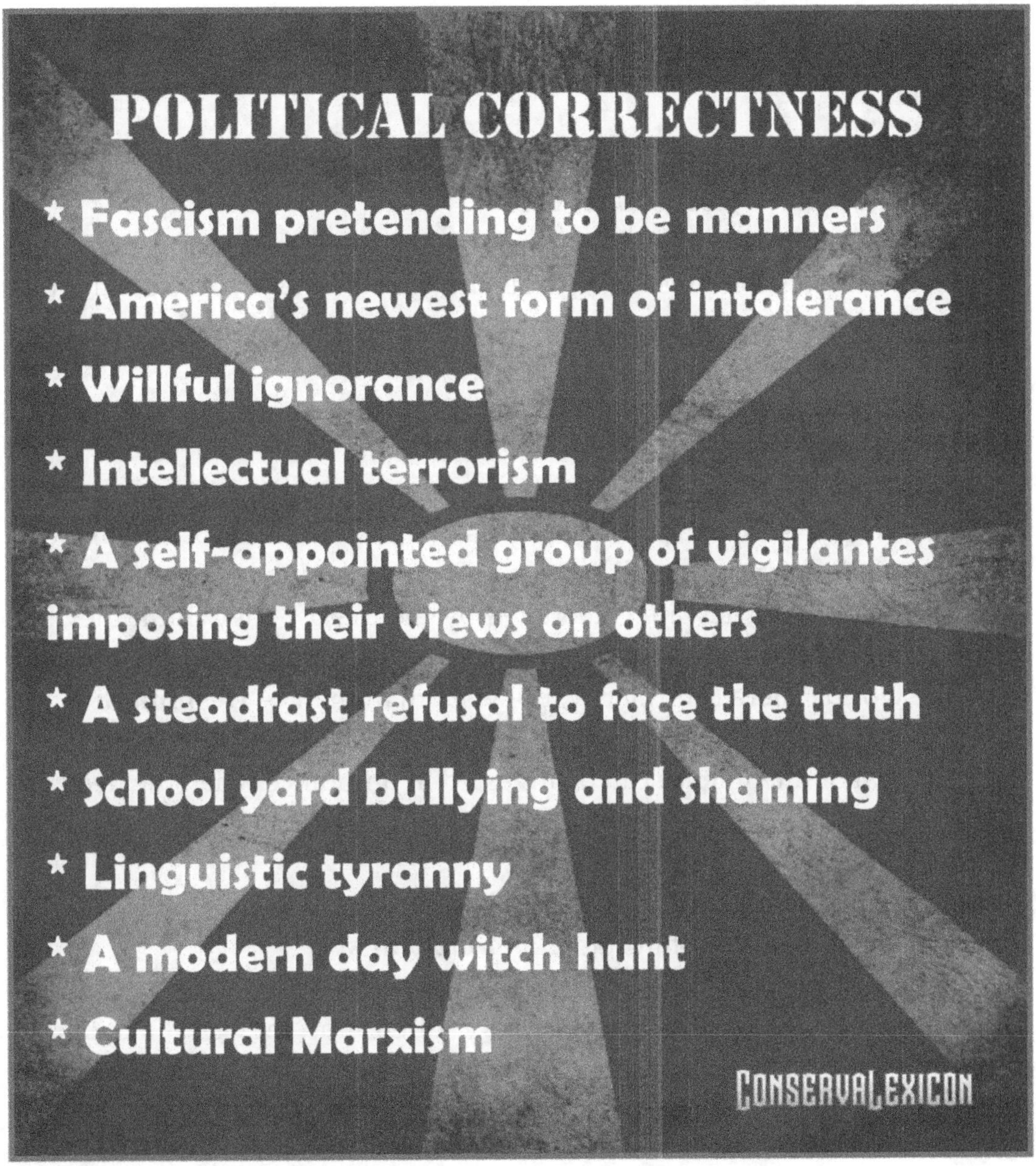

Quotes

"Beware lest you lose the substance by grasping at the shadow." – **Aesop**

"Man has such a predilection for systems and abstract deductions that he is ready to distort the truth intentionally, he is ready to deny the evidence of his senses only to justify his logic." – **Dostoevsky**

"It's easier to fool people than to convince them that they have been fooled." – **Mark Twain**

"If you tell a lie big enough and keep repeating it, people will eventually come to believe it." – **Joseph Goebbels**

"Whoever controls the present controls the past. Whoever controls the past controls the future" – **George Orwell**

"In a time of universal deceit, telling the truth is a revolutionary act." – **George Orwell**

"Nobody today is normal, everybody is a little bit crazy or unbalanced, people's minds are running all the time. Their perceptions of the world are partial, incomplete. They are eaten alive by their egos. They think they see, but they are mistaken; all they do is project their madness, their world, upon the world. There is no clarity, no wisdom in that!" – **Deshimaru**

"A great deal of intelligence can be invested in ignorance when the need for illusion is deep." – **Saul Bellow**

"We do not err because truth is difficult to see. It is visible at a glance. We err because this is more comfortable." – **Solzhenitsyn**

"The great enemy of the truth is very often not the lie – deliberate, contrived, and dishonest – but the myth – persistent, persuasive, and unrealistic." – **John F Kennedy**

"Education is not merely neglected in many of our schools today, but is replaced to a great extent by ideological indoctrination." – **Thomas Sowell**

"In the famous liberal two-step, they leap from one idiotic point to the next, so you can never nail them. It's like arguing with someone with Attention Deficit Disorder." – **Ann Coulter**

"Lack of transparency is a huge political advantage. And basically, call it the stupidity of the American voter, that was really critical to get for the thing to pass." – **Jonathan Gruber, Obamacare architect**

"Enough with the PCBS" – **Joe Schaller**

SAGAN'S BAMBOOZLE

Oh, the irony of Carl Sagan's famous quote. In 1990 Sagan warned that computer models forecasted a doomsday scenario for mankind due to carbon dioxide emissions. Carl was captured by the bamboozle and became the charlatan he so much feared. His quote below is now a spot-on summation of man made climate change theory.

"One of the saddest lessons of history is this: if we've been bamboozled long enough, we tend to reject any evidence of the bamboozle. We're no longer interested in finding out the truth. The bamboozle has captured us. It's simply too painful to acknowledge, even to ourselves, that we've been taken. Once you give a charlatan power over you, you almost never get it back. So the old bamboozles tend to persist as the new ones rise."
Carl Sagan, *The Demon-Haunted World*, 1995

ACADEMIC BIAS: Nearly identical to media bias, with similar four to one ratios of liberal to conservative professors and scholars. Claims are widespread on campus of discrimination against those who hold a conservative ideology and arguments that research has been corrupted (junk science) by a desire to promote a progressive agenda.

ACCUSATION vs EVIDENCE: "Tell a lie often enough and it becomes the truth" can be an effective propaganda tool for character assassination. Accusation-driven rather than evidence-based reporting has a cumulative ability to shape public opinion, similar to historical revisionism. File it under the Orwellian tactics of PC Cultural Marxism.

"If you are evidence-based you lead with the lack of evidence for explosive or insidious charges. That becomes the news. If you are accusation-driven, the news is that certain people are making charges. With the details we may learn that there is no evidence, but the frame in which that discovery is made remains "he-said, she-said". – **Jay Rosen,** professor of journalism.

AESTHETIC RELATIVISM: With similarities to moral relativism, "beauty is in the eye of the beholder" represents a decline in universal aesthetic standards, with no way of determining quality or inferiority. Scatological becomes meaningful when artistic statements are made merely for shock value. Defenders of artistic relativism see it as a harbinger of tolerance by the open-minded, rather than its incoherence and uncritical intellectual permissiveness. File it under PCBS.

AGENT PROVOCATEUR: The undercover agent who infiltrates a group such as a political party or activist group, pretending sympathy with its aims, and gets the members to do precisely those things that they can be punished or put away for.

AVATAR BLUES: "James Cameron's completely immersive spectacle "Avatar" may have been a little too real for some fans who say they have experienced depression and suicidal thoughts after seeing the film because they long to enjoy the beauty of the alien world Pandora." – **CNN.** . . See "eco-angst", "liberal bubble", and "utopia".

BANDWAGON EFFECT: A conformity phenomenon. The rate of uptake of beliefs, ideas, fads and trends increases the more they have already been adopted by others. As more people come to believe in something, others also "hop on the bandwagon" regardless of the underlying evidence.

BIGOTRY: Making a judgment of someone without knowing the facts. For the politically correct, accurately judging content of character is often considered bigotry. A bigot also wishes to deny others the same rights that he has. It is the hallmark of the environmental zealot.

BIMBO ERUPTION: A term coined by the 1992 Bill Clinton campaign in response to numerous accusations of illicit sexual behavior and harassment including Juanita Broaddrick's rape allegation. Hillary Clinton and "feminists" now maintain we should believe such accusations without question.

BLACKLISTING: A blacklist is a list or register of people who are being denied a particular privilege. It is an element of political correctness and Neo-McCarthyism and commonly found in the liberal institutions of Hollywood, media, academia and bureaucracy. I have personally been blacklisted in radical left Gallup NM by a media establishment which likes to dish it out but can't take it.

BLIND FAITH: An assertion with insufficient evidence. A belief without true understanding, perception or discrimination. Commonly seen among green activists.

BLIND FAITH, DUPLICITY and IGNORANCE: The recipe for cooking up false narratives.

CAMPAIGN FINANCE REFORM: A PC euphemism for controlling free speech. If the goal is to get money out of politics, the real solution is to get politics out of money. In other words, shrink government

CHICKEN LITTLE ALARMISM: The history of environmentalism is distinguished by distortions, exaggerations and flat-out lies in all of the following; acid rain, ozone hole, radon, asbestos, oil spills and natural seeps, DDT, rainforests, land stewardship, public transportation, uranium mining, radiation exposure, second-hand smoke, recycling, landfills, organic food, GMOs, endangered species and global warming.

CENSORSHIP: The suppression of speech, public communication or other information which may be considered objectionable, harmful, sensitive, politically incorrect or inconvenient as determined by governments, media outlets, authorities or other institutions.

CHRISTIAN CRUSADES: A defensive maneuver ultimately requiring offense to thwart the persistent attacks of the Islamic Crusades.

CNN DIPLOMACY: Foreign policy driven by television news coverage and political polling, associated with President Clinton's 44 military overseas dispatches in eight years. There had been only eight in the previous 45

years. The role of the American soldier changed from homeland defender to nomadic peacekeeper. The media gave Clinton a free pass on his excessive foreign policy.

COEXIST: A belief system based on moral equivalence dogma claiming all religions are ultimately equal. Ironically the followers are primarily secular liberals with their real agenda to rid the world of all religious ideologies in favor of a secular godless one.

COLLECTIVE DELUSIONAL BEHAVIOR: A condition of mass hysteria in which a large group of people exhibit similar physical or emotional symptoms, such as anxiety or extreme excitement. Also called 'epidemic hysteria'. – **TheFreeDictionary.com**. There is little doubt the American Left, particularly those in media and academia suffering from Trump Derangement Syndrome, have descended deeper and deeper into this psychotic disorder.

COMING OUT (of the closet): When homosexuals "come out" by discussing their sexual preferences in the workplace it is considered a courageous act. For the rest of us it is considered sexual harassment.

CONFEDERATE FLAG: A symbol of Democrat Party racial oppression since 1861. Indeed, to be consistent, all historical symbols of pro-slavery, white supremacist, KKK segregationist, Civil Rights Act-opposing Democrats should be banished to history museums with a reminder that they waved those banners until very recently.

CONFIRMATION BIAS: The tendency for people to seek out information that conforms to their pre-existing view points, and subsequently ignore information that goes against them, both positive and negative. Avoiding confirmation bias is an important part of rationalism and in science in general. This is achieved by setting up problems so that you must find ways of disproving your hypothesis.

CONSPIRACY THEORIES: A conspiracy is a secret plan by a group to do something unlawful or harmful. A conspiracy theory is considered to be a belief that some covert but influential organization is responsible for a circumstance or event. Sometimes a conspiracy claim is made when entities are exposed of corruption. Several conspiracy "theories" have proven to be true, which only reinforces an ever growing suspicion in Federal overreach. More often than not, theories such as chemtrails (contrails) are merely a form of intellectual bullying.

COUNTERING DISINFORMATION and PROPAGANDA ACT: Quietly inserted inside the 2017 NDAA, the CDPA greenlights the government to crack down with impunity against any media property, particularly websites, it deems as "propaganda" and provides substantial amounts of money to fund an army of "local journalist" counterpropaganda, to make sure the government's own fake news drowns that of the still free "fringes".

COUNTRY CLUB REPUBLICANS: Moderate establishment Republicans eager to fold before Democrats and even attack conservative Republicans such as Ted Cruz and Rand Paul. Country clubbers accept Democrats' belief that the ruling class and big government knows what's best for the country.

CREATE A CRISIS: The modus operandi of Cloward-Piven, Saul Alinsky, yellow journalism and Rahm's (Emanuel) Rule, "You never want a serious crisis to go to waste". Real or manufactured crises can provide cover for distributing benefits to targeted special interest groups.

CULT OF PERSONALITY: Arises when mass media, propaganda, or other methods are used to create an idealized, heroic, and at times worshipful image, often through unquestioning flattery and praise.

CULTURAL MARXISM: The fundamental transformation of society by subversion of Western culture to create a society fully dependent on government. For cultural Marxists, no cause ranks higher than the breakdown of the nuclear family, which they despise as a dictatorship and the incubator of sexism and social injustice.

DEMAGOGUE: By manipulating the emotions, prejudices and passions of listeners, often employing deceit, demagogues are able to sway an audience into contemptible thoughts and actions.

DEMOCRATIC SOCIALISM: Politically correct for "socialism". There is absolutely no difference between "democratic socialism" and "socialism". The term is used solely to lull the average American into accepting socialism, the path to communism.

DISINFORMATION: Coined by Joseph Stalin. Whereas misinformation is unintentionally false, disinformation is intentionally false or inaccurate information that is spread deliberately.

DOGMA: A set of beliefs accepted on faith; that is, without rational justification or against rational evidence. A dogma is a matter of blind faith.

DOG WHISTLE POLITICS: The "dog-whistle effect" had its origins in the field of opinion polling in which subtle changes in question-wording sometimes produce remarkably different results. The modern dog-whistle strategy has advanced to the point of collective paranoia; politically incorrect "code words" that only a certain group who are "in-the-know" will take away the secret, intended message. Words such as "thug" or "entitlement" are derogatory words tantamount to using the N-word. This strategy allows the liberal elite to freely assign racist, sexist, homophobic, Islamophobic etc. labels.

DOUBLE STANDARD: The "go-to guy" for liberal bias. Since their cause is just, and "whatever advances the cause" is their morality motto, any bigoted, dishonest, hypocritical transgressions by the Left are justified and to be glossed over and ignored with no accountability, including inciting violence.

DUMBING DOWN: The consequence of rewarding the lazy, uneducated and uninformed. Call it liberalism or socialism, for all its intentions, good or bad, it produces a dumbed-down society of low information voters waiting for the government to cure all its ills.

ECO-BUZZWORDS: A buzzword is an important-sounding, usually technical word or phrase often of little meaning used chiefly to impress dimwits. Environmentalists have become the most common source of these vague, contradictory, fuzzy terms hyping their religious-political-bureaucratic snake oil. Here are a few of the most common: * biodegradable * biodiversity * carbon footprint * carbon offsets * eco-friendly * eco-footprint * free range * global weirding * going green * greenhouse gases * green initiative * green living * natural * off-gridder * renewable resource * organic * recyclable * sustainability *.

ECO-FOOTPRINT GUILT: A symptom of liberal neurosis. It's when you could have taken the time to pick up that plastic bottle, carry it home, clean it and put it in your recycle bin, but you consciously made that irresponsible choice to ignore it, and now you feel that twinge of guilt that you have just impacted our environment in an adverse way.

ECO-SHAMING: You didn't pick up that plastic bottle? You don't use those smelly, sticky reusable bags for groceries? Shame! Shame on you!

ELITE MEDIA BUBBLE: The habitat of coastal mainstream media, an echo chamber skewing their outlook on politics and culture - out of touch with the mood and values of heartland America. The problem is one of groupthink pack mentality and confirmation bias, compounded by an eighty percent or more liberal predominance in media, with a resultant homogeneity of viewpoints producing uncritical consensus.

ENLIGHTENMENT DELUSION: A delusion is a belief or false idea that is not true, typical of a mental disorder. Enlightenment is the absence of ignorance and delusion. There are no short-cuts to enlightenment, and what is sometimes perceived as enlightenment thru meditation or drugs is often merely a grandiose delusion. The path to true enlightenment requires a disciplined effort of education which leads to understanding.

ENVIRONMENTAL DUPLICITY QUOTE: "... To do that we need to get some broad-based support, to capture the public's imagination. That, of course, entails getting loads of media coverage. So we have to offer up scary scenarios, make simplified, dramatic statements, and make little mention of any doubts we might have. This 'double ethical bind' we frequently find ourselves in cannot be solved by any formula. Each of us has to decide what the right balance is between being effective and being honest." - **Stephen Schneider,** Professor of Environmental Studies, Stanford, 1989

ENVIRONMENTAL DUPLICITY THEOREM: There is no form of "clean" or "alternative" energy that environmentalists won't decide to oppose if it becomes practical and affordable on a large scale. – **Steven Hayworth, AEI**

EQUAL RIGHTS: A situation in which people have the same opportunities in life as other people, without being treated in an unfair way because of their race, sex, sexuality, religion, or age. Modern politically correct "equal" rights grants special treatment for selective groups.

EUPHEMISMS: People often prefer to soften their speech with euphemism: a mixture of abstraction, metaphor, slang and understatement that offers protection against the offensive, harsh or blunt. Since they often distort and mislead "to make lies sound true and murder respectable", as George Orwell put it, they are one of the primary components of political correctness.

FACT CHECKER: Self-proclaimed fact checkers check factual assertions to determine the veracity and correctness of statements, yet in their feigned above-it-all objectivity often prove to be even more dishonest, such as politifact.org, proven to carry a leftist bias. This opens up an entirely new arena for fact checker checkers.

FAKE NEWS: Since the election of Donald Trump, "fake news" suddenly became buzzwords, yet media bias, misinformation, disinformation, confirmation bias, sensationalism, junk science, and propaganda have been prevalent for over a century. What has changed is the brash proliferation of liberal bias in media, academia, Hollywood, and bureaucracy.

FAIRNESS DOCTRINE: The Fairness Doctrine was a policy of the U.S. Federal Communications Commission (FCC), introduced in 1949, that required the holders of broadcast licenses to both present controversial issues of public importance and to do so in a manner that was—in the Commission's view—honest, equitable, and balanced. The FCC eliminated the Doctrine in 1987. Since 2005, despite the preponderance of left wing bias in the mainstream media, democrats have considered reinstatement of the Doctrine five times in an attempt to stifle all conservative speech.

FAKE CRISES: Fake science plus fake news can create a manufactured crisis, thus providing cover for a distribution of benefits to targeted special interest and grievance groups. Virtually all environmental "crises" are at the very least exaggerated and often completely fraudulent.

> **FACTOID:** Something fictitious or unsubstantiated that is presented as fact, designed especially to gain publicity and accepted because of constant repetition. Nazi socialist Joseph Goebbels put it this way, "If you tell a lie big enough and keep repeating it, people will eventually come to believe it".

FALLACIES, LOGICAL: Errors in reasoning and untruths in which there is an attempt to marginalize your opponent's position with a rhetorical device to distract or evoke emotion rather than providing a genuine argument. Logical fallacies include anecdotes, appeal to emotion, appeal to nature, straw men, ad hominem, moral equivalence, rationalization, loaded questions, ambiguity, false premise, willful ignorance, slothful induction, cherry picking, red herring and moving the goalposts. Over 300 logical fallacies can be found on *logicallyfallacious.com.*

FALSE NARRATIVE: A complete narrative pattern is perceived in a given situation, however it is false or inaccurate information (misinformation). A false narrative may be constructed with false premises, political correctness, straw men, junk science or intentional deception (disinformation). Common in environmental propaganda campaigns.

FALSE PREMISE: An untrue proposition that forms the basis of an argument, thus the conclusion is likely in error. It is a standard liberal democrat trick. After a false premise is created, such as "cops murder blacks at will", then with help from their buddies in the mainstream media they brand everyone who does not embrace their false premise a hater, divisive, intolerant, bigoted, "denier" and mean-spirited.

FALSIFIABILITY: The ability of a theory to be disproved by an experiment or observation. The ability to evaluate theories against observations is essential to the scientific method, and as such, the falsifiability of theories is key to this and is the prime test for whether a proposition or theory can be described as scientific.

FEARMONGERING: The spreading of frightening and exaggerated rumors of an impending danger, or needlessly arousing public fear about an issue. It is commonly used politically as emotional blackmail and to stoke cultural anxiety in order to dictate policy. Nowhere has it been used more effectively than in the environmental movement.

FEDERAL DEFICITS CORRELATION: Congress controls spending. Over the past 100 years there has been a striking correlation between a democrat controlled Congress and skyrocketing federal deficits, particularly since the 1995 republican control and resultant deficit declines. Contrary to PC notions, there is no deficit correlation by party of the president.

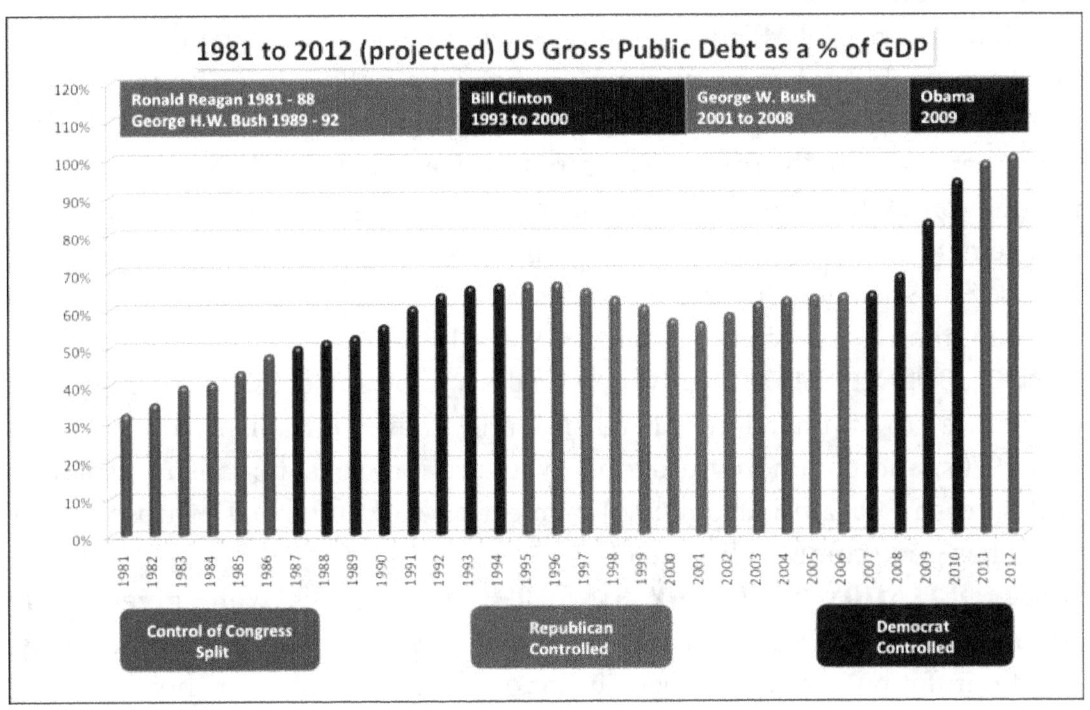

FIRST AMENDMENT ATTACKS: In 2015 Hillary Clinton went so far as to say her goal is to "change the First Amendment, in order to further empower the political class to regulate the quantity, content and timing of political speech about the political class."

FRANKFURT SCHOOL: The pioneers of political correctness and Cultural Marxism who fled Germany in 1933 and led by Georg Lukacs came to the United States. Herbert Marcuse may be the most important member of the Frankfurt School in terms of the origins of political correctness because he was the critical link to the counterculture of the tumultuous 1960s.

GASLIGHTING: Political gaslighting is increasingly used to describe the left's efforts to push a false view of reality and to convince mainstream Americans that their common sense views are somehow extreme. This is a far more insidious tactic than political spin. Spin merely attempts to shift the interpretation of a real situation by presenting it in a different light. Gaslighting presents a completely false alternative to reality and is intended to erode the confidence of the target in his or her own perception. – **Timothy Daughtry**

GAYWASHING: The act of adding something to your product, advertisement or TV show to make it gay to make sure you're being politically correct. – **urbandictionary.com**

GENDER WAGE GAP MYTH: Yes, construction workers are paid more than hotel maids, but when comparing similar jobs with similar hours, several studies including the US Department of Labor reveal the 23-cent gender wage gap is actually five to six cents and even that is primarily due to negotiation skills as well as individual choices being made by both male and female workers, such as college majors and willingness to work long hours. So when you hear someone say "77 cents on the dollar", it's no different than "97 percent of scientists say". It's a lie.

GONZO JOURNALISM: A highly personal style of subjective reporting with similarities to "immersion journalism" and "new journalism" of the 1960s and 1970s, and commonly utilizing exaggeration, sensationalism, profanity and sarcasm. Origin is from 1970 connection to Hunter S Thompson. "Yo, CNN has gone completely gonzo!"

GRADE INFLATION & TROPHY SYNDROME: 'A' grades were given to 15 percent of college students in 1960. That has risen to 43 percent today. Grade inflation promotes ego inflation, the opposite of healthy self-confidence. The "everybody gets a trophy" mentality basically says that you're going to get rewarded just for showing up. That won't build true self-esteem; instead, it builds this empty sense of "I'm just fantastic, not because I did anything but just because I'm here."

GREENWASHING: A form of spin when an organization deceptively claims to be "green" thru advertising and marketing, in an attempt to brand themselves as eco-friendly. Greenwashing provides an effective placebo for many who suffer from "eco-footprint guilt".

GROUPTHINK: A pattern of thought characterized by self-deception, forced manufacture of consent, and conformity to group values and ethics, done in

GRUBERING: Pertaining to Obamacare architect-campaigner Jonathan Gruber. Grubering is when politicians or their minions engage in a campaign of exaggeration and outright lies in order to "sell" the public on a particular policy initiative. The justification for grubering is that the public is too "stupid" to understand the topic and, should they be exposed to the true facts, would likely come to the "wrong" conclusion.

a way that discourages creativity or individual responsibility. The group is more concerned with maintaining unity than with objectively evaluating their situation, alternatives and options. The group, as a whole, tends to take irrational actions or overestimate their positions of moral righteousness.

HANDS UP, DON'T SHOOT!: The mainstream media's 2014 false narrative of Ferguson, Missouri which became a racial activist slogan and fueled anti-police resentment and violence. It is an example of how a fake news lie told repeatedly will "stick".

HATE CRIME: Hate crimes are an absurd, politically correct construct which suggests that crimes committed for reasons of ethnic or gender hatred are somehow more reprehensible than crimes that are committed for other reasons. A politician who supports such laws earns votes from the minority voters who are supposedly protected by such laws. Whites, yer out of luck.

HATE SPEECH: Any negative or critical view of liberalism, its goals, its core constituents, or its activities no matter how radical, outlandish or arbitrary.

HERD BEHAVIOR: Describes how people are influenced by their peers to adopt certain behaviors or follow trends. Unique behavioral characteristics emerge when people are in large groups.

HITLER WAS A SOCIALIST LIBERAL: The PC liberal notion is that Hitler was a right-winger. NAZI stands for National Socialist German Workers Party. As a democratic socialist Hitler supported public education with state sponsored curriculum, gun control, labor unions, nationalized healthcare, abortion, euthanasia death panels, blamed the one percent (Jews), loathed free speech, and pioneered the environmental movement.

HYPERBOLE: Exaggerated statements. The consequence of "crying wolf" with embellished rhetorical overkill, seen routinely in our sensationalistic liberal complex, is that nobody takes you seriously anymore.

INDOCTRINATION: To teach someone to fully accept the ideas, opinions, and beliefs of a particular group without consideration of other ideas, opinions, and beliefs.

INDOCRINATION U: The Left's War Against Academic Freedom: David Horowitz's 2007 book culminating his 2003 campaign to promote intellectual diversity and a return to academic standards in American universities.

INTELLECTUAL DIVERSITY: Diversity of ideas which are virtually forbidden on campus, mainstream media and public institutions due to conflicts with the abject conformity required by political correctness.

JOURNALISM STANDARDS: 1. Truth and Accuracy; Getting the facts right is the cardinal principle of journalism. 2. Independence; Journalists must be unbiased independent voices. 3. Fairness and Impartiality; Stories should be balanced and add context. 4. Humanity; Journalists should do no harm. 5. Accountability; Errors must be corrected.

JUMP THE SHARK: A term to describe a moment when something that was once great has reached a point where it has crossed over into stupidity and uselessness and will now decline in quality and popularity. For a politician, bureaucrat, scientist, journalist or academic, a point where they have lost all credibility.

JUNK SCIENCE: Untested or unproven theories when presented as scientific fact. It is faulty scientific data and analysis used to advance special interests and hidden agendas often for financial or political gain. Junk science is commonly found among the cultures of green activists, bureaucrats, politicians, academia and media.

KOOL-AID DRINKER: Someone blinded by faith. To "drink the kool-aid" means to make a wholehearted, unconditional commitment to a cause without researching it. It originates from the followers of Jim Jones' religious cult who traveled to Guyana and committed suicide by drinking poisoned Kool-Aid. Common usage is associated with many environmental causes and liberal politics founded on emotion, faith and pseudoscience.

KU KLUX KLAN: Contrary to the characterization portrayed by the left, the KKK was a terrorist cult aligned with the pro-slavery Democrat Party in 1865. Over three thousand blacks were killed by the original KKK however what most people don't know is that over one thousand whites were also killed, and they were republicans. Both the 1910s-20s and 1950s-60s KKK revivals were also initiated by democrats.

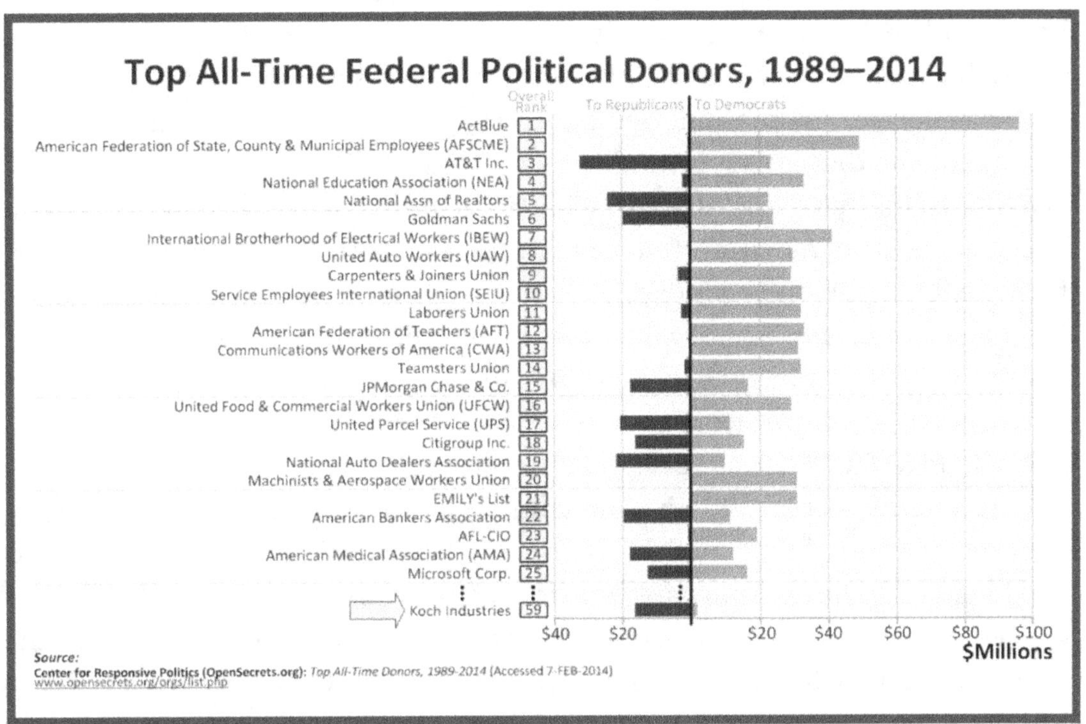

KOCH BROTHERS: The "evil" billionaires Charles and David Koch are common scapegoats for liberal democrats despite winning 792 awards since 2009 for environmental quality, operational safety, community service and philanthropy. They even received awards from the EPA and USFW and donate hundreds of millions of dollars for cancer research, hospitals, the fine arts and libertarian groups. Since they are oil tycoons the left insists they "are waging a war against anything that protects the environment."

LAMESTREAM MEDIA: Coined by journalist Bernard Goldberg to describe the clueless mainstream media that repeat superficial, discredited liberal claptrap.

LANGUAGE ACTIVISM, LANGUAGE POLICE, PC POLICE, SENSITIVITY ENFORCERS: Imposition of a "correct" political language by creating new words (Hispanic, sexism, victimization, social justice), or redefining words (discrimination, diversity, budget cuts) with the goals of deconstructing American culture and producing socialist ways of thinking and behaving.

LIBERAL CREEP: Liberal bias that gradually creeps or distorts an entry, definition, explanation, description, or historical account (revisionism). Example; the ferocity and savageness of the Native Americans towards American settlers has gradually been downplayed, while the relocation of the Cherokee has been gradually inflated to the point that some liberal textbooks treat it as an atrocity comparable to the Holocaust. Similarly, there has been an increase in denial of the many technological and spiritual improvements the settlers brought to previous inhabitants.

LIBERAL DELUSIONAL DISORDER: Delusions are irrational beliefs, held with a high level of conviction, that are highly resistant to change even when the delusional person is exposed to forms of proof that contradict the belief. It is most noticeable in liberals, most likely because there are more issues where the beliefs and policies held by liberals are not supported by truths and facts but are more supportive of emotional agendas.

LIBERAL PLATITUDES and CLICHES: Commonly used by liberals to avoid real arguments. A platitude is a meaningless statement directed at quelling emotional unease. Like a cliché it betrays a lack of original thought and provides a shallow, unifying wisdom over difficult topics. Examples: "Violence never solved anything"; "Diversity is strength"; "Save the planet"; "No war for oil"; "The one percent"; "The Constitution is a living document".

LIBERAL RELIGION STIGMA: For liberals, optimum meaning lies in a fulfillment of the ideals of justice – social justice thru redistribution of wealth, and environmental justice thru regulations. Liberal ideology ultimately rests on an act of faith and heretics are not tolerated. It is expedient for liberals that their movement not be seen as a religion since it thereby escapes the accusations of dogmatism and intolerance that are routinely made against conventional religions.

LIBERAL SELF-DECEPTION: "The liberal mind pretends it is intelligent by being open-minded. But open-minded is empty-headed, and the failure to see distinctions when lines are drawn in the sand of consciousness is reminiscent of Obama drawing a false red line in Syria… The liberal mind fails to make distinctions and decisions…. Black Lives Matter, transgenders – the causes multiply like rabbits in a cage. Not that the liberals really care about any of their causes. They just pretend because it reflects on themselves and allows them to feel better about themselves as good people. They want to feel indignant about how others treat others rather than examining their own failures." – **David Lawrence**

MARTIN LUTHER KING: Contrary to the liberal narrative, Dr. King was a Republican. Democrats were opposed to all the civil rights legislation of the 1950s and 1960s not to mention their pro-slavery history, Jim Crow laws and KKK affiliation.

MCCARTHYISM and VENONA PROJECT: In 1995 the Venona Project files were declassified and made available to the general public. They revealed that Joe McCarthy had underestimated the Soviet espionage threat. There were likely far more than the Project's confirmed 350 Americans who had secret relationships with Soviet intelligence, several in sensitive and high-level positions. Despite his vindication, the formerly beloved McCarthy is still vilified by the cult of politically correctness to this day.

MEDIA BIAS: The perception that the media is reporting the news in a partial or prejudiced manner. Media bias occurs when the media seems to push a specific viewpoint, rather than reporting the news objectively. Keep in mind that media bias also occurs when the media chooses to ignore significant news or an important aspect of the story (bias by omission). Numerous studies reveal a four or five to one liberal to conservative ratio of reporters, journalists and media professionals.

MICROAGGRESSIONS: Acts or words that are perceived to be insulting by a person who is looking to be insulted, whether or not that was the intent of the transgressor. They are usually a symptom of a persecution complex. Not only that, social scientist Dr. Stanley Hurt claims that modern human beings exist in a climate of near-continuous psychological danger, surrounded by potentially offensive situations known as "nanoaggressions". The widespread hospital practice of asking patients for their date of birth? That's right, it's a nanoaggression.

MEDIA VETTING BIAS: A comparison of the vetting of Barack Obama in 2008 with that of Donald Trump in 2016 reveals a huge double standard. It was not fashionable to report on Obama's 30-year history associating with Marxists and other questionable and radical characters, considering it rumor, innuendo and conspiracy theories. Seventy-one percent of the coverage of Obama's 2008 campaign was positive or neutral.

Comparatively, sixty-one percent of Trump's coverage was oppositional. Trump was fact-checked 135 times by Politifact to 48 times for Hillary Clinton in the same period. With Trump, nothing is too salacious, conspiratorial, or out-of-bounds for the press.

MINORITY RIGHTS: "The defense of minority rights is acclaimed today, virtually by everyone, as a moral principle of a high order. But this principle, which forbids discrimination, is applied by most of the 'liberal' intellectuals in a DISCRIMINATORY manner: it is applied only to racial, sexual orientation or religious minorities. It is not applied to that small, exploited, denounced, defenseless minority which consists of businessmen. Yet every ugly, brutal aspect of injustice toward other minorities is being practiced toward businessmen. Indeed, the smallest minority on earth is the individual." – **Ayn Rand**

MOB MENTALITY: A form of groupthink. The study of mob mentality or crowd hysteria is used to analyze situations that range from problems during evacuations to public gatherings that turn violent.

MORAL EQUIVALENCE: Typically, a logical fallacy used in political debates which seeks to draw comparisons between unrelated things to make a point that one is just as bad or good as the other.

NATIONAL CLIMATE ASSESSMENT BIAS: The NCA conducts a survey every four years. Obama's 2014 NCA overly focused on the supposed negative impacts from climate change while largely dismissing the positives. They foresaw an increasing frequency and magnitude of heat waves leading to growing numbers of heat-related deaths. Science suggests just the opposite though. Heat mortality has actually declined for several decades. This is one of many examples of intentional deception by our federal government in their efforts to expand the scope and power of EPA regulation and control.

NAZI PARTY LIBERALS: The left portrays the Nazis as a radical right-wing movement however the exact opposite is true. The National Socialist Party were socialists and opposed capitalism. They supported nationalization of corporations and industry, industry profit-sharing, price fixing, progressive taxation, welfare entitlements, a national bank, Keynesian economic policies, central planning, government supported labor unions, gun control, government controlled health care, abortion, euthanasia, affirmative action (for native Germans), state control of the press, public school indoctrination, expropriation of land, pro-animal rights, and were pioneers of eco-fascist environmentalism.

NEWZAK: A blend of news and Muzak. It describes the drone and constant buzz of omnipresent media – unchallenging, inessential, and without depth.

OPPOSITION RESEARCH: The practice of investigation and the collection of information into the dealings of political opponents in order to discredit them publicly. Fusion GPS was the Democrat-funded opposition firm which played a key role in the 2017 Russian collusion investigation of the Trump administration.

OPTICS: Primarily "bad optics". The viewing lens of public perception when the media creates and spins a story which may have political repercussions.

ORWELLIAN: Attitude and policy of government control by propaganda, surveillance, denial of truth, politically correct misinformation, censorship, and manipulation of the past.

PATHOLOGICAL SCIENCE: Nobel laureate Irving Langmuir's "science of things that aren't so". It is the specialty of self-styled public interest groups, whose agenda too often is not protection of public health or the environment, but intractable opposition to whatever research, product, or technology they happen to dislike. This is not a harmless diversion: When their machinations give rise to overregulation or even bans of safe and useful products or processes, such as GMO, fracking and nuclear energy, all of society is the poorer for it.

PAX ROMANA MYTH: For two centuries beginning in 31 B.C., the Roman Empire was peaceful and prosperous due to a huge, powerful central government that kept everyone in line. European statists pine for a return to the Pax Romana – never mind that it never happened. The 200-year 'Pax' was filled with tyranny, assassinations, terror, rebellion, foreign wars, and civil wars. All this is clearly documented.

PCBS: Adds emphasis to "politically correct" and "bullshit". With the daily bombardment of deception we face in modern media, academia, bureaucracy and pseudoscience, an acronym expansion is fitting. As more and more non-racist non-sexist Americans take umbrage to being labeled "racist!" and "sexist!" by the left, the response is "Enough with the PCBS!" and thus, Hillary and democrats lose.

PHOBIA PC MISNOMERS: A phobia is an irrational fear of something. Judging the behavior and character of individuals and cultures is rational and normal. Disapproving of promiscuous cultures as well as intolerant violent religions is totally rational and has little to do with fear.

Homophobic and Islamophobic labels are examples of politically correct deceptive terms used to confuse the issue and control the debate.

POLITICAL CORRECTNESS:

1. A scheme of social engineering and propaganda seeking to impose a uniformity of thought and behavior.

2. PC for short (or BS), political correctness is the politically correct term for Cultural Marxism, a systematic method to punish dissent and to stigmatize social heresy. Its trademark is intolerance, classifying its adversaries as haters, or mentally ill.

3. As the new age psychological bully, PC can be any true statement that has been transformed into a lie to control or mislead the weak minded or used as a weapon of intimidation to silence any criticism of a leftist authoritarian political agenda.

4. PC is the conscious, designed manipulation of language intended to change the way people speak, write, think, feel, and act, in furtherance of a liberal agenda.

5. PC is also the modus operandi for revisionist history.

POLITICAL CORRECTNESS AVATARS: Diversity, Tolerance, Sensitivity and Inclusion.

POLITICAL CORRECTNESS, GEORGE CARLIN: "Political Correctness is fascism pretending to be Manners" is a brilliant piece by George Carlin which can be viewed on YouTube.

POLITICAL INCORRECTNESS:

    1. For the most part, factually correct. **2.** Shinola.

POLITICALLY CORRECT MANIFESTO: Whoever is declared the biggest victim gets to be the biggest bully.

POPULISM vs PRINCIPLES: Populism is a doctrine often used in political campaigns that appeals to the interests and conceptions (such as hopes and fears) of commoners. It is an emotional and anti-intellectual appeal. Principles are basic truths, laws or assumptions. Nixon was populist, Reagan was principled. Trump vs Cruz was an example of emotional populism vs intellectual conservative principles. Populism is a building block for progressivism, and populists are ultimately progressives.

POLYANDRY and POLYGAMY: Marry your bowling team and keep your spouse as well – the next move for redefining marriage. After all, shouldn't they have the "right to love" as well? Who would deny them that?

POST-TRUTH: Oxford Dictionaries 2016 word of the year: "relating to or denoting circumstances in which objective facts are less influential in shaping public opinion than appeals to emotion and personal belief." This is what Pope Benedict called "the dictatorship of relativism". A post-truth society is one in which truth takes a back seat to emotion—where feelings effectively replace facts. A post-truth culture also leads us to equate disagreement with hatred and can lead us to ignore reality altogether.

PROPAGANDA: Information, especially of a biased or misleading nature, used to promote or publicize a particular political cause or point of view. Propaganda is a powerful weapon used to dehumanize and create hatred toward a supposed enemy by creating a false image in the mind.

PSEUDO-IDEALISM: Coined by Australian biologist Jeremy Griffith to describe apparently charitable behavior that on scrutiny is revealed as selfish because the giver is engaging in it only so that he can feel good about himself. It is a characteristic commonly found among the left and it constitutes their inherent dishonesty.

PUBLIC RADIO: Taxpayer funded media with a persistent liberal bias even after being outed. KGLP Gallup's signature program Democracy Now features anti-capitalist Amy Goodman, an identity politics, eco-hysteria and warfare sociology crusader.

RACIAL ATTITUDE EVOLUTION: Contrary to the prevailing liberal paradigm, the decades which showed by far the most remarkable economic and social gains made by blacks were the 1940s and 1950s, prior to the Civil Rights Movement, Civil Rights Acts and War on Poverty welfare programs of the 1960s. The 1970s saw a reversal of those gains, including the devastating breakdown of the previously endurant black family.

RATIONALIZATION: "… is a cover-up, a process of providing one's emotions with a false identity, of giving them spurious explanations and justifications—in order to hide one's motives, not just from others, but primarily from oneself… When a theory achieves nothing but the opposite of its alleged goals, yet its advocates remain undeterred, you may be certain that it is not a conviction or an "ideal," but a rationalization… 'Nobody can be certain of anything' is a rationalization for a feeling of envy and hatred toward those who ARE certain." – **Ayn Rand**

REACHING ACROSS THE AISLE: Politically correct for "asking twice as much as what you want and then compromising for half". One hundred years of progressive democrats reaching across the aisle and republicans reaching back has expanded government to the brink of socialism.

RED PILL & BLUE PILL: Derived from the 1999 film *The Matrix*, red pill and its opposite, the blue pill, represent the choice between the sometimes painful truth of reality (red pill) and the blissful ignorance of illusion (blue pill). "Red Pillers" primarily identify as libertarian and seek to roll back the achievements of Cultural Marxists, social justice warriors, political correctness and radical feminists. It is associated with the men's rights movement, who believe that women are actually the privileged group instead of men.

REGNERUS STUDY CENSORSHIP: The extensive peer-reviewed study on homosexual parenting by Mark Regnerus revealed rather clearly that children raised by gay or lesbian parents on average are at a significant disadvantage when compared to children raised by the intact family of their married, biological mother and father. These results were no surprise to researchers yet what was just as significant as the study was the bitter attacks from pro-homosexual activists smearing the reputation of Regnerus in attempts to silence any such research. A politically correct and complicit media, academia and bureaucracy assisted in the Orwellian censorship.

REVISIONIST HISTORY: A major component of the dumbing down process, revisionism is a liberal indoctrination tool to reinterpret history in order to conform with a politically correct ideology.

SACRED COW: A figurative sacred cow is something that is considered immune from question or criticism. In the Gallup NM establishment, the Navajo Nation is a sacred cow.

SAFE SPACE: A place where college students can go if they have been subjected to ideas that differ from the progressive narrative. Presumably, this allows them to recover from the trauma; free from any lasting damage resulting from exposure to ideas that conflict with their leftist professors.

SEXUAL HARASSMENT: The accusation when heterosexual men attempt "coming out" by discussing their sexual orientation with women in the workplace.

SHAMING: Historically, public derision and stigmatization of those engaging in culturally taboo activities, usually to modify behavior by inducing guilt or to assign blame. The term that sparked the current surge, "slut-shaming" goes back millennia as a preventive measure to the breakdown of the nuclear family and society as well as STD prevention. "Fat-shaming" is a politically incorrect contemporary method of reducing obese people's excessive health care costs which are paid for by healthy people. Nowadays anyone who is slightly insensitive or not PC enough can be led to a public character lynching (shaming) without due process. What a shame.

SHEEPLE: A term that highlights the herd behavior of people by likening them to sheep, a herd animal. The term is used to describe those who voluntarily acquiesce to a suggestion without critical analysis or research.

SLOTHFUL INDUCTION: A logical fallacy of poor pattern recognition. Slothful induction is the "sticking your head in the sand" defense, despite overwhelming evidence to the contrary. It is commonly found among the green activist cult. "Just because all 73 climate change computer models and doomsday predictions considerably overshot the mark doesn't mean we aren't on the eve of destruction."

SNOPES.COM: A left-wing "fact-checking" site known for twisting facts and definitions to validate progressive notions under the guise of neutral examination of the facts. Snopes was chosen by Facebook as a source of vetting for "fake news", putting it in the position of censoring access to material on the biggest single source of news for Americans. – **Thomas Lifson,** American Thinker

SOCIO-CULTURAL ENGINEERING: Cultural transformation by forceful and coercive government intervention into society and family life so as to bind people into a 'better' existence compliant with a politically correct moral code. Familiar examples include dictating our food choices, affirmative action, mandatory recycling, demonizing smokers and micromanaging personal energy consumption.

SPIN: To provide an interpretation of something such as a statement or event, especially in a way meant to sway public opinion.

SPIN DOCTOR: A spokesperson employed to give a favorable interpretation of events to the media, especially on behalf of a political party.

SUPERSTITIONS, POLITICAL: The ability to hold fervent beliefs, in defiance of evidence, that explain how the world works – and why liberal solutions must be adopted. *Refer to the appendix for Kate Bachelder's top ten list of liberal superstitions.*

> **STRAW MAN ARGUMENT:** An informal fallacy based on mischaracterizations and the misrepresentation of an opponent's argument and requiring that the audience be ignorant or uninformed of the original argument.

SWIFTBOATING: The public disclosure of a politician's claims to phony war heroism and undeserved medals. The Left's politically correct definition which can be found in Wikipedia is something like "a harsh attack by a political opponent that is dishonest, personal, and unfair." Swiftboating has become an appropriation by the Left, twisting a term describing honorable behavior involving self-sacrifice by American veterans into an epithet which when directed your way by liberals immediately labels you as some sort of treacherous turncoat. – **Russ Vaughn, Viet Nam veteran**

TABLOID OR YELLOW JOURNALISM: The practice of seeking out sensational news for the purpose of boosting a newspapers circulation. It exploits, distorts or exaggerates news which is luridly or vulgarly sensational such as doomsday "the sky is falling" predictions.

TABOOS, PROMISCUITY: Taboos are social customs prohibiting or forbidding certain behaviors, discussions of a particular practice, or forbidding association with a particular person, place, or thing. For thousands of years, cultural promiscuity taboos have served the purpose of ensuring children's birthrights to their biological mother and father as well as prevention of sexually transmitted disease. What seemed obvious to primitive man ("duh!") has now become a violation of political correctness with the obvious consequence of fatherless children and STI epidemics.

TALK RADIO: How is it that mainstream media is so liberally biased yet liberal talk radio has been an utter failure? Liberalism is primarily based on emotion so the lack of intellect makes any prolonged monologue or dialogue insufferably boring. Even leftist NPR must be subsidized for survival. On the other hand, dozens of conservative talk radio hosts enjoy large audiences.

THOUGHT-TERMINATING CLICHÉ: A short definitive-sounding expression thrown into a debate to end all discussion or thought about the topic of that debate. It is used in totalitarian societies to quell dissent and more generally to mask the fact that the person using it cannot mount an effective argument or effectively address the counter-argument. – **Conservapedia.** Allegations of a microaggression are sometimes utilized to terminate a discussion and the clichés may be of varying intensity from "everyone is entitled to their own opinion" to a play of the race card - "Racist!"

TOLERANCE PARADOX: Arises when a tolerant person holds antagonistic views toward intolerance, and hence is intolerant of it.

TONE POLICING or TONE ARGUMENT: The ultimate derailing tactic - a "call for civility" method of silencing the opposition. It occurs when an argument is dismissed or accepted on its presentation, such as perceived crassness, hysteria or anger. The "victim" has the tables turned on them, becoming the "victimizer".

TRIGGER WARNING: A phrase posted at the beginning of various posts, articles, or blogs. Its purpose is to warn weak minded people who are easily offended that they might find what is being posted offensive in some way due to its content.

Trigger Warning - This is a politically incorrect definition of political correctness – "A term used for whiny overly sensitive pansies who need everything sugar-coated for them."

WEAPONS OF MASS DESTRUCTION: Contrary to the false liberal narrative, 1998 was the year of the WMD alarmists. George Bush took office in 2001 and the Iraq invasion began in 2003. It was Bill Clinton who laid out the connection between Iraq, WMD and Al Qaeda in 1998, bombed Iraq in order to "degrade" Hussein's WMD capabilities and then provided such a strong rationale for going to war against Hussein that the far left was distressed at his turn toward warmongering.

WHITEWASH: To gloss over or cover up vices, crimes or scandals or to exonerate through biased presentation of data. Example; the Democrat Party's whitewashing of their racist history to create a politically correct appearance of inclusion, integration and diversity.

WILLFUL IGNORANCE: The state and practice of ignoring any sensory input that appears to contradict one's inner model of reality. At heart, it is almost certainly driven by confirmation bias.

WITCH HUNT: The Puritans engaged in the search and persecution of supposed witches, a process of societal purification. Modern day witch hunts, typically of the left, also engage in purification by utilizing identity politics to demonize and bully those who do not conform to their politically correct orthodoxy.

ZINN, HOWARD: Cult figure author of the 1980 propaganda, *A People's History of the United States*. Utilizing the tactics of Cultural Marxism, Zinn believed historians should embrace bias and selectivity as tools for the utopian pursuit of social justice – a moral obligation to shape material in ways that will advance certain causes, even at the expense of truth. His hateful leftist fantasy was that America has always been racist, oppressive, warmongering, and exploitative, and that it must be subverted, beginning in the classroom.

TEN COMMANDMENTS OF RATIONAL DEBATE AND THEIR LOGICAL FALLACIES

1. THOU SHALT NOT ATTACK THE PERSON'S CHARACTER, BUT THE ARGUMENT. *(AD HOMINEM)*

2. THOU SHALT NOT MISREPRESENT A PERSON'S ARGUMENT IN ORDER TO MAKE IT EASIER TO ATTACK. *(STRAW MAN FALLACY)*

3. THOU SHALT NOT USE SMALL NUMBERS TO REPRESENT THE ALL. *(HASTY GENERALIZATION)*

4. THOU SHALT NOT ARGUE THY POSITION BY ASSUMING ONE OF ITS PREMISES IS TRUE. *(BEGGING THE QUESTION)*

5. THOU SHALT NOT CLAIM THAT BECAUSE SOMETHING OCCURRED BEFORE, IT MUST BE THE CAUSE. *(POST HOC/FALSE CAUSE)*

6. THOU SHALT NOT REDUCE THE ARGUMENT DOWN TO TWO POSSIBILITIES. *(FALSE DICHOTOMY)*

7. THOU SHALT NOT ARGUE THAT BECAUSE OF OUR IGNORANCE, A CLAIM MUST BE TRUE OR FALSE. *(AD IGNORANTUM)*

8. THOU SHALT NOT LAY THE BURDEN OF PROOF ONTO HIM THAT IS QUESTIONING THE CLAIM. *(BURDEN OF PROOF REVERSAL)*

9. THOU SHALT NOT ASSUME "THIS" FOLLOWS "THAT" WHEN THERE IS NO LOGICAL CONNECTION. *(NON SEQUITUR)*

10. THOU SHALT NOT ARGUE THAT BECAUSE A PREMISE IS POPULAR, THEREFORE IT MUST BE TRUE. *(BANDWAGON FALLACY)*

CHAPTER FIVE

IDENTITY

IS IT 'WHITE PRIVILEGE' OR 'RAISED BY BIOLOGICAL MOTHER AND FATHER PRIVILEGE'?

USA out-of-wedlock births by race

Asian/Pacific Islander	17%
White	29%
Hispanic	53%
American Indian	67%
Black	72%

U.S. Dept of Health & Human Services

Median household income by race (thousands)

Indian-American ethnicity	$86
Filipino-American ethnicity	$77
Asian	$69
Egyptian-American ethnicity	$63
Pacific Islander	$59
White	$57
Hispanic	$39
American Indian	$39
Black	$33

U.S. Census Bureau

Joe Schaller

Quotes

"Our deeds determine us, as much as we determine our deeds." – **George Eliot**

"The great virtue of a free market system is that it does not care what color people are; it does not care what their religion is; it only cares whether they can produce something you want to buy. It is the most effective system we have discovered to enable people who hate one another to deal with one another and help one another." – **Milton Friedman**

"I look to a day when people will not be judged by the color of their skin, but by the content of their character." - **Martin Luther King Jr**

"I'll have those niggers voting Democrat for 200 years." – **Lyndon Baines Johnson**

"Racism is not dead, but it is on life support – kept alive by politicians, race hustlers and people who get a sense of superiority by denouncing others as 'racists'." – **Thomas Sowell**

"Feelings" and "compassion" are two of the most often used liberal terms. "Character" is no longer a liberal word because it implies self-restraint. "Good and evil" are not liberal words either as they imply a moral standard beyond one's feelings." – **Dennis Prager**

"End results that work that don't involve government threaten liberals." – **Rush Limbaugh**

"The legacy of slavery, Jim Crow, discrimination in almost every institution of our lives, you know, that casts a long shadow, and that's still part of our DNA that's passed on." – **Barack Obama**

"Indeed, liberals and white supremacists are the only people left in America who are neurotically obsessed with race. Conservatives champion a color-blind society." – **Ann Coulter**

"In short, liberalism is based on one central desire: to look cool in front of others in order to get love. Preaching tolerance makes you look cooler, than saying something like, "please lower my taxes". – **Greg Gutfeld**

"When you are so obsessed with identity politics it's not healthy because you're constantly worried about how you're perceived as opposed to your achievements. Once your identity becomes your achievement then you run into serious problems." – **Greg Gutfeld**

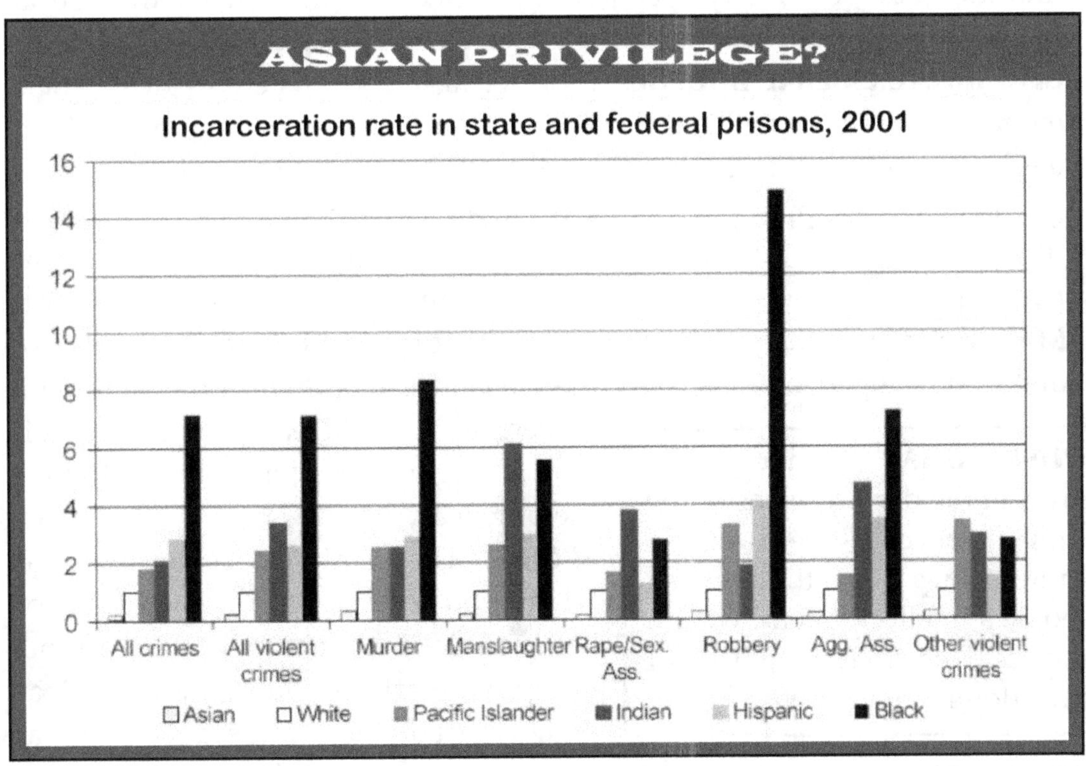

ACCULTURATION: The process of learning and adapting to the practices and customs of a new culture. Acculturation of immigrants, refugees and indigenous peoples are associated not just with changes in daily behavior, but with numerous measures of psychological and physical well-being. Acculturation requires more adaptation than assimilation.

ADVERSITY.NET: "A non-profit educational organization dedicated to the elimination of prejudice and discrimination – including the elimination of divisive racial preferences and quotas." I have used them as a resource for several definitions below.

AFFIRMATIVE ACTION: Political correctness in the form of institutionalized racism, classism and sexism. It is an unconstitutional form of reverse discrimination that sets racial, gender and class quotas, judging a person's credentials by race, class or gender rather than merit. It's intent was to lift minorities out of poverty, yet who benefited the most from the special treatment of affirmative action? It was rich black kids and women.

AGING HIPPIE LIBERAL DOUCHE: A former hippie with stereotypical beliefs, who may or may not still externally show their hippieness, and have liberal beliefs. This phrase was coined on an episode of South Park. An example of a possible aging hippie is a man in his late fifties/early sixties, a full beard, but groomed, long strait hair, usually braided or tied into a pony tail, and openly speaks out their beliefs in the way of an activist. - **urbandictionary**

ANCHOR BABY: Politically incorrect for 'automatic birthright citizenship'. Among developed nations, only the US and Canada still offer automatic citizenship to children born on their soil. Not a single European country follows the practice.

ANTI-SEMITISM: Primarily class envy. In the dark recesses of the human psyche we are so screwed up by the Jewish people's intellect, talent, wealth and resilience that the poison of envy dominates.

APORIA: That sinking feeling you get when you realize that something you believed in isn't actually true. In our deceptive world of information overload and contradictory messages from an activist media, academia and bureaucracy, aporia has become a common slap-in-the-face wake-up call.

ASSIMILATION: Involves being absorbed into the new culture. People can assimilate without being acculturated. The Mormons of Utah are not completely acculturated to contemporary American society but they are assimilated.

BARBARY PIRATES: One of America's first confrontations with the Muslim world occurred in the late 1700s with Tunis, Morocco and Algeria. John Adams and Thomas Jefferson were astonished at the excessive tribute required for safe passage of US merchant ships. The Tripolitan ambassador declared that all nations which had not acknowledged the prophet were sinners, whom it was the right and duty of the faithful to plunder and enslave. The two founders were horrified by the envoy's religious justification for greed and cruelty.

BLACK CRIME: The skyrocketing rise of crime among blacks had a direct correlation with political correctness and the 1964 War on Poverty with its perverse incentives which tore apart black families. Evidence reveals blacks are not targeted by police, they simply commit far more crimes, both petty and grand.

CHECK YOUR PRIVILEGE: Refers to which class or collective identity you have been assigned. Are you a member of an "official victim" class or an "official oppressor" class. Are you to be sympathized with or vilified.

CISGENDER PRIVILEGE: While cisgender refers to someone's sex and gender identity appearing to align, cisgender privilege speaks to how perceived gender/sex alignment means not having to think or address topics that those without cisgender privilege have to deal with.

Examples from University of Oregon transgender-cisgender "research guide": 1. "I am a size and shape for which clothes I feel comfortable wearing are commonly made." 2. "My potential lovers expect my genitals to look roughly similar to the way they do, and have accepted that before coming to bed with me." The guidelines reveal that capitalism is to blame.

CLASSISM: Class discrimination. It is prejudice or discrimination on the basis of social class. The class envy of the "one percent" exhibited by Occupy Wall Street is an example of classism.

CONTENT OF CHARACTER: Criteria for judging individuals and cultures prior to the era of the institutional cult of political correctness. Dr. Martin Luther King is rolling over in his grave.

CRITICAL RACE THEORY: If you are white you are a racist. "Color blindness" is also racist. Racist cops arrest black people for no reason, prosecutors are trying them for no reason, juries are convicting them, judges are sentencing them, parole boards are releasing them, and cops are rearresting them all for no reason what-so-ever except for the fact they are black.

CULT: Divergent definitions include systems of religious, political or social veneration and devotion directed toward a particular figure or object; as well as social groups, large and small, with novel beliefs and practices often considered to be of a socially deviant nature.

CULTURAL APPROPRIATION: Hey paleface, are you authorized to wear that headdress? A politically correct concept which views the adoption or use of elements of one culture by members of a different culture as a largely negative phenomenon. Indicative of a group persecution complex which does nothing but support segregation, promote racism and hinder progress in the world. PC run amok. Halloween will never be the same. America is an appropriated culture in itself, with virtually ALL sub-cultures appropriating from each other. Thus, the melting pot - *E pluribus unum.*

CULTURE: The beliefs, customs, attitudes, behaviors etc. characterizing a particular society or group of people, large and small. Culture is transmitted through language, ritual, institutions, and art, from one generation to the next.

CULTURAL/MORAL RELATIVISM: In contrast to ethnocentrism cultural relativism is the philosophical belief that all cultural views are equally valid. Moral relativism rejects the idea of universal right and wrong. In a relativist society we have no right to judge or punish anyone. In my own relativist version of the truth I maintain that relativism is false and nothing but PCBS.

CULTURAL TRIBALISM: Conformity to a way of thinking or behaving in which people are loyal to a social group. Members tend to possess a strong feeling of identity. Tribal identity ultimately creates the segregation of multiculturalism.

DEMOCRAT SYMBOLS OF RACISM: Contrary to politically correct beliefs, the Confederate flag represented the Democrat Party. While the Republican Party was founded primarily to oppose slavery, the Democrat Party fought them and tried to keep and even expand slavery. In fact, democrats have fought to oppress blacks for hundreds of years. Other symbols of democrat racism include those associated with Jim Crow laws, the Ku Klux Klan and the current symbol and mascot of the Democrat Party, the jackass, which in all fairness to the cult of political correctness should be erased as a hurtful microaggression to all minorities.

DISPARATE IMPACT: Any test, job criterion, educational statistic, or crime statistic in which minorities are rated more poorly than whites. The presumption is that ANY test, statistic, crime report, or educational admission standard under which minorities perform poorly is somehow inherently racist – **Adversity.Net**

DIVERSITY: An excuse to discriminate. "In the 1990s the racial quota industry co-opted the term "diversity" to have a distinctly political pro-quota meaning." – **Adversity.Net**…. In the real world, be careful what you wish for - the KKK, pedophiles, drunkards, transient panhandlers and Islamic jihadists are all examples of diversity. In Hollywood, diversity means black.

Trigger Warning The PC police have deemed the following Robert Putnam study a microaggression to be stricken from academic records.

DIVERSITY and INCLUSION: Diversity is when people of different skin colors and ethnic groups all think exactly the same. Inclusion is when those same people get together and include only themselves. – **Greg Penglis**

DIVERSITY RESEARCH (Robert Putnam): The greater the diversity in a community, the fewer people vote and the less they volunteer, the less they give to charity and work on community projects. In the most diverse communities, neighbors trust one another about half as much as they do in the most homogeneous settings. The study, the largest ever on civic engagement in America, found that virtually all measures of civic health are lower in more diverse settings.

Banned phrase- "birds of a feather flock together".

DYSPHORIA: The opposite of euphoria – a general state of anxiety, restlessness, lack of energy, vague irritation, depression, and anger. Dysphoria is most often associated with gender and ethnic identity confusion.

ECHO CHAMBER, MSM: Media conformity – an element of cultural tribalism; someone in the mainstream media will make a claim, a phrase, or a buzzword, and suddenly it is repeated over and over again by mass media. Sources go unquestioned and opposing views are often censored or underrepresented.

EQUAL OPPORTUNITY: A corrupted concept meaning, "we hire the right numbers of people from each of the government-specified racial and sexual categories". – **Adversity.Net**…. In contrast to forced equality, opportunity for everyone is a basic premise of a free market society.

EQUAL OPPORTUNITY HARASSER: If a preferred minority treats ALL of his/her employees badly than he/she may escape prosecution for reverse discrimination.

EQUAL PAY ACT 1963: Guarantees that men and women in the same job with the same level of seniority and experience are paid the same amount. If there are disparities, a lawyer is the person to seek, not a politician, bureaucrat, activist or journalist.

ETHNIC DIVERSITY: Racism in a politically correct disguise which causes people to be condemned or praised based on their ethnic membership. Ethnic diversity is a goal of affirmative action.

ETHNICITY: Stresses the traditional, rather than the physiological characteristics of a group, such as language, however race is involved so the advocacy of ethnicity means racism plus tradition or conformity.

ETHNOCENTRISM: In contrast to cultural relativism, ethnocentrism is the belief that your native culture is the most natural or superior way of understanding the world.

FEMINISM, DIFFERENCE: Asserts that there are physiological, emotional and intellectual differences between men and women that do not, or should not, be considered equally.

FEMINISM, NEW: Holds that women should be valued in their role as child bearers, both culturally and economically, while not being viewed as a "home maker" in the broader sense of the meaning. Its main aim is to promote the idea that women are individuals with equal worth as men; and that in social, economic and legal senses they should be equal, while accepting the natural differences between the sexes.

FEMININE SIDE, IN TOUCH WITH: Contemporary men are encouraged to express their feelings more. On the flip-side modern feminism encourages women to adopt male characteristics. Lost in the PC cult's fear of stereotypes is step one; women must first get in touch with their feminine side and men their masculine side.

FORCED BUSING 1970s: Supported by only a thin majority of black parents, they eventually discovered that forced integration of schools by busing students to other neighborhoods undermined parental involvement in faraway schools, took away the community feeling they had for neighborhood schools, had no appreciable effect on black educational achievement, increased racial tension and animosity, and drove white families out of the cities, all at a very great expense to taxpayers.

GENDER IDENTITIES: Genderqueer, pansexual, transgender, trannydyke, trannyfag, boi, boydyke, trannyboy, multigendered, polygendered, queerboi, transboi, transguy, transman, half-dyke, bi-dyke, stud, stem, trisexual, omnisexual, multisexual, heteroflexible, FTM, MTF and butch dyke. You'll have to use your imagination.

GENDER NEUTRAL LANGUAGE: A denial of XY male chromosomes and XX female chromosomes determining sexual identity. Gender neutrality enforces the idea that we should avoid giving roles to genders and sexes in schools, the workplace, places of worship and other institutions. Gender neutral locker rooms? - finally, men get what they have always wanted.

GENTRIFICATION: The buying and renovation of houses and stores in deteriorated urban neighborhoods by upper- or middle-income families or individuals, thus improving property values but often displacing low-income families and small businesses.... "If you are a minority, the government defines gentrification as 'bad' -- especially if it means that more 'whites' are moving into your neighborhood. But if you are 'white', the government defines gentrification as 'good' as long as it means that you have to leave the neighborhood so that more minorities can live there." – **Adversity.Net**.... Spike Lee does not want gentrification of white people into his neighborhood.

GRIEVANCE INDUSTRY: Coined by Bill O'Reilly; opportunistic activists, agitators and lawyers profit from false claims of racial, gender, class and environmental injustice. The PC media legitimizes the grievance hustlers instead of challenging them, enabling power to ideological fanatics. Racial agitator Al Sharpton rakes in big bucks as a leader of the racial grievance industry.

HATE GROUPS: Stoking fear and hatred in the name of racial, gender, class, environmental or gay sensitivity is diabolical and must be exposed and confronted. Some of those groups include; Southern Poverty Law Center (the worst), Antifa, NAACP, ACLU, Dept of Homeland Security, Service Employees International Union, Anti-Defamation League, MoveOn.org, and Black Lives Matter.

HOMOPHOBOPHOBIA: A fear or dislike of those who do not condone a homosexual lifestyle. "I hate homophobes. It is so sick that they hate someone because of a lifestyle choice".

HOMOSEXUALITY, APA 1973 DECISION: After three years of intense political pressure and intimidation "to discredit psychiatry" from gay activists, 33 percent of American Psychiatric Association members voted to remove homosexuality from its official list of psychiatric disorders. For over a hundred years the APA had regarded homosexuality as a perversion, deviant behavior and mental illness. There was no scientific breakthrough or set of facts that stimulated the change, only the claim that homosexuals were content with their sexual orientation, and that as a group they appeared to be well-adjusted. That rationale could just as well be made by pedophiles and other, ahem, abnormal behaviors.

HOMOSEXUALITY, IDENTICAL TWIN STUDIES: Eight major studies of identical twins in Australia, the U.S., and Scandinavia during the past two decades all arrived at the same conclusion: gays were not born that way. If an identical twin has same-sex attraction the chances the co-twin has it are only about 11 percent for men and 14 percent for women. Because they have identical DNA, it ought to be 100 percent.

HOMOSEXUAL PARADOX OF NATURAL SELECTION: How can a trait like male homosexuality, if it has a genetic component, persist over evolutionary time if the individuals who carry the genes associated with that trait are not reproducing.

HYPHENATED-AMERICANS: A phrase popularized by Theodore Roosevelt during World War I to criticize Americans who had loyalties to the countries of their ancestors. For most Americans, the essence of being an American does not include the use of a hyphen because we do not need the added "security" of belonging, or having allegiance to, more than one place, country or ancestry. America is enough for us and we simply have no need for anything "more".

IDENTITY and IDENTIFYING: Identity is the qualities, beliefs, etc., that make a particular person or group different from others. Identifying is the practice of psychological orientation of the self in regard to something (as a person or group) with a resulting feeling of close emotional association. Viewers often identify with movie characters. There are some who identify with other races, ethnicities and the opposite gender.

IDENTITY APPROPRIATION: Whereas cultural appropriation is viewed as a negative phenomenon, appropriating gender identities is a politically correct positive. Thus, transgender identities gain preferential treatment and access. I'm not quite sure what the term would be if one decided to identify as a black lesbian in a wheelchair – schizophrenic appropriation?

IDENTITY CRISIS: A period or episode of psychological distress in which a person's sense of identity becomes insecure, often occurring in adolescence but sometimes in adulthood.

IDENTITY DISORDERS: Strong "cross-gender identification" is defined as "gender dysphoria". There is also "species dysphoria" – the sense of being an animal stuck in a human body – and Body Integrity Identity Disorder (BIID), the strong sense that a body part or parts don't belong on/in one's body (e.g., legs, eyes). All three disorders are defined by "feelings". There's no more proof that gender dysphoria has a biological basis then there is that species dysphoria or BIID does. Telling schoolchildren it's normal to live as the opposite sex is child abuse. It warps their sense of reality. – **Selwyn Duke**

IDENTITY POLITICS: Political arguments that focus upon and exploit the interest and perspectives of groups with which people identify to forward an agenda. Also, political activity or movements based on or catering to the ethnic, gender, racial, sexual, religious, class or social interests that characterize a group identity. Gender warfare, class envy, gay rights, race hustling and even environmentalism are examples of identity politics. Whereas the dividing lines in the GOP are primarily over policy, democrats have become the party of identity, which not only fuels polarization, it requires it.

ILLEGAL ALIEN: A foreigner who does not owe allegiance to our country and who has violated our laws and customs in establishing residence in our country. He or she is therefore a criminal under applicable U.S. laws. Politically incorrect for "undocumented democrat". – **Adversity.Net**

IMMIGRANT, UNDOCUMENTED: An oxymoron. An immigrant is synonymous with "permanent legal resident". – **Adversity.Net**

INCLUSION: or Politics of Inclusion is politically correct for racial quotas and preferences. Inclusion in this context is based upon the dubious (and constitutionally indefensible) assumption that persons of certain colors, genders, sexual orientations and ethnicities are entitled to proportional representation in all jobs, schools, all walks of life – regardless of their qualifications. – **Adversity.Net**

INDIGENOUS: Any given people claiming a region as their traditional tribal land. However, American Indians are not one ethnicity, culture or race.

They are made up of hundreds of separate tribes of many different origins and, similar to most peoples around the world, they at some point migrated and "invaded" new lands. In the American Southwest assigning indigenous labels can be tricky considering Northern Canadian Athabaskans (Navajo and Apache) emigrated thousands of miles southward to the Southwest circa 1500 around the same time the Spaniards settled in Central America and then emigrated to the Southwest from the south circa 1600.

INDIGO CHILDREN: The chosen ones, here to raise the vibration of the planet, leaving a trail of consciousness they have pioneered with their aura of indigo waves. Only the dysfunctional and helpless qualify.

INTEGRATION: Motivated by equal opportunity for all, integration is a two-way societal process where there are cross influences from differing cultures and both change a small bit to accept the minority culture into the majority culture.

INTERSECTIONALITY: Whoever shouts the loudest and claims victimization on account of more facets of their identity can expect to get what they demand, regardless of the quality or even logic of what they have to say. – **James Kirchick**

INVOLUNTARY VICTIMHOOD: Where mass groups of individuals, either by race, religion, ethnicity, political belief, education level, or any other characteristic, are grouped together and made victims for political gain of the Left, whether those individuals would choose to be labeled victims or not. – **Greg Penglis**

ISLAMIC SHARIA LAW: Religious-political legal system including deterrent punishments ordained by Allah. Under Islamic law there is no separation of church and state. Sharia guides all aspects of Muslim life including daily routines, familial and religious obligations, and financial dealings. The Sharia system is totalitarian and incompatible with the US Constitution. Unlike other religions, Islam is the only major religion that prescribes coercive violence at its core.

JIHAD: "To war against non-Muslims to establish the religion," is the duty of every Muslim and Muslim head of state.

JUDEO-CHRISTIAN VALUES: Distinguished primarily by the Ten Commandments and embodied in the Declaration of Independence and US Constitution. Judeo-Christian values are in total contrast to the toxic values of fascism, communism and totalitarian Islamic Sharia law.

LIBERAL INSECURITY: Liberals are by nature insecure people desperately trying to socially legitimize a fundamentally illegitimate ideology. – anonymousconservative.com

LIBERALS: Advocates of statism and opponents of freedom. They do not want to know or to admit that they are the champions of dictatorship and slavery, nor that their only principle is that every problem can be solved by the magic power of brute force.

MANSPLAINING: Explaining without regard to the fact that the explainee knows more than the explainer, typically done condescendingly by a man to a woman. Often an indication of a persecution complex of the explainee.

MELTING POT: E pluribus unum (out of many, one) is the historically exceptional notion of American identity as one formed not by the accidents of blood, sect, or race, but by the unifying beliefs and political ideals enshrined in the Declaration of Independence and the Constitution: the notion of individual, inalienable human rights that transcend group identity. Prior to the welfare state, immigrants escaped cultural and racial oppression, abandoning their previous nationalities while still retaining ethnic pride and integrating into a new American culture. Integration-assimilation was also the motivation for the 1954-68 Civil Rights Movement.

METRICS: The term the corporate quota pushers use to define "measures of diversity". – **Adversity.Net**

MISANDRY: We often hear of misogyny, a contempt of women, yet much of modern feminism has devolved into a cult of misandry, a contempt of men. Many feminists are indeed sexist – close-minded, manhating sheep, indoctrinated to see "oppression" everywhere.

MOTIVATED REASONING: How we fool ourselves thru groupthink. Motivated reasoning lets your gut emotions shape your thinking or arguing in an identity protective fashion – to protect who you are, what collectivist group you belong to, your religious beliefs, or your political views, such as emotional liberals blindly dismissing the science of nuclear power, historical economic failures of statism-progressivism, or lack of global warming evidence.

MULTICULTURAL SALAD: The racial identity politics of modern political correctness encourages multicultural segregation over integration. Immigrants often come to America seeking all the freedoms and benefits without any desire of abandoning their failed national culture nor have any desire for social contact with any outside their own ethnicity, even seeking to alter the American legal system to conform to their own cultural norms. Multiculturalism as we know it is not about respecting or celebrating the salad bowl of cultural or ethnic diversity, but about indicting American civilization for its imperial, colonial, xenophobic, and racist sins.

MULTICULTURALISM: Also known as cultural pluralism. It is the doctrine that simultaneously (and incoherently) propounds the equality of all ethnic groups (cultural relativism), and stridently attacks all aspects of Western thought as corrupt (racist, classist, sexist, etc.). Rather than celebrate diversity, modern multiculturalism endorses a species of identity politics predicated on victimization. It fosters segregation rather than integration. Multiculturalism is anti-individualistic in the sense that it expects each person to agree with the perceptions, thoughts, and judgments of his ethnic-racial group in order for his own perceptions, thoughts, and judgments to be legitimate.

MULTICULTURALISM, EUROPEAN: In 2011, the United Kingdom, Germany, France and the famously progressive and permissive Netherlands declared multiculturalism as a failure and sought obligatory integration, assimilation and acceptance of British, German and Dutch values.

MULTIRACIAL MARRIAGE: Sociologists have traditionally viewed multiracial marriage as a benchmark for the ultimate stage of assimilation of an ethnic-racial group in society. America now has among the highest percentage of multiracial marriages in the world, along with 87% approval of black-white marriages.

MUSLIM CULTURE: Followers of Islam. Muslim history is distinguished for piracy, slave trading and jihad crusades against Byzantine and European Christians, Jerusalem and any other non-Islamic infidels they could find.

MUSLIM INBREEDING: Generations of accepted inbreeding of first cousins sanctioned by Muhammad may well have done virtually irreversible damage to the Muslim gene pool, including extensive damage to Muslim's intelligence, sanity, and health. This has placed a tremendous health care and societal burden on European countries with large Muslim populations.

NATURE vs NURTURE: Nurture is the notion that we develop behavioral traits almost exclusively from environmental influences. Nature says "It's biological" or "I was born this way" or "There's a genetic link", thus justifying a claim to "normality". The heritable trait argument has been used for ADHD, criminal behavior, substance abuse, rape, domestic violence, homosexuality, pedophilia, psychopathy and just about any dysfunctional behavior one can imagine. In other words, how convenient!

NEW YORK VALUES: Folks don't much like big-city Northeasterners. That's partly because New York City has a long history as a corrupt liberal politico-media-big labor complex. Overall, New York values run counter to those of America's grassroots conservatism and much of America's Heartland views Gotham as less a melting pot of diversity and more a noisy, alien, arrogant and even threatening multicultural cesspool – a place they can't relate to.

NORMIES: An ironic term used by snobbish and elitist PC conformists (retreads of beatniks and hippies), who consider their own intolerant collectivist culture as being nonconformist, rebel and hipster. They use "normie" to describe individualistic, independent and successful people typically guilty of "white privilege".

NORMOPATHY: A symptom of collectivist thought and the antithesis of individualism. Normopathy is a mania found in people who are focused on blending in and conforming to social norms. A person who is normotic is often unhealthily fixated on having no personality at all, and only doing exactly what is expected of society. – **Christopher Bollas**

OBAMA RACIAL CONFLAGRATION LEGACY: His presidency was supposed to unite us, however Barack Obama stayed true to his quasi-Marxist upbringing and chose to exploit and exacerbate racial tensions for political objectives, and with predictable results – anger, chaos, and violence. Cops were murdered, neighborhood's torched, and innocent lives ruined. Before Obama, race was becoming a nonissue. Now it's *the* issue. Race is everything and everything is racial.

OPPRESSION OLYMPICS or COMPETITIVE VICTIMHOOD: When two or more groups compete in a one-upmanship dynamic to prove themselves more oppressed, more authentic, and thus more correct.

PASSIVE TOLERANCE: The idea that simply living in an area of high diversity simply rubs off on you, making you more tolerant of ethnic diversity. Several studies reveal that just witnessing diverse interaction by those who live in diverse neighborhoods results in higher levels of passive tolerance. This partly explains the World Values Survey standing of the US as most racially tolerant in the world and also reveals the dangers of segregation and non-assimilation found in societies of multiculturalism.

PEJORATIVE: A word or phrase that has negative connotations or that is intended to disparage or belittle. Not that long ago "socialist" was considered an insult to leftists. Despite the negativity, pejoratives are often accurate descriptions, such as:

Chattering classes; often used by pundits and political commentators to refer to a politically active, socially concerned and "highly" educated section of the "metropolitan middle class", especially those with political, media, and academic connections.

Che chic; a 'dumbing down' phenomenon. Brutal Marxist henchman Che Guevara has been glorified as a fashion trend.

Lifestyle anarchist; anarchists who dress the look or live in certain ways, but who don't really act on the basic tenets of anarchism at the expense of class struggle.

Pinko; originally a person regarded as sympathetic to communism.

San Francisco values; a secular progressive culture and moral degradation which grew out of the hippie counterculture.

PRIVILEGE THEORY: Some are more equal than others. Despite Asian-American achievement levels far greater than whites, privilege theory is still almost exclusively "white privilege". When demographic correlations are analyzed though, the primary indicator of achievement and happiness is "raised by biological mother and father privilege."

PROFILING: Detective work. Profiling is a politically incorrect investigative tool used by law enforcement agencies to identify likely suspects and analyze patterns that may predict future offenses and/or victims.

PROFILING, RACIAL: Is performed every day by government employers when they demand that employees and contractors list their race and ethnicity on their applications. The U.S. Census is a big racial profiler. The quota industry wants you to believe there is a good form of racial profiling (employer racial quotas), and a bad form of racial profiling (police apprehending minority criminals). – **Adversity.Net**

PROGRESSIVE STACK: A "stack" is a list of speakers who are commenting or asking questions in a public meeting. Apparently there is a flaw in our traditional representative democracy, the majority is heard while non-dominant groups are silenced. The "majority culture" means white people, men, and young adults. Author Jim Goad satirically puts it this way: "The concept of intersectionality is also related to the "progressive stack", which assumes that white males at all times bear noxious degrees of unearned power, which is why they have to get to the back of the line and let all the legless black lesbians speak first."

PSEUDOFEMINISM: Feminism which encourages women to think in terms of weakness and helplessness, in need of rescue by an external entity providing special privileges rather than equal opportunity. Physical, intellectual and emotional deviations of men and women resulting from divergent X and Y chromosomes are ignored. Adopting male characteristics is encouraged.

QUOTAS: The notion of racial quotas is so obviously an expression of racism that no lengthy discussion is necessary. If a young man is barred from a school or a job because the quota for his particular race has been filled, he is barred by reason of his race. Telling him that those admitted are his "representatives," is adding insult to injury. To demand such quotas in the name of fighting racial discrimination, is an obscene mockery.

RACE-BAITING: The unfair use of statements about race to try to influence the actions or attitudes of a particular group of people.

RACE CARD: Falsely accusing another person of being a racist in order to gain some sort of advantage. Similarly, the gender card and the class card. Thomas Sowell coined the term "race card fraud".

RACIAL IDENTITY: The basis for racism. Similar to ethnic identity, PC notions of racial identity determine one's value rather than content of character, with the consequence of separatism and segregation whether intended or not. If you determine your own worth by the color of your skin, you will

---

RACIAL TOLERANCE INDEX: Racist? Compared to what? In a global research project, the World Values Survey studied 80 countries over three decades revealing the most and least racially tolerant. The United States ranks as the most tolerant along with Canada, United Kingdom and Australia although our status under the Obama administration declined. For the dregs of racial and ethnic intolerance try India, Egypt, Iran, Korea or France.

---

certainly judge others accordingly.

RACIALISM: 1. Consistently acting under the assumption that the actions of others are racially motivated whenever they concern members of separate races. 2. Favoring quotas and preferences which favor specific minorities. The quota industry would have you believe that racialism equals "good" discrimination. Don't be fooled, racialism has exactly the same meaning as racism. – **Adversity.Net**

RACISM: Racial identity. Racism is prejudice and discrimination based in social perceptions of biological differences between peoples and the notion that one's race determines one's identity. It is the belief that one's convictions, values and essence are determined not by the judgment of one's mind or content of character but by one's anatomy or "blood."

RACISM, DEMOCRAT PARTY: The pro-slavery party of Jim Crow laws and the Ku Klux Klan opposed all civil rights legislation of the 1950s and 60s.

RACISM, INSTITUTIONAL: Any system of inequality based on race such as affirmative action, tribal membership, or Southern democrat Jim Crow laws.

RACISM, SYSTEMIC: The foundation of individual and institutional racism; it is the value system which is embedded in a society that supports and allows discrimination. The World Values Survey racial tolerance index determined the US to have the least systemic racism in the world, prior to the 2008 election of Obama.

REDNECK: Authentic - the real McCoy, judging others by content of character rather than superficial qualities. The opposite of a redneck might be a liberal elitist snob. "The glorious absence of sophistication." – **Jeff Foxworthy**. "A sense of self and a way of life." – **Gretchen Wilson**, songwriter, "Redneck Woman".

REPARATIONS FOR SLAVERY: The movement to provide black Americans with "reparations" for slavery is based upon the dubious, legally indefensible assumption that white Americans living today have somehow mysteriously and unfairly benefited from oppression of black Americans during the pre-1865 slavery days. – **Adversity.Net**

SAME-SEX DIVORCE: A 2004 study of registered partnerships in Sweden reported that gay male couples were 50 percent more likely to divorce than were heterosexual couples. Lesbian couples were nearly three times more likely.

SAME-SEX MONOGAMY: The defining characteristic of the gay community is promiscuity. That is why monogamy in gay relationships is estimated at about 25 percent and their divorce rate so high. You won't hear "commitment" thrown around much at a gay wedding.

SEX DETERMINATION: The sex of an individual is determined by a pair of sex chromosomes. Females have two of the same kind of sex chromosome (XX), and are called the homogametic sex. Males have two distinct sex chromosomes (XY), and are called the heterogametic sex. The trillions of cells in your body contain either all XX or all XY. As of yet there are no chromosome transplants available.

SEX and GENDER: Historically "sex" and "gender" have been used interchangeably – not anymore. "Sex" refers to biological characteristics and "gender" now refers to the individual's and society's perceptions of sexuality and the malleable concepts of masculinity and femininity.

SEXUAL FLUIDITY: Sexual preferences are not set in stone and can change over time, often depending on the immediate situation the individual is in. Like any other social trait, sexual preferences, attitudes, behaviors and identity can be flexible to some degree.

> **SEXUAL LIBERATION and CASUAL SEX:** Components of the 1960s to 70s women's liberation movement allowing men to finally get what they had long wanted.

SEXUAL ORIENTATION: Regarding one's preference in sexual partners. Some forty or so sexual orientations comprise various psychiatric and pop psychology lists ranging from Androphilia to Zoophilia. Historically orientation has not been the problem; the consequences of promiscuity in whatever expression is mankind's dilemma.

SHAKEDOWN: A form of extortion, the act of taking something from someone by using threats or deception. It may be coercion or intimidation for personal gain such as Jesse Jackson's racial shakedowns of businesses for alleged discrimination.

SLAVE TRADE FACTS: The universal institution of slavery was primarily a product of Arabs, followed by Portuguese, Spaniards, Dutch and British. Virtually all of the enslavement of Africans was carried out by other Africans, who then sold to the slave traders. Only six percent of the slave trade to the Western Hemisphere was to colonial North America, with most going to Brazil and the Caribbean.

SOCIAL CONSTRUCTIONISM vs BIOLOGICAL DETERMINISM: Social constructionism is the theory that social identifiers, like race and gender, are created by society rather than biology. Biological determinism is the belief that biology determines such characteristics as behavior, ability, likes and dislikes – "boys will be boys". Evidence from numerous studies on species, world cultures, rape, cognitive abilities, brain anatomy, hormones, hormone treatments and Turner's Syndrome strongly suggest gender identity is almost entirely based on genetics with gender roles rooted in real, measurable, biological differences between men and women.

SODOMITE: Oh my, so politically incorrect. A sodomite is a promiscuous homosexual engaging in sodomy. It is a synonym for homosexual yet homosexuals are not necessarily promiscuous and can even be celibate. There should be a differentiation rather than all lumped under "gay".

SPECIAL TREATMENT: Favoritism, preferential kindness or allowance, as opposed to equal opportunity. Identity activists such as feminists often seek special treatment. When preferential treatment is based on race and gender it is essentially discriminatory.

STEREOTYPING: One of the symptoms of groupthink. A stereotype is a preconceived notion, usually exaggerated or oversimplified, about a group of people. They can be negative or positive and not necessarily inaccurate. Examples: The rich are greedy; Jews are successful, intelligent and skilled negotiators; PC liberals act on bleeding-heart emotion rather than intellect.

SUNNIS and SHI'ITES: The two major sects of Islam. Sunnis comprise about 90 percent of all Muslims and are relatively tolerant, believing in rule by tradition and consensus. The Shi'ites are the radical reformers who, like fundamentalist Christians, are convinced the world is going to hell. Shi'ites are given to dire proclamations, the cutting off of hands in the public square, and believe in rule by imams; those divinely appointed, sinless, infallible successors of Muhammad.

SUPPLIER DIVERSITY PROGRAM: A term used by private corporations and government agencies to indicate that they award contracts and subcontracts to minorities ahead of non-minorities – **Adversity.Net**

TRANSGENDER: Refers to gender identity and gender expression rather than physical sex characteristics or even sexual orientation. The notion is so vague it can be used at the spur of the moment to demand access to previously exclusive gender territories. Ladies Night Happy Hour discount? Go for it, dude.

TRANSGENDER, APA 2012 DECISION: Similar to the APA 1973 decision on homosexuality, after decades of classification as a mental disorder the American Psychiatric Association reclassified "gender identity disorder" with a new term "gender dysphoria" – no longer an illness or disorder. Many years of lobbying by LGBTQ activists paid off. It shouldn't be long before there is another effort to reinvent the state of 'being pedo' from the mental illness of 'pedophile' to another normal human variant.

TRIBAL ECOLOGY MYTHS: "Indians were, in truth, the pioneer ecologists of this country" – Stewart Udall. Not exactly. American Indians transformed the landscape and manipulated ecosystems, sometimes beneficial, sometimes harmful, such as deforestation and "buffalo jumps". Land and water rights along with free market trade were the most effective means for survival.

UNCLE TOM SYNDROME: Considered to be a coping mechanism where individuals use passivity and submissiveness when confronted with a threat, leading to subservient behavior and appeasement, while concealing their true thoughts and feelings. Considering that the original Uncle Tom was beaten to death for refusing to betray his fellow slaves, there is an irony that those racial minorities of strong character who would stray off the "Democrat plantation" by exhibiting individualistic, self-sufficient, independent behavior would be branded with the Uncle Tom pejorative.

UNIFORM GUIDELINES UGESP: Federal "Uniform Guidelines on Employee Selection Procedures" dictate that employers (federal, state, local and private) must devise employment tests and selection procedures which guarantee that the "correct" proportion of protected races are hired and/or promoted. They call this process "reducing adverse impact". In their guidelines the Feds go to great lengths to disguise their goal of racial quotas. – **Adversity.Net**

UNLAWFUL IMMIGRANT DEFICIT: An extensive Heritage Foundation 2010 study utilizing US Census Bureau data revealed the average American unlawful immigrant household paid $10,334 in taxes annually. They also collected $24,721 in government benefits and services for a net annual deficit to lawful taxpayers of $14,387.

WAR ON MEN: 94% of industrial accidents; 92% occupational fatalities; 97% combat casualties; 90% of homeless; 80% of suicides; 77% of murder victims, under 42% of college enrollment; 10% awarded child custody; half as likely to commit child abuse as mothers; big losers in Obamacare premiums; female sexual assault victims declined by 58% from 1994 to 2010; less than half the federal funding for prostate cancer research as for breast; since 1973 average full-time earnings have decreased, compared to 32% increase for women.

WARFARE SOCIOLOGY: The neo-Marxist way of looking at things thru the lens of identity class war. Rich over poor, capital over labor, whites over blacks, men over women, heterosexuals over homosexuals. Everywhere they look they see classism, racism and sexism.

WHITE GUILT: The individual or collective guilt felt by liberal white people for past transgressions by their ancestors. Skin color is the basis for judgement, making white guilt a form of racism.

WHITE PRIVILEGE: A form of race-baiting. "I am about to attempt to bully you into submission using logical fallacies and your own sense of decency as a club." Evidence reveals the primary correlation to success and mental health is "raised by your biological mother and father privilege".

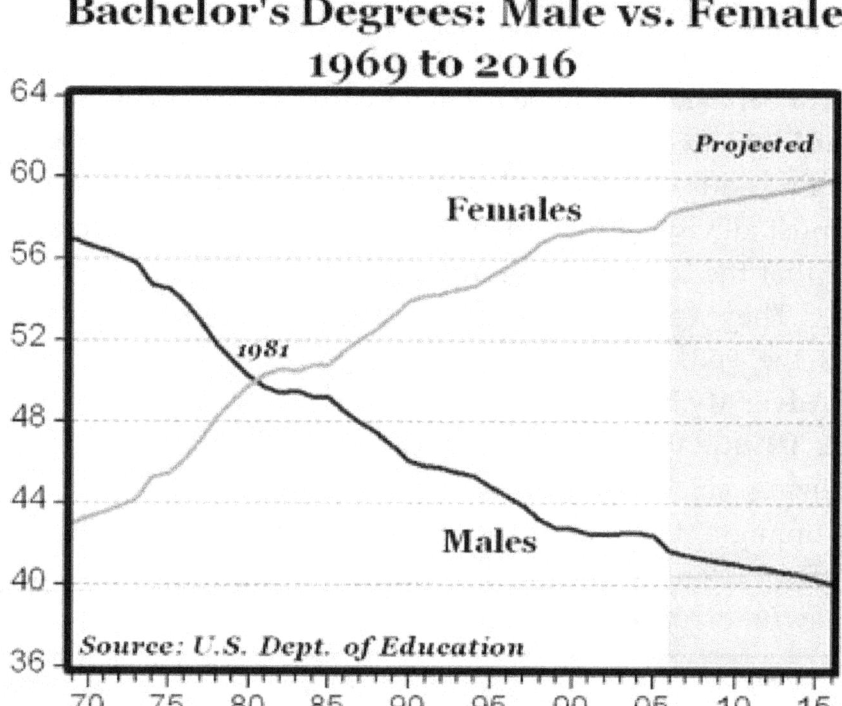

ConservaLexicon

ACTIVISM

"Something's just not right—our air is clean, our water is pure, we all get plenty of exercise, everything we eat is organic and free-range, and yet nobody lives past thirty."

Alex Gregory, **The New Yorker**

Quotes

"Americans are so enamored of equality that they would rather be equal in slavery than unequal in freedom." – **Alexis de Tocqueville**

"The urge to save humanity is almost always only a false face for the urge to rule it." – **H L Mencken**

"The whole aim of practical politics is to keep the populace alarmed – and hence clamorous to be led to safety – by menacing it with an endless series of hobgoblins, all of them imaginary." – **H L Mencken**

"Silence in the face of evil, is itself evil: God will not hold us guiltless. Not to speak is to speak. Not to act is to act." – **Dietrich Bonhoeffer**

"Don't expect to build up the weak by pulling down the strong." – **Calvin Coolidge**

"When fascism comes to America, it will come in the name of anti-fascism." – **Huey Long**

"I know a lot of people without brains who do an awful lot of talking." – **The Scarecrow, from the Wizard of Oz**

"The threat of environmental crisis will be the international disaster key to unlock the New World Order." – **Mikhail Gorbachev**

"The activist is not the man who says the river is dirty. The activist is the man who cleans up the river." – **Ross Perot**

"If you see a snake, just kill it - don't appoint a committee on snakes." – **Ross Perot**

"Activism is a way for useless people to feel important, even if the consequences of their activism are counterproductive for those they claim to be helping, and damaging to the fabric of society as a whole." – **Thomas Sowell**

"Global warming is just the latest in a long line of hysterical crusades to which we seem to be increasingly susceptible." – **Thomas Sowell**

"Envy plus rhetoric equals "social justice". – **Thomas Sowell**

"It's amazing how much panic one honest man can spread among a multitude of hypocrites." – **Thomas Sowell**

"For me the protection of Planet Earth, the survival of all species and sustainability of our ecosystems is more than a mission. It is my religion and dharma." – **Rajendra Pachauri, former chairman of the IPCC**

"One of the most powerful religions in the Western World is environmentalism. Environmentalism seems to be the religion of choice for urban atheists." – **Michael Crichton**

"The fate of mankind, as well as of religion, depends upon the emergence of a new faith in the future. Armed with such a faith we might find it possible to resanctify the earth." – **Al Gore quoting deChardin**

"Conservatives think liberals are stupid. Liberals think conservatives are evil." – **Charles Krauthammer**

"Liberals think moralizing is fine. They just want to have a monopoly on the franchise." – **Jonah Goldberg**

"You can't save the earth unless you're willing to make other people sacrifice." – **Dogbert,** Dilbert comic strip by Scott Adams

"Gay marriage is one of those trick arguments. Marriage should not be a legal institution – that's the argument you should be having. If marriage didn't exist, would you invent it? Would you go 'Baby! This shit we got together, it's so good we gotta get the government in on this shit. We can't just share this commitment tweenst us. We need judges and lawyers involved in this shit." – **Doug Stanhope**

ACTIVIST CHARACTER BULLYING: Spreading the idea that anyone opposing your agenda should be hated. Activist bullies try to frame the narrative through attacks on your character that take the form of name-calling, heated rhetoric and intimidation with generous use of identity politics. If you object to tax hikes, you hate the poor. If you promote traditional marriage, you are homophobic.

ALARMIST: Someone who is considered to be exaggerating a danger or prophesying calamities, often with a profit motive, and so causing needless worry or panic. Alarmism is the mechanism of survival for the climate crisis industry, EPA bureaucracy and "big green" activism.

ALARMIST INTEGRITY QUANDARY: Violation of the public trust is a serious offense. Once scientific, academic, media, bureaucratic and political alarmists are "all in" by investing their credibility in something purely theoretical which turns out to be a hoax, an act of courage by admission of guilt is required to restore the public trust. The other recourse is an attempt to save face by continuing the charade for fear of fraud exposure, loss of credibility, and/or monetary loss – until the inevitable collapse of their house of cards.

ALINSKY, SAUL: 'Rules for Radicals' and the Cult of Alinsky utilized Neo-Marxist tactics of cultural manipulation. True revolutionaries do not flaunt their radicalism, Alinsky taught. They cut their hair, put on suits and infiltrate the system from within. Alinsky viewed revolution as a slow, patient process. The trick was to penetrate existing institutions such as churches, unions and political parties. Both Barack Obama and Hillary Clinton are disciples of the cult of Alinsky. See Appendix for a list of Alinsky's rules.

ALT-RIGHT ALT-LEFT: Claimed to be a sort of anti-orthodox conservativism that promotes white identity, however as America has moved farther and farther left no one seriously believes it. But on the other side an "Alternative Left" is no longer an "alternate" wing of the Democrat Party or traditional liberalism. Radical extremist globalist, anti-capitalist, and man-caused climate change views now drives their trajectory.

ALTRUIST: PC for do-gooders and bleeding heart liberals. Altruism says man has no right to exist for his own sake, service to others is the only justification of his existence, and self-sacrifice is his highest moral duty, virtue and value.

AMERIPHOBIA: Related to oikophobia. "Liberals tend to not look fondly on our Founding Fathers (most of whom were true abolitionists), or our Declaration or Constitution. They tear down America because of our sins. In contrast, conservatives look fondly at America for her ideals and values, which led to the ending of slavery and eradication of many other historical ills. Americans are not the dictators of the world, but the liberators of humanity from the hands of dictators. That is simply a fact!"-- **David S Whitley**, *The Jihad of Liberalism*

ANARCHO-PRIMITIVISM: The rise of the "future primitive", the ultimate Luddites. Anarcho-primitivists advocate a return to non-civilized ways of life through deindustrialization, abolition of the division of labor or specialization, and abandonment of large-scale organization technologies.

ANTIFA: Claimed to mean "anti-fascism" by activists and rioters, however is anti-First Amendment, anti-capitalist, and anti-personal freedom. Antifa harbors a social superiority with a lack of civility and intellect. "When fascism comes to America, it will come in the name of anti-fascism." – **Huey Long**

APOCALYPSE ABUSE: Extrapolating only the most horrendous trends, while systematically ignoring any ameliorating or optimistic ones, offering worst-case scenarios in the guise of balanced presentations. – **Ronald Bailey**, *Eco-Scam*

APPEAL TO NATURE: An argument or rhetorical tactic in which it is proposed that "a thing is good because it is "natural", or bad because it is "unnatural". Often used in green marketing campaigns as well as the propaganda campaigns of ecologists. An appeal to nature is indeed a foundation principle of the entire green movement.

BEAT GENERATION: The beat movement and generation of the 1950s and early 60s was, more than anything, non-conformist rebels and ramblers. The "beatnik" adherents were generally apolitical and indifferent to social problems, embracing originality and individuality, and advocating personal release, purification and illumination through the heightened sensory awareness induced by jazz, drugs, sex or Eastern religions. They were the precursors to the more political hippie and environmental movements.

BIG GREEN or GANG GREEN: Well-funded non-profit environmental organizations partnering with corporations to finance the climate change industry by way of political contributions to the Democratic Party.

BIG SCIENCE: In government-supported science the temptation to influence policy and appropriations by manipulating scientific conclusions is irresistible.

CARBON OFFSETS SCAM: The Stockholm Environment Institute determined that the Joint Implementation carbon offsetting mechanism of the Kyoto Protocol enabled global GHG emissions to be massively *higher* than they otherwise would have been. In 2011 the global carbon trading market was worth $176 billion. The carbon credits scheme has been abused by countries such as Russia and the Ukraine as a moneymaking scam.

CARPETBAGGER: An outsider who seeks private gain from an area often by meddling in its business or politics. The global warming scare has been cover for a massive transfer of funds from taxpayers to green carpetbaggers, thanks to headline-seeking politicians and activists trying to take credit for "solving" a problem that doesn't exist.

CARSON, RACHEL: The environmentalist queen of green genocide. Carson exploited her reputation as a well-known nature writer to advocate and legitimatize positions linked to a darker tradition in American environmental thinking. She encouraged some of the most destructive strains within environmentalism: alarmism, technophobia, failure to consider the costs and benefits of alternatives, and the discounting of human well-being around the world. Carson's proselytizing and advocacy raised substantial anxiety about DDT and led to bans in most of the world and to restrictions on other chemical pesticides. But the fears she raised were based on gross misrepresentations and scholarship so atrocious that, if Carson were an academic, she would be guilty of egregious academic misconduct. When properly applied DDT is safe and effective. Carson's observations have been condemned by many scientists. Her legacy is the deaths of 50 million to malaria since 1972, most of the victims' poor children in Africa.

CHAVEZ, CESAR: The Martin Luther King of Chicanos was deeply opposed to illegal immigration in order to protect his UFW union from Mexican "strikebreakers", essentially demanding that the sovereignty of the United States be respected. UFW representatives brutally beat hundreds of Mexican aliens, whom Chavez referred to as "wetbacks", to keep them from crossing the border.

CIVIL RIGHTS MOVEMENT: Supporting civil-rights reform was not a radical turnaround for congressional republicans in 1964, but it was a radical turnaround for Lyndon Johnson and the democrats. Not one democrat in Congress voted for the Fourteenth Amendment, Fifteenth Amendment or the Civil Rights Act of 1875. It was republicans who began the process of desegregation and it was republicans who were primarily responsible for the passage of the 1964 Civil Rights Act. It was democrats who subsequently created the "democrat plantation" by enslaving minorities to the welfare state with their War on Poverty.

CLIMATE CONFUSION: Middle Ages "weather witchcraft", 1975 "global cooling", 1985 "global warming", 2010 "climate change", 2015 "climate chaos/disruption".... 2020 either "oops, never mind" or "weather witchcraft".

CLIMATE CRISIS INDUSTRY: Social entrepreneurship and engineering at its worst, it is corporate-government cronyism, a major force for progressive statism. As an economic driver, insurance companies value it at $1.5 trillion including a $27 billion per year consulting industry that handles "reputation management" to link any and all crises to climate change. The climate crisis industry can survive only by relying on the coercive powers of government. - follow the money. In the end, billions will face premature mortality from energy poverty.

CLIMATE ALARMIST; says "the sky is falling, do something!"
CLIMATE REALIST; says "if a warming planet, whether man-made or natural cycles, has a net benefit to mankind, why should we be alarmed if there is no crisis?"

CLIMATE-INDUSTRIAL COMPLEX: Scientific societies universally claim to be high-minded promoters of science, however the reality is very different and many act like lobbying organizations or labor unions. They often form committees to investigate scientific issues. These committees usually come to the same conclusion: We need more money. – **Norman Rogers**, Heartland Institute

COLLECTIVE MUNCHAUSEN SYNDROME: A theory explaining the mass hysteria surrounding the Donald Trump presidency associated with social justice warriors. Munchausen disorder is when somebody feigns a medical illness or injury to garner sympathy and empathy. SJW's respond in a collective manner of faux-fear, more than just mass hysteria. They have a specific goal which is: "Oh my god, we're such victims." – **Gad Saad**, evolutionary psychologist

COMMONER: An ordinary person, without rank or title.

COMMUNITY ORGANIZER: Lobbyist and/or rabble rouser for more government spending, more entitlements, and more preferential treatment (quotas) for certain privileged minorities. They also advocate class envy and income redistribution. – **urbandictionary.com**

CONSENSUS, 97 PERCENT MYTH: A bogus study by green alarmists supported by yellow journalists and democrats, which claims overwhelming support by scientists of global warming theory. Several other studies reveal only a tiny percentage that believe man is the primary cause for warming since 1950.

CONSENSUS, ONE OR TWO PERCENT: An analysis by Friends of Science of the four main studies to document alleged warming consensus, revealed only 1.2 percent or thirteen scientists out of 1,117 agreed with the Intergovernmental Panel on Climate Change (IPCC) view that human activity is the primary cause of global warming since 1950.

CONSERVAPEDIA: A conservative and Christian alternative to Wikipedia, developed as an online encyclopedia free from liberal bias.

CONSERVATIONIST: A person who wants to protect natural resources without trampling on everyone else's property rights. Typical

CONSERVATION REFUGEE: The idea of separating man from nature forms the core of the conservation movement. Conservation refugees are peoples driven out of their traditional lands when those lands are set aside for parks and sanctuaries. The applied conservation models of arrogant ENGOs often clashes with indigenous knowledge of the environment.

conservationists are hunters, fishermen, campers, and hikers.

CORNUCOPIANS vs DOOMSAYERS: Cornucopians argue that humanity faces no real problems; technological and institutional advances have and will continue to make it possible to address any shortages. The doomsayers viewpoint, still shared by modern environmentalists, argues the human dilemma in Terrible Toos terms: There are *too* many of us! We consume *too* much! We rely *too* heavily on technology, which we understand *too* poorly! – **Fred Smith**. Despite overwhelming evidence to the contrary, doomsayers dominate the published literature, media, academia, and bureaucracy.

COUNTERCULTURE: A way of life and set of attitudes opposed to or at variance with the prevailing social norm. The late 1960s counterculture opposed capitalism.

COUNTER COUNTERCULTURE: The new campus counterculture embraces Milton Friedman/Ayn Rand conservative values counter to the prevailing progressive establishment norms including 1. Individual freedoms with personal responsibility. 2. Free market capitalism over fascist crony corporatism. 3. Fiscal responsibility over unsustainable debt. 4. Content of character over racial-gender-class identity. 5. Limited government over progressive statism (socialism).

COVFEFE: *"Despite the constant negative press covfefe"*. A twitter tweet typo by President Trump in June 2017 which created media hysteria and immediate pop culture status. ConservaLexicon chooses to define covfefe as not just fake news but a symbol of the collective paranoia and loathing of commoners by the elite Left.

CRY-BULLY: The poster child of politically correct social justice warriors, hybrids of victim and victor, often engaging in identity politics, and using feelings over facts…. "Someone who uses the perceived righteousness of a social justice cause as a pretext to abuse others, and then plays the victim when confronted about that abuse." – **urbandictionary.com**

DARK MONEY FUNDS: A term used to describe funds given to nonprofit organizations. A net annual amount of $46 million supports conservative think tank efforts opposing global warming activism. On the other hand, out of hundreds, five environment-specific groups alone raise more than $1.6 billion per year (Greenpeace, The Nature Conservancy, World Wildlife Fund, National Wildlife Federation, and the Sierra Club) promoting global warming alarmism.

DHMO HOAX: Did you know your city's reservoirs have extremely high levels of dihydrogen monoxide? The DHMO hoax has been used as an educational tool to illustrate the scientific illiteracy, gullibility and hysteria of green activists, thus encouraging critical thinking and avoidance of the 'appeal to nature'. Dihydrogen monoxide (DHMO or H_2O) is water.

DOOMSDAY PREDICTIONS: Media, academic, political, bureaucratic, corporate and evangelical activist prophets rake in $billions frightening the gullible with contemporary Chicken Little fables of ozone depletion, acid rain and the grandest whopper of all, global warming - or cooling - or climate change- or chaos - whatever.

DOOMSDAY PREDICTION, AL GORE 2016: World CO_2 emissions have not decreased and that means the world was toast in 2016. Mankind ceased to exist. Praise be Algore!

DOUBLE STANDARD: "All animals are equal, but some animals are more equal than others." – **George Orwell**, Animal Farm.

ECO-ANGST: "The moment a new bit of unpleasant ecological information about some product or other plunges us into despair at the planet's condition and the fragility of our place on it." – **The New York Times.** . . It's a matter of perception over reality. When Chicken Little alarmists leave us worried that the sky really is falling and we are more afraid than evidence warrants, the perception gap creates a danger all by itself.

ECO-FUNDAMENTALISM: Common sense environmentalism transformed into an extreme ideology and social movement that advocates for the subordination of democratic principles and individual rights to the whims of the Green lobby. The "health" of the environment is illogically elevated beyond the health of man. Reasoned questioning of its mantras is regarded as a form of blasphemy. There is no greater threat to the people of this planet than the retreat from reason we see all around us today.

ECO-IMPERIALISM: Coined by Paul Driessen, it refers to the forceful imposition of Western environmentalist views on developing countries. Environmentalists legitimize the well-being of the environment over the well-being of humans, engendering poverty, death and even environmental degradation in the process.

ECOLOGY: Proclaims that city smog and filthy rivers are not good for men (though they are not the kind of danger that the ecological panic-mongers claim them to be). These are scientific, technological problems though, not political ones, and can be solved only by technology. Even if smog were a risk to human life, we must remember that life in nature, without technology, is wholesale death.

ECOTOURISM: Like "sustainable tourism", an oxymoron. It is a form of tourism involving visiting fragile, pristine, and relatively undisturbed natural areas, intended as a low-impact alternative to standard commercial tourism, however the transportation alone for all tourism leaves an environmental footprint. Even nature hikes can be destructive, contributing to soil impaction, erosion and plant damage as well as scaring away animals and disrupting their feeding and nesting sites. Rather than be hypocritical those concerned about saving the planet might want to stay at home, sell the car and watch travel documentaries on TV.

ELITISM: The belief or attitude, whether real or imaginary, that some individuals – "elitist snobs" - who form an elite are those whose influence or authority is greater than that of commoners; or whose extraordinary abilities render them especially fit to govern. Elitists typically insert themselves into positions of power on governing boards. A.k.a. "conceit of the anointed", pertaining to people elected to public office.

ENDANGERED SPECIES ACT: The Endangered Species Act passed in 1973 because the public believed the recovery of endangered or threatened species was important. Since that time, over 1,100 species have been listed, but only 27 species have been delisted. Unfortunately, none of these 27 species recovered because of positive actions instituted by the federal government under the ESA. In addition, there have been numerous reports of financial loss and hardship because of the ways in which the federal government implements the ESA. The unintended consequence of the ESA has been landowners ridding their property of the species and habitat rather than suffering bureaucratic consequences.

ENGO: Environmental non-government organization. ENGOs are now a multi-billion dollar industry financed not just by private foundations but more and more by corporate sponsorship and governments, creating conflicts of interest. There are hundreds of ENGOs such as the World Wildlife Fund and Nature Conservancy. These organizations can act outside the formal processes that government institutions must comply with.

ENLIGHTENMENT: The absence of ignorance and delusion. Subjective introspection may facilitate the path however the human action of intellectual exertion and effort thru research, investigation, examination and analysis are the keys to enlightenment. The recipe is ten parts elbow grease to one part navel-gazing.

ENVIROMARXIST: An environmental activist who believes that Marxist economics (carbon taxes, wealth distribution, etc) should be applied to remedy the situation.

ENVIRONMENT: The surroundings or conditions in which a person, animal, or plant lives or operates, especially as affected by human activity. The vagueness allows for broad interpretation by those who wish to control others by force and coercion.

ENVIRONMENTAL: Relating to the natural world and the impact of human activity on its condition.

ENVIRONMENTAL ENDEAVORS FUND: An euphemism for a tax which goes to a slush fund used for "anything we want to impose on our fellow citizens in the name of political correctness".

ENVIRONMENTAL HEALTH: Specifically addresses the physical, chemical and biological factors external to a person that can potentially affect health. Unlike many vague "environmental" terms, environmental health concerns the environment's impact on something which is typically excluded as a component of the environment – people. The world's number one environmental health hazard according to the World Health Organization is indoor air pollution from wood, coal and dung burning stoves.

ENVIRONMENTALISM: Common sense practical survival techniques practiced by mankind for thousands of years, with none greater than the access of clean water (which was greatly enabled by fossil fuels in the 19th century). Adapting to one's environment thru preservation, restoration or improvement is not a complicated concept.

ENVIRONMENTALISM, SECOND-WAVE: The first-wave of environmentalism proved to be primarily Chicken Little alarmism. The second-wave proposes that private owners offer the best defense against environmental degradation. Simply by protecting their property – trees, animals, fish, grazing areas, rivers - they incidentally protect the earth for the rest of us. – **Ronald Bailey**, 1995

ENVIRONMENTAL JUSTICE: The politically correct term for eco-fascism, a totalitarian government that requires individuals to sacrifice their interests to the well-being and glory of the "land".

ENVIRONMENTAL MOVEMENT: The political movement that seeks to protect the environment. Ecology as a social principle condemns cities, culture, industry, technology and the intellect, and advocates men's return to "nature," to the state of grunting sub-animals digging the soil with their bare hands.

ESTABLISHMENT, THE: Denotes a dominant group or elite that holds power or authority in a nation or organization. The Establishment may be a closed social group which selects its own members or specific entrenched elite structures, either in government or in specific institutions. Bureaucrats, media, academia, Hollywood and Wall Street comprise our contemporary leftist progressive establishment.

FASCIST ECOLOGY: In 1934, a year after the Nazis took power, they declared that the Third Reich had ushered in a new era of environmental stewardship. They foresaw a new age of "organic" land use planning that stressed long-term sustainability over short-term profitability. The green policies of the German socialists, like the green policies of today, were riddled with contradictions and impracticalities yet that did not disturb them since every bit of green legislation justified and involved a further extension of planning and state intervention. They were the pioneers of eco-fascism.

FREE SPEECH: Our First Amendment rights to free speech means we will not be arrested, fined or otherwise sanctioned by government for expressing ourselves on our own time in places that are solely our business. This does not extend to saying or doing anything you wish at work, where codes of conduct are designed to attract customers and workers rather than chase them away. Imagine your waitress lecturing you on abortion rights, or your football hero flipping you the finger right before kick-off.

FRENCH REVOLUTION: The 'Revolution of 1789' was the classic manifestation of modern leftism and served as the model for still more modern revolutions around the world more than a century later. As that revolution proceeded its aims grew more ambitious, with its most fervent partisans demanding nothing less than the total transformation of society. – **Llewellyn H Rockwell Jr**, Mises Institute

GAIA EARTH WORSHIP: Neopaganistic veneration of natural phenomenon utilizing faith based junk science to the point of delusional superstitions. Gaians claim that the earth is a sentient super-being, an ancient goddess spirit, deserving of worship and reverence. It is the foundation of environmental activism with modern origins in 1930s Nazi Germany. Gaia worship is at the very heart of today's environmental policy.

GAY MAFIA or VELVET MAFIA: Any organized group of homosexuals who use extortion and other illicit methods to exert a controlling influence over a particular industry or field, such as scientific research. Commonly found in the media, academia and Hollywood.

GENERATION Z: Born from 1995 to 2010. "These kids have never known economic growth. Every three or four generations you get a shift away from whatever destruction is taking place. Eventually a generation's gonna be born that is going to reject the ways its parents and grandparents lived. And Generation Z could be that generation. The Millennials are not. The Millennials have signed on to it [that America is the problem of the world] hook, line, and sinker. The Millennials are buying every lie they're being told. They're soaking up every misconception and every distortion that they're being fed." – **Rush Limbaugh**

GLOBAL COOLING SCARE 1970s: During the 1970s the media promoted global cooling alarmism with dire threats of a new ice age. Extreme weather events were hyped as signs of the coming apocalypse and man-made pollution was blamed as the cause. The media hype was found in newspapers, magazines, books, and on television – *'In Search Of' with Leonard Nimoy, 'The Coming Ice Age', 1978* (on YouTube).

GLOBAL WARMING MYTHS: * The USFWS estimates the global polar bear population at 20,000, up from 5,000 in the 1960s. * International sea level experts report no sea level rise in 50 years. * NASA satellite instruments reveal the polar ice caps have not receded at all since 1979. * Antarctic sea ice reached record high levels in 2014.

GLOBAL WARMING PETITION PROJECT: Signed by 31,487 American scientists, including 9,029 with PhDs. The petition rejects greenhouse gas theories of catastrophic heating of Earth's atmosphere and disruption of the Earth's climate, while also acknowledging the substantial scientific evidence that CO2 increases produce many beneficial effects on the environment.

GOLDWATER RULE: Since 1973, the American Psychiatric Association and its members have abided by a principle commonly known as "the Goldwater Rule," which prohibits psychiatrists from offering opinions on someone [such as a president] they have not personally evaluated. Simply put, breaking the Goldwater Rule is irresponsible, potentially stigmatizing, and definitely unethical. – **Maria A Oquendo MD**. Sadly, many modern mental health professionals have turned to activism and apply the rule only to the left.

GORE EFFECT: The connection between unseasonable cold weather and global warming activism events - happens every time. Not only that, after Al's 2006 movie with catastrophic predictions, the hurricane pause and global warming pause immediately followed.

GREEN ACTIVISM: A politically correct mechanism with roots in Nazi Germany utilizing "useful idiots" to advance an anti-industry anti-capitalist crony-corporatist socialist agenda expanding statist power and control by force and coercion. Alarmism, junk science, groupthink, propaganda, intimidation and indoctrination are featured. In contrast, traditional activism in America involved citizen watchdogs and whistle blowers holding government accountable to oversight and transparency.

GREEN ACTIVIST: An environmentalist is legitimately concerned about their surrounding local environment and environmental health concerns. A green activist has primarily an anti-capitalist, anti-fossil fuel political agenda on a globalist scale and rooted in faith, a faith which blinds them to that which is scientifically observable, and to that which is clearly seen as common sense to bona fide environmentalists.

GREEN INITIATIVE: "Going green" buzzwords such as "sustainable" and "eco-friendly" used as PR ploys for greenwashing a business image by representing practical policies and programs which have been commonly implemented for centuries as "green initiatives". Unfortunately, "green" rarely means "energy savings" or "energy efficiency".

GREEN LOBBY: Insurance companies estimate the value of the climate crisis industry at over $1.5 trillion. In Washington, the more "green" companies spend on lobbying, the more they receive from the government in loan guarantees - in 2013 $13 billion was guaranteed to solar energy companies, with companies such as Sun Edison and Abengoa filing bankruptcy after $billions in subsidies. Twenty-four of the twenty-six on the EPA advisory panel received grants totaling $190 million, thus receiving taxpayer money to lobby for more taxpayer spending.

HIPPIES, LIBERTARIANS and THE TEA PARTY: The fundamental core values of the mid-1960s hippie counterculture movement were 1. A craving for independence. 2. A celebration of individuality. 3. Joy in the freedom of self-sufficiency. 4. An acceptance of the natural order of things. The Tea Party and Libertarians are the social movements in contemporary America that can rightfully claim to be the ideological heirs. Sadly, by the late 1960s the hippie counterculture ideals became contaminated by big government socialists. The hippies lost their way, forgot their roots, embraced statism and a nanny state progressing to a bully state marked by collectivism, dependency, force and coercion, all in an attempt to control others.

HUNGER FALLACY: The childhood hunger lobby would have us believe one of five American children are hungry or "food insecure". If we limit the USDA sample to households with children it becomes ten percent and the weekly food spending by those households is 95% of the USDA Thrifty Food Plan. Only one or two percent of those families reported that "children were hungry" or "skipped meals". The evidence reveals that poor food choices are the only problem, and that the number one health problem of low-income children is, you guessed it, obesity.

IMAGINE: John Lennon's globalist anthem for ushering in plans of world socialism, unipolar government, substituting God with materialism, erasing national identity, crowd-sharing, rationing, collective thought void of individuality, and voluntary slavery – all sung to the tune of tens of millions dead in the former Soviet Union.

INTIMIDATION TACTICS: The new age activism of Big Green, velvet mafia, feminazis, race hustlers and anarchists relies on intimidation, threats and violence to advance their cause. Many "scientific" organizations, such as the American Psychiatric Association, fold under the pressure and compromise on their principles, thus losing credibility. Bureaucrats in particular are easily intimidated.

ISLAMOFASCISM: The faith of Islam as a cover for totalitarian ideology, embodied by several fundamentalist sects such as the Islamic State (ISIS), Wahhabis, Hezbollah and Muslim Brotherhood.

IVORY TOWER: If you're in an ivory tower, you live in a world of ideas separate from the realities of most people's lives. Your university philosophy department might be your ivory tower, where discussions about theory are the most important things in life. It's a privileged situation to be in, since ordinary people tend to have more mundane priorities, concerns, and struggles. The phrase most often describes academia.

JESUS, POLITICALLY INCORRECT: Jesus loved people and was opposed to religious-political dogma and programs that kept people in bondage and used them for their own ends rather than helping them to grow. He was totally committed to people's spiritual and personal growth and was strongly opposed to anything that hindered that growth such as social engineering (political correctness). People were offended with Jesus because He violated their understanding of religion and piety.

JUDICIAL ACTIVISM: Is when judges allow their personal views about public policy, among other factors, to guide their decisions. When the Supreme Court invents "constitutional rights" out of thin air they have crossed the line that separates judging from legislating.

JUNKSCIENCE.COM: One of my early inspirations; since 1996 Steve Milloy's website has led the fight debunking junk science. "We were the first web site with comprehensive overviews of various global warming issues."

LANDFILL MYTHS: The Environmental Protection Agency has declared landfills create absolutely no environmental harm and that landfill space is abundant nationally, requiring far less space than green activists would have us believe. Landfills become recreational parks, gardens, industrial parks and golf courses when covered. In a place like Gallup NM with so much open land, clay soil, dry climate, minimal leaching and the relative space required for landfills so small it's absolutely mindboggling that we waste so much energy and expense sending our trash forty miles away, or that we would even pay someone a landfill cost.

LEFTIST IDEOLOGY, destruction of: There are three questions that would destroy most of the arguments on the left. 1. "Compared to what?" 2. "At what cost?" 3. "What hard evidence do you have?" There are very few ideas on the left that can pass all three of those. – **Thomas Sowell**, economist.

LIBERAL BUBBLE: A comfortable, supportive and self-esteem enhancing environment reinforced by mainstream media, Hollywood, academia, bureaucracy and other self-righteous elite, all constructed by liberals for themselves. Their institutional high ground enables them to dismiss their conservative opponents as ill-informed, crude, bigoted and evil. Rather than experiencing their isolation from the rest of us as 'disorientation' - a state which connotes confusion and uncertainty - most liberals experience their differences with the rest of society as a sign of their advanced intelligence and consciousness. At best, they are perplexed at how long it is taking everyone else to catch-up with their enlightened state of understanding. – **Thomas Lifson**, American Thinker

Warning to liberals. The harsh realities outside the delusional confines of the warm fuzzy bubble can be devastating to some, and to others a slap-in-the-face wake-up call. Prepare to have your bubbles burst.

LIBERAL ELITE: aka limousine liberals. Those who claim to support the rights of the poor and working class yet are themselves members of the upper class, or upper middle class, and therefore out of touch with the real needs of the people they claim to support and protect.

LIBERAL INTOLERANCE: Liberals claim to want "tolerance" but in fact they are extremely intolerant of anyone who believes differently than they do. Just visit any college campus.

LIBERAL JIHAD: "The longer I live, the more I see the similarities between the ideology of liberals and the Islamists they so often defend. You either think like them, believe like them or feel their wrath. You either convert to their side, or face the penalties of their faith system: pay them homage by bowing down in political correctness to their idols or remain fearfully silent

-- otherwise you will be what is called behind closed doors as an "example." If that doesn't work, they will move to option three, the slow death of a million cuts known as the political vendetta aka character assassination."-- **David S Whitley**, The Jihad of Liberalism

LIBERTARIANS: Hippies of the right touting "more freedom, less government". In the philosophical battle for a free society with individual freedoms, many libertarians tie capitalism to the whim-worshipping subjectivism and chaos of anarchy, yet at the heart of libertarianism is the limited government and free market capitalism principles of Milton Friedman as well as the rational self-interest and productivity principles of Ayn Rand objectivism. The notion that gay marriage figures into freedom and less government is contradictory.

LOYALIST: A person who remains loyal to the established ruler or government, especially in the face of a revolt. During the American revolutionary period the Loyalists were colonists who supported King George III and the British cause. They opposed the Patriots.

LUDDISM: A technophobic social movement of British artisans in the 19th century who organized in opposition to technological advances in the textile industry. Luddites rejected new technologies that impacted the structure of their established trades, or the general nature of the work itself.

MALLARD FILMORE: As the lone conservative comic strip in a big pond of liberals, Bruce Tinsley created Mallard for what he saw as the conservative underdog. The strip is for "the average person out there: the forgotten American taxpayer who's sick of the liberal media and cultural establishments that act like he or she doesn't exist," Tinsley says.

MALTHUSIANISM: In 1978, the Reverend Thomas Malthus argued that humanity had a propensity to reproduce far faster than the food supply could increase. Thus, some portion of humanity would always be condemned to starvation. First-wave environmentalists embraced this notion, arguing that humanity and technological civilization are heedlessly using up the earth's resources. Despite man's technological advances allowing resource access and adaptation to our environment, doomsayers of the Left still persist with a "crisis of the month" media mentality.

MARX, KARL: Anti-Semite who considered blacks inferior and Mexicans contemptible. His communist ideology in the 20th century alone was responsible for more than 100 million murders. "Intellectuals" still find Karl Marx's ideas of communism as praiseworthy and attractive.

MONSANTO: Similar to the Koch brothers and Big Oil, Monsanto Company has become a pop cultural bogeyman and the face of corporate evil to bizarre-world liberals. Their crime? As leaders in biotechnology they have brought durable biotech crops of beans, corn, grains and cotton to millions of impoverished in developing countries around the world.

MORALITY: What is morality, or ethics? It is a code of values to guide man's choices and actions—the choices and actions that determine the purpose and the course of his life. Ethics, as a science, deals with discovering and defining such a code.

MORAL POSTURING: Similar to virtue signaling; acting as if you are morally enlightened, while anyone who opposes you is deplorable.

MUCKRAKER: One who investigates and publishes scandal and allegations of corruption among political and business leaders.

NAVEL-GAZING: Self-indulgent or excessive contemplation of oneself to the point of being narcissistic, or a single issue at the expense of a wider view. Navel-gazing is an old hippie practice passed on to our self-absorbed Millennials.

NEO-LUDDISM: The modern Luddite movement has connections with radical environmentalism as well as the human population control, wilderness preservation, rewilding and simple living associated with Deep Ecology, eco-anarchism, anarcho-naturism, and Gaia earth worshippers.

NEO-PURITANS: New age witch-hunters - ultra-progressives legislating against "sin", oxymoronically in the name of liberalism - bullying, controlling, freedom-hating, totalitarian, nanny state oppressors. Sinners are publicly branded as "racist, sexist, classist, homophobic, Islamophobic, bigoted, deniers, anti-science, xenophobic, nativist, classist, wastrels and insensitive." Fossil fuels, fracking, pipelines, GMO, landfills, non-organic? These be the wicked ways of heretics!

OBJECTIVISM: The philosophy of Ayn Rand, advocating independent thinking, rational self-interest, individual rights, laissez-faire capitalism and reason over faith. There is no greater moral good than achieving happiness, accomplished by productivity, moral integrity and respect for the rights of others. Objectivism has been an inspiration for the Libertarian and Tea Party movements.

OCCUPY WALL STREET: Pure capitalism is a form of anarchism. OWS are self-proclaimed anarchists with an anti-capitalist Marxist agenda of a classless society attained by massive government intervention thru class warfare and redistribution of wealth. Confused? That's their trademark.

OPENMINDEDNESS: A genuine willingness to consider the evidence before rejecting the idea; being receptive to arguments or ideas. Social and environmental justice warriors' censorship, intolerance, and demands of conformity to their agenda increasingly reveals that in the real world the Left is close-minded, while the Right allows dissent.

ORGANIZING FOR ACTION: Obama's post-presidency has set up a shadow government to not only protect his threatened legacy, but to sabotage the incoming administration. The leftist nonprofit OFA says it trains young activists to develop "organizing skills", however Obama's army of agitators, numbering over 30,000, have primarily developed "rioting skills".

ORGANIC FOOTPRINT: Numerous studies prove no consistent differences in nutritional content between organic and conventionally grown crops. Organic farming methods require considerably more land though, and that makes its environmental footprint considerably larger. Organic foods offer an effective placebo to some.

OVERGRAZING SNUB: For decades desertification from overgrazing on the Navajo Nation was considered America's worst environmental disaster yet green activists turned a blind eye in the name of political correctness.

OVERPOPULATION: A problem that has been misidentified and misdefined. The term has no scientific definition or clear meaning. The problems typically associated with overpopulation (hungry families, squalid and overcrowded living conditions) are more properly understood as issues of poverty. Despite a tripling of the world's population in the past century, global health and productivity have exploded. Today human beings eat better, produce more, and consume more than ever before in the past. – **Nicholas Eberstadt**

PACIFISM: "The necessary consequence of man's right to life is his right to self-defense. In a civilized society, force may be used only in retaliation and only against those who initiate its use. All the reasons which make the initiation of physical force an evil, make the retaliatory use of physical force a moral imperative." – **Ayn Rand**

PANTHEISM: The underlying theology of Neopaganism and Gaia earth worship, based on the conviction that what Christianity has traditionally denounced as idolatry and superstition actually represents a profound and meaningful religious worldview and, secondly, that a religious practice based on this worldview can and should be revitalized in our modern world.

PARALYZING FATALISM: Identified by the World Health Organization as a condition caused by "persistent myths and misperceptions about the threat of radiation." The fear mongering and propagation of ignorance by anti-nuclear activists has caused more harm to affected populations of radioactive fallout than the actual accident. Examples include Fukushima, Chernobyl, Three Mile Island and the chemical contamination at Love Canal. Residents assume a role of "chronic dependency" and develop an entitlement mentality.

PCKKK: The Ku Klux Klan was historically a terrorist cult of the Democrat Party, killing over a thousand white Republicans as well as over three thousand blacks. Modern-day witch-hunters and soft terrorist groups of force and intimidation hide behind the shield of political correctness while crying racist! sexist! homophobe! Islamophobe! denier! heretic! The "boy who cried wolf" tactic has worn thin though, and Americans have cried bullshit! on the intolerant left – thus, Trump. The collectivist lynch-mob mentality includes Black Lives Matter, LGBTQ, MoveOn.org, Earth and Animal Liberation Fronts, Greenpeace, EPA, labor unions, Democrat leaders, college campuses, aging hippie liberals, and your garden-variety protest/rioters. Their overwhelming hostile presence in locales such as the Bay Area, Hollywood, Eugene, Boulder and King County WA has bullied many conservatives into the closet.

PEACEFUL PROTEST: Nonviolent action expressing disapproval of various Constitutional-governmental policy issues or advocating human rights.

PLACEBO EFFECT: A fake treatment can sometimes improve a patient's condition simply because the person has the expectation it will be helpful. The environmentalist cult is abundant with placebos such as mandatory recycling, organic foods and renewable energy. Wishful thinking can be a blinding elixir, even an addiction.

POVERTY PIMP: An individual or group benefiting unduly by acting as an intermediary on behalf of the poor, the disadvantaged, or some other "victimized" groups.

PRECAUTIONARY PRINCIPLE: A popular concept in environmental circles, which states that we should avoid technologies which carry potential risk for harm. The trouble is that you also add risk when you prevent society from technological benefits. In the real world, costs must always be weighed against benefits. That's the way everyone lives their lives, every day.

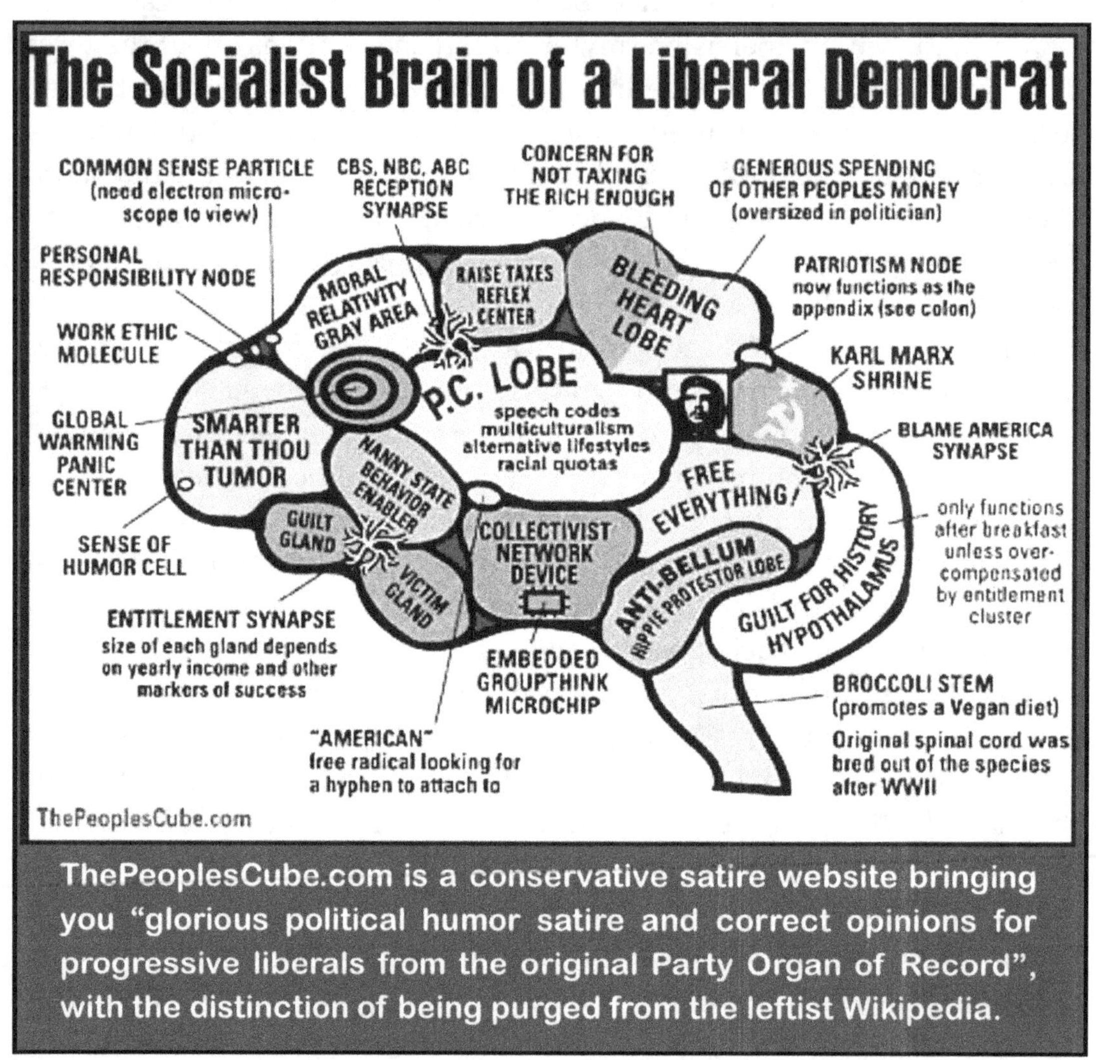

ThePeoplesCube.com is a conservative satire website bringing you "glorious political humor satire and correct opinions for progressive liberals from the original Party Organ of Record", with the distinction of being purged from the leftist Wikipedia.

PREDICTIONS, failed environmental: 1. Global Cooling 2. Overpopulation 3. Mass Starvation 4. Resource Depletion 5. Mass Extinction 6. Renewable Energy 7. Global Warming – **Robert Tracinski**

PROGRESSIVISM: The belief that you can get something for nothing, that you can get the government to take something by force from other people and give it to you. Historically the unintended consequence of progressivism is an unsustainability of debt which robs from the young, relatively poor, to give stuff to the old, relatively wealthy. Constructing a collectivist utopia requires that human nature be altered and therein lies the rub, something the Pilgrims at Plymouth Colony quickly realized nearly 400 years ago.

PROSELYTIZE: To try to persuade people to join a religion, cause or group. Proselytizing is common in the secular proxy religion of environmentalism.

PUBLIC TRANSPORTATION: Like many green endeavors such as organic farming and recycling, mass transit offers earth worshippers a placebo - it just feels right. The U.S. Bureau of Transportation and Bureau of Energy statistics reveal transportation energy use per passenger mile is less for an average car than heavy rail, trolley bus and city bus and half as much as light rail. The New Mexico Rail Runner Express offers just another cautionary tale of the unintended consequences of green fantasies. The slower than highway NMRRE train is subsidized $30,000 per passenger per year by the state taxpayers.

RACE HUSTLER: An individual who projects himself into the media spotlight as a spokesperson for a racial group in order to exploit a racial situation to serve their own interests. Al Sharpton and Jesse Jackson are the classic examples.

RACE PIMP: A race monger. They feed off racial tension and they live and die by racism. They offer nothing new, nothing good, nothing to repair, only conflict between the races. They are socially irresponsible, and think nothing of destroying innocent people's names if it means furthering their own finances and level of fame. – *urban dictionary*

RADIATION HYSTERIA: Thanks to advances in technology modern uranium mining, processing and reclamation has achieved high safety levels protecting workers and public. Considering the tremendous economic gains the Navajo Nation could reap from uranium mining as well as nuclear energy, it is sad to see the perpetuation of poverty and social disorders enabled by media, academia, bureaucrats and "big green" activists.

RADIOPHOBIA: The irrational thinking and hysteria over radiation. We hear scary stories of what "could" happen and of remote possibilities that never happen but make good news stories.

RAIN FOREST CRISIS: In the 1980s, we were told that the clear-cutting of the Amazon jungle was an environmental and human threat. It turned out that the claims of the volume of destruction were exaggerated, and disaster was never imminent.

RECYCLING, MODERN: An invention of big industry without any prodding from the government. On the other hand, government imposed recycling has proven to waste resources, use more energy, do more environmental harm than good and be very costly. Yet, how can it be wrong, when it feels so right?

RENEWABLE ENERGY UTOPIAS: In 1971 China was a renewable utopia, deriving 40 percent of its energy from renewables. Today China gets a trifling .23 percent of its energy from unreliable solar and wind. Africa is now the renewable utopia getting 50 percent of its energy from renewables.

RESISTANCE, The: Resistance means facing up to tyranny, usually at some personal risk. In 2017 progressives have embraced the term "resistance" to signify their strategy to bring down the elected POTUS. But the real resistance in the US, the one that has been going on for decades, is the resistance to the social and cultural engineering efforts from the Left. Their power in those spheres is far more sweeping than the powers of President Trump over the federal government, where the bureaucrats themselves often are hostile to his goals. – **Thomas Lifson**, American Thinker.

RURAL BLIGHT: Climate protection, which is implemented against nature with technological means, is a paradox. The ironic consequence of wind farms and other renewable energies is the destruction of landscapes and wildlife, a devastation of nature and our environment.

SANGER, MARGARET: Founder of Planned Parenthood and contributor to the eugenics movement, specifically "to exterminate the Negro population".

SECULAR RELIGION: Political ideologies such as liberalism and environmentalism mimic the forms of religious institutions with their own sacred texts and taboos, crusades, inquisitions and doomsday scenarios. The political correctness that undergirds it, meanwhile, can be traced back to the past century's liberal Protestantism as well as the Puritan witch-hunters.

SELF-ACTUALIZATION-LIBERATION-TRANSCENDENCE: "No one is more interesting to anybody than is that mysterious character we all call 'me', which is why self-liberation, self-actualization, self-transcendence, etc., are the most exciting games in town." – **Robert Anton Wilson**

SLACKTIVISM: Feel-good measures, in support of an issue or social cause, that have little physical or practical effect, other than to make the person doing it feel satisfied that they have contributed.

SOCIAL ENTREPRENEURSHIP and ACTIVISM: A social engineering movement to drive social change and transformation. While microentrepreneurs are limited in their power to affect wide-ranging processes, social entrepreneurship as a popular concept offers a rational and socially acceptable crony method to disguise radical aims for social change and allow experimentation with marginal ideas. All social entrepreneurs are activists but not all activists are social entrepreneurs. The $1.5 trillion climate crisis industry went from religion to activism to social entrepreneurship-cronyism to social engineering, with an end goal of global socialism. The insidious consequence is energy poverty and premature mortality for billions of impoverished around the world.

SOCIAL JUSTICE WARRIORS: Extremists of the new age of political correctness. SJW's often hide behind the social justice movement to advance their own personal political agenda. They are sure to adopt politically correct stances of their social circle, using logical fallacies which are not well-thought-out. Much of their passion goes into speech and culture policing directed at victimless crimes that violate their moral taboos.

SOROS, GEORGE: The real life version of "Dr. Evil" who despises capitalism and loves social engineering. According to Rachel Ehrenfeld, the billionaire financier "uses his philanthropy to deconstruct the moral values and attitudes of the Western world, rejecting the notion of ordered liberty, in favor of an ideology of rights and entitlements."

SPOTTED OWL: The mascot of failed green activist policies. Economically productive forests in Oregon and Washington have been transformed over 30 years to an overgrown mass of dead or dying trees infested with pests and disease. Consequently, the resulting wildfires have killed the spotted owls, the forests that all animals rely on, the logging industry, and taken away the common sense management that previously kept our forests thriving for more than 160 years.

STAGE-TWO THINKING: Before acting on an event's initial (stage-one) anticipated results, it's best to engage in stage-two thinking by first asking, "and _then_ what will happen?", to determine long-term repercussions. – **Thomas Sowell,** _Applied Economics_. Lack of this cognitive skill is indicative of an undeveloped frontal lobe commonly found in the progressive statist brain.

TEA PARTY: Not a party, but a grassroots movement. Very simply, three guiding principles give rise to the freedom necessary to pursue and live the

American Dream: Personal Freedom, Economic Freedom, Debt-free Future. Core values include: Fiscal Responsibility, Constitutionally Limited Government, Free Markets. TEA means Taxed Enough Already.

TECHNOPHOBIA: The fear or dislike of advanced technology or complex devices. Commonly found in the environmental movement. Genetically modified organisms (GMO) and hydraulic fracking are examples.

TERRORISM: Intimidating or coercing a civilian noncombatant population by targeting them using acts dangerous to human life, or to affect the conduct of a government by mass destruction, assassination or kidnapping.

TOLERANCE, THE LIBERAL RELIGION: A Pew Research survey revealed that 88 percent of "consistently liberal" Americans list tolerance as their most important value in teaching their children. However, tolerance is about accepting the often-difficult differences between you and someone you strongly disagree with, and respecting that person's right to an opposing point of view. Obviously, liberals only tolerate things they agree with, and what they really practice is a selective tolerance. They embrace the faith of tolerance, but it is a selective faith and ironically often excludes the religious. – **Paul G Kengor,** professor of political science.

TRAGEDY OF THE COMMONS: Public lands and waters may be overgrazed and overfished. The simple time-tested solution is to convert the public resource into private property. Overgrazing on the public owned Navajo Nation is a prime example.

USEFUL IDIOTS: Coined by Vladimir Lenin. Those people perceived as propagandists for a cause whose goals they are not fully aware of, and who are used cynically by the leaders of the cause.

VALUE/VIRTUE: "Value is that which one acts to gain and keep, virtue is the action by which one gains and keeps it." – **Ayn Rand**

VIRTUE SIGNALING: Saying you love something or, more often than not, hate something to show off what a virtuous person you are, instead of actually trying to fix the problem. "I hate Fox News, they are so bigoted and uncompassionate."

WATCHDOG, CITIZEN: Informs the public regarding the decision-making processes of the elitist government-media-academic complex by fact-checking, interviewing and investigating and then alerting others when a problem is detected. Watchdogs give a voice to the powerless commoners by standing up to those who abuse their positions of power for political or financial gain.

WATERMELONS: Green on the outside, red on the inside. "Watermelons" are former socialists who diverted their political efforts away from economic central planning and channeled them into the environmental movement.

WOKE or WOKE AF (as f*):** A state of perceived intellectual superiority, particularly regarding social justice – seeing racism and oppression in virtually everything. "Get woke and stay woke, yo!"

Scott Adams is the creator of the *Dilbert* comic strip. His support of Donald Trump in 2016 triggered media hysteria with headlines such as these:

"Dilbert has gone fascist: The strange unrequited love Scott Adams seems to have for Donald Trump." - Salon

"How Dilbert's Scott Adams got hypnotized by Trump" - Bloomberg

HATE GROUPS: A product of Cultural Marxist and Saul Alinsky strategies of identity politics and political correctness, with goals of advancing the power of the state over the individual. Some of the groups who stoke fear and hatred in the name of some "sensitivity" by advancing false narratives ("hands up, don't shoot"), while also promoting an anti-conservative agenda of controlling others while taking away their freedoms include: Alt-Right, Antifa, Black Lives Matter, La Raza, Southern Poverty Law Center, NAACP, ACLU, SEIU, Moveon.org, and Anti-Defamation League. That's not all; dozens of feminist, LGBT, and environmental activist groups, as well as a large portion of our alarmist mainstream media use those same "fake news" deceptive tactics, with the consequence of inciting hate and violence. All of this is strangely reminiscent of our early American Puritan witch-hunters.

ConservaLexicon

CHAPTER SEVEN

SCIENCE

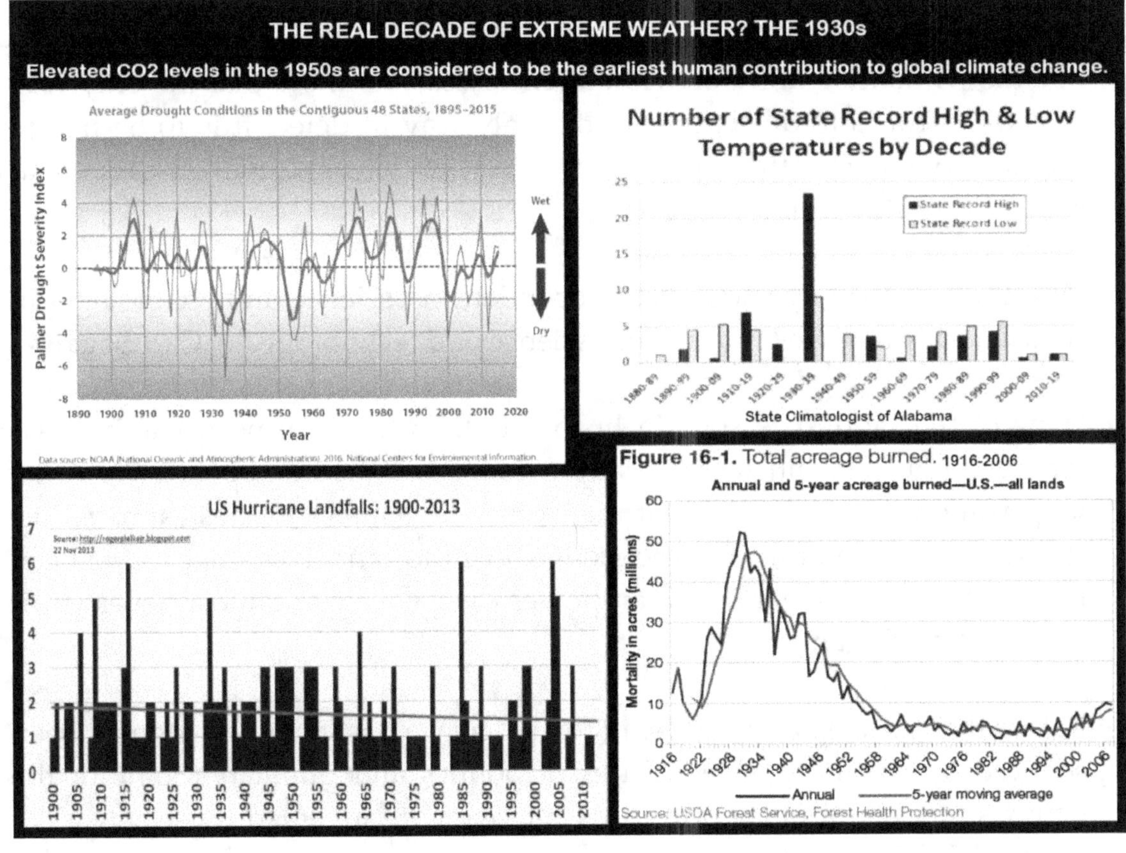

<h1 style="text-align:center">Quotes</h1>

"The foolish reject what they see, not what they think; the wise reject what they think, not what they see." – **Huang Po**

"I can calculate the motion of heavenly bodies, but not the madness of people." – **Isaac Newton**

"Science commits suicide when it adopts a creed." – **Thomas Huxley**, biologist

"We do not believe any group of men adequate enough or wise enough to operate without scrutiny or without criticism. We know that the only way to avoid error is to detect it, that the only way to detect it is to be free to inquire. We know that in secrecy error undetected will flourish and subvert." – **J Robert Oppenheimer**

"We live in a society exquisitely dependent on science and technology, in which hardly anyone knows about science and technology." – **Carl Sagan**

"One of the saddest lessons in history is this: If we've been bamboozled long enough, we tend to reject any evidence of the bamboozle. We're no longer interested in finding out the truth. The bamboozle has captured us. It's simply too painful to acknowledge, even to ourselves, that we've been taken. Once you give a charlatan power over you, you almost never get it back." – **Carl Sagan**

Rather than serving as a cleansing force, science has in some instances been seduced by the more ancient lures of politics and publicity. Some of the demons that haunt our world in recent years are invented by scientists." – **Michael Crichton**, 2005

"On the one hand, as scientists we are ethically bound to the scientific method, on the other hand, we are not just scientists, but human beings as well. And like most people, we'd like to see the world a better place, which in this context translates into our working to reduce the risk of potentially disastrous climatic change. To do that, we need to get some broad-based support, to capture the public's imagination. That, of course, entails getting loads of media coverage. So we have to offer up scary scenarios, make simplified, dramatic statements, and make little mention of the doubts we might have. Each us us has to decide what the right balance is between being effective and being honest." – **Stephen Schneider**, 1988, "well-respected" climatologist and Professor of Environmental Biology and Global Change, Stanford U

"Climate change is the perfect pseudoscientific theory for a big government politician who wants more power. Why? Because it is a theory that can never be disproven." – **Ted Cruz**

ABENGOA MOJAVE SOLAR PLANT: In contrast to Ivanpah's dry cooling, the 2015 Abengoa project utilizes 700 million gallons of water annually for more efficient sun power, creating yet another California green boondoggle.

AIR POLLUTION, INDOOR: The world's and Navajo Nation's greatest environmental health hazard (WHO) and killer of 4.3 million people every year. It is caused by wood, coal and dung burning stoves used by those in fuel poverty. Virtually ignored by green activists since affordable fossil fuel energy is the solution.

AIR POLLUTION, OUTDOOR: Thanks to our advanced technology in fossil fuel energy the United States is ranked in the top six of over 90 countries for clean air quality by the World Health Organization in 2015. Carbon emissions (CO2) does not contribute to outdoor air pollution.

AIR QUALITY: Even before Congress passed the Clean Air Act Amendments of 1970, air quality had been improving for decades. Since 1970 "criteria pollutants" (carbon monoxide, lead, sulfur dioxide, nitrogen oxides, ground-level ozone, particulate matter) have declined significantly, even though the generation of electricity from coal-fired plants has increased by over 180 percent.

ALTERNATIVE ENERGY: A euphemism for "woefully inadequate substitute".

AMBIENT AIR POLLUTION: Particulate matter air pollution, or smog. The World Health Organization ranks the US in the top six percent for least ambient air pollution in urban areas.

ANECDOTAL EVIDENCE: The basis for most modern social and environmental justice activism. An anecdote is a short and amusing but serious account, which may depict a real or fake incident or character. Anecdotal evidence is an informal account of evidence in the form of an anecdote. The term is often used in contrast to empirical scientific evidence – it is evidence that cannot be investigated using the scientific method. The problem with arguing based on anecdotal evidence is that it is not necessarily typical; only statistical evidence can determine how typical something is. Misuse of anecdotal evidence is an informal fallacy. Isolated extreme weather events are often used as anecdotal "proof" of man-made climate change.

ANTARCTIC ICE RECORD: NASA satellite records reveal the Antarctic Sea ice levels continue to set record highs, baffling climate bureaucrats.

BIOFUEL SCAM: The production of ethanol and use of ethanol-fueled vehicles requires tremendous amounts of water and results in up to 80 percent more damage to air quality including 50 percent more CO2 emissions. Overall, bioenergy pollutes water supplies and degrades soils, while promoting land-grabbing and the destruction of forests for

CANCER VILLAGES: Over 400 in China, many associated with unsafe mining and manufacturing of rare earth metals for solar panels, wind turbines, electric car batteries as well as recycled American plastics, paper and e-waste processing. Cancer rates have risen 80 percent over the last 30 years making it China's leading cause of death. Virtually ignored by green activists.

monoculture agriculture and plantations.

CARBON DIOXIDE: CO2 is a clear odorless gas and the foundation of life on earth. The EPA regards it as a pollutant.

CARBON CYCLE, OCEANS: The ocean stores fifty times more carbon dioxide than does the atmosphere. CO2 dissolves into cold ocean water at high latitudes and emits it into the tropical atmosphere. In other words, as the planet warms the oceans produce higher CO2 emissions.

CARBON EMISSIONS: A misnomer for "carbon dioxide emissions" and an indoctrination tool used to mislead the weak-minded. Most people think of carbon as black carbon soot, an entirely different pollutant which is most common in Third World countries using wood burning stoves.

CARBON EMISSIONS, RENEWABLE ENERGY: Forty-six percent of US renewable energy is from biomass (wood, biofuels, biomass waste) which emits CO2 when burned.

CARRINGTON EVENT: In 1859 the largest recorded geomagnetic solar storm occurred, causing telegraph systems to fail. A Carrington-sized storm today would be far more disastrous. Other solar phenomena include 11-year solar cycles, sunspots, coronal mass ejections, solar flares, solar proton events (SPE), prominences, and solar winds. Of course, any claims that solar events could affect the Earth's climate are silly, since we all know that only man is responsible for climate changes.

CHICKEN LITTLE SCIENCE: Embarrassing climate alarmist predictions. Here is a list of failed alarmist forecasts from well over a decade ago; sea level rises, increased hurricanes-tornadoes, drought, desertification, wildfires, global cooling (1970s), global warming, coastal flooding, crop failures, food riots, climate refugees, disappearing ice caps-glaciers, "snow falls and skiing are now just a thing of the past". Not only have all the predictions failed, for most of them the exact opposite has occurred.

CLEAN ENERGY: Does not exist.

CLIMATE CHANGE BUSINESS JOURNAL: How to profit off of hysteria and the world's largest business scam in history, at the expense of the poor and powerless. CCBJ provides market research on the Climate Change Industry.

CLEAN CHINA? Nuclear energy is cleanest, safest and among the most practical. As the US quietly closes nuclear reactors, China plans to build over 100 in the next decade.

CLIMATE CHANGE INDUSTRY: Climate Change Business Journal estimates the Climate Change Industry is a $1.5 trillion dollar escapade, which means four billion dollars a day is spent on our quest to change the climate. That includes everything from carbon markets to carbon consulting, carbon sequestration, renewables, biofuels, green buildings and insipid cars. As a comparison, global retail sales online are worth around $1.5 trillion also, so all the money wasted on the climate is equivalent to all the goods bought online.

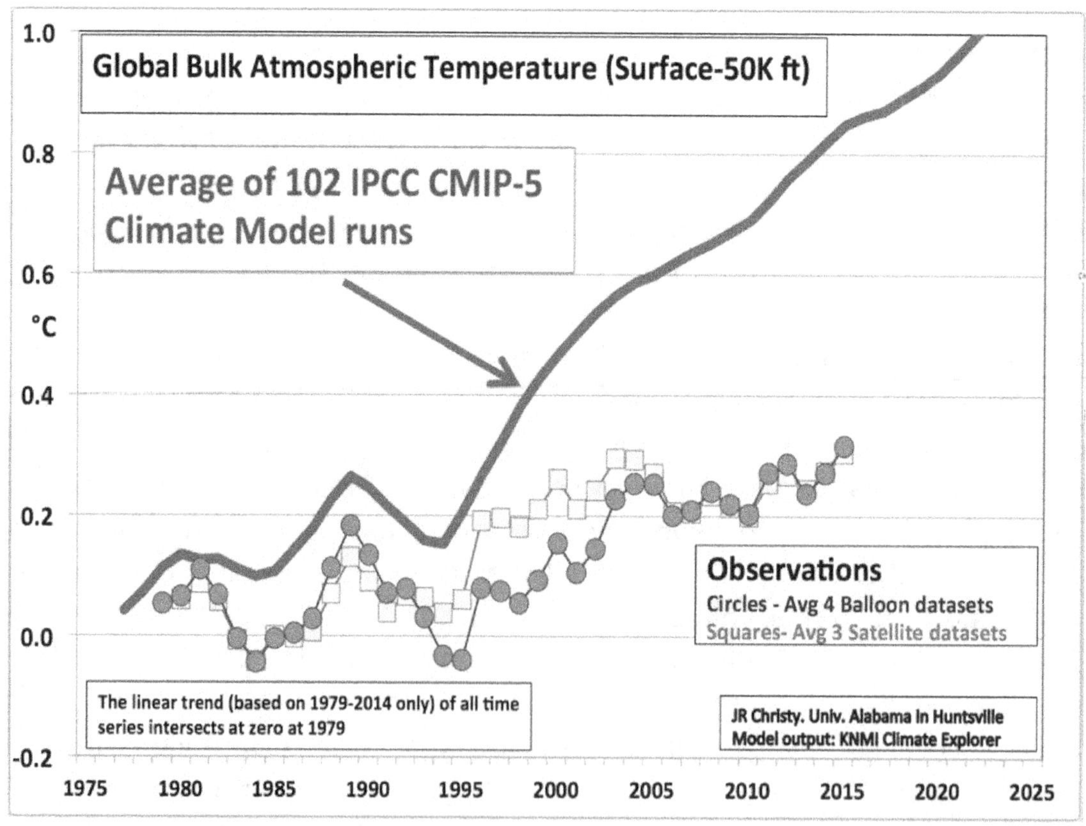

CLIMATE COMPUTER MODEL QUANDARY: Climate scientists have just one method to measure global CO2 impact, computer models. Analysis of 102

computer model predictions over 30 years revealed an average global warming overstatement of three to four times what occurred in the real world. All of them overshot the mark. A gambler would likely become quite wealthy by betting on the opposite of whatever predictions are made by the climate crisis industry.

CLIMATE FINANCE: Financing channeled by national, regional and international entities for climate change mitigation and adaptation projects and programs. $100 billion a year is pledged by developed nations for 'climate related matters' at the expense of improved public health, education and economic development. This effectively means telling the world's worst-off people suffering from fuel poverty, tuberculosis, malaria or malnutrition, that what they really need isn't medicine, mosquito nets, micronutrients, control of pestilence or affordable energy, but a solar panel.

CLIMATE-RELATED DEATHS: Since there is no intrinsically perfect global temperature, the key statistic is whether the climate is becoming more or less livable. The EM-DAT climate mortality data reveals that a naturally volatile and dangerous global climate system has been made more livable thru development and technology powered by cheap, reliable, fossil fuel energy.

CLIMATE SCIENCE DAFFYNITIONS – Jim Kress:

peer review: The act of banding together a group of like-minded academics with a funding conflict of interest, for the purpose of squeezing out any research voices that threaten the multi-million dollar government grant gravy train.

settled science: Betrayal of the scientific method for politics or money or both.

denier: Anyone who suspects the truth.

climate change: What has been happening for billions of years, but should now be flogged to produce 'panic for profit.'

data-evidence: Unnecessary details. If anyone asks for this, see "denier," above.

climate scientist: A person skilled in spouting obscure, scientific-sounding jargon that has the effect of deflecting requests for "data" by "deniers". Also skilled at affecting an aura of "smartest person in the room" to buffalo gullible legislators and journalists.

CLIMATE PARASITES: Modern indulgence sellers and rainmakers - opportunistic frauds who prey on superstition and natural disasters respectively to separate honest people from their money.

CLIMATE STATISM: Excessive power and representation of environmentalists and bureaucrats in our government creating a clear and present danger of energy and economic restrictions imposed in the name of controlling Earth's perpetually fickle climate. Those restrictions perpetuate poverty, disease and death and make it difficult to respond and adapt to future changes.

CO2 REDUCTION POVERTY: Green policies hurt the poor and working class the most. Soaring electricity, vehicle, transportation, heating and appliance costs, opposition to modern mining and drilling techniques, and blocking infrastructure projects leave a heavy footprint on the less fortunate.

COAL ENERGY JOBS vs GREEN JOBS: According to the US Energy Information Administration, it took 5,000 solar energy employees in 2016 to produce the same amount of energy as one coal job.

COAL POWER: Localized coal burning electrical generating plants dramatically improved urban environmental conditions in the late 19th century by replacing the widespread use of horses and their manure pollutants. Indoor and outdoor air pollution from coal and wood burning stoves was reduced and access to clean water was tremendously enhanced.

CRONY SOLAR SWINDLE: Without both explicit and hidden large government subsidies paid for by citizens the solar industry would collapse as is currently happening in Europe. Competitive claims by crony solar company proposals ignore the costs associated with unreliability, water usage and backup fossil fuel plants since solar farms generate such a tiny amount of energy only during daylight hours. The cost is passed on to the utility customers with the connivance of the government. As with virtually all green projects it is the poor who suffer the most.

DDT BAN: An example of pathological science. The insecticide DDT was banned in 1972 following Rachel Carson's pseudoscientific studies on bird's eggs. Since then over 50 million humans have died from malaria, most of the victims poor children in Africa. DDT effectively controls malaria by killing the mosquitoes that carry the disease. DDT poses a threat to neither humans nor the environment when properly applied.

In 2006 the WHO reinstated DDT as part of its effort to eradicate malaria.

ECO-FASCISM: or "fascist ecology" is a totalitarian government with origins in Nazi Germany that requires individuals to sacrifice their interests to the well-being and glory of the "land". Violation of property rights, crony corporatism, population control, creation of vast wilderness zones, energy control and elimination of fossil fuels are distinguishing features of environmental fascism. The method is one of bureaucratic force and coercion typical of our Environmental Protection Agency and Bureau of Land Management, with propaganda and indoctrination provided by complicit media, academic and political activist institutions.

ELECTRIC CAR POLLUTION: Whether powered by coal, solar or wind, each leave a larger environmental footprint than gasoline. Electric cars release only ten percent less CO2 in their lifetimes and the process of mining, manufacturing and disposing of toxic battery materials leaves a massive footprint as well. On the positive side, despite being so expensive the wealthy owners of plug-in cars receive large tax credits.

ENVIRONMENTAL CORRECTNESS: EC is just as authoritarian and mindless as political correctness, and for the same reason. Leftist orthodoxy needs to suppress dissent, or it will collapse. Rachel Carson's DDT myth continued to be enforced for some forty years in the name of EC.

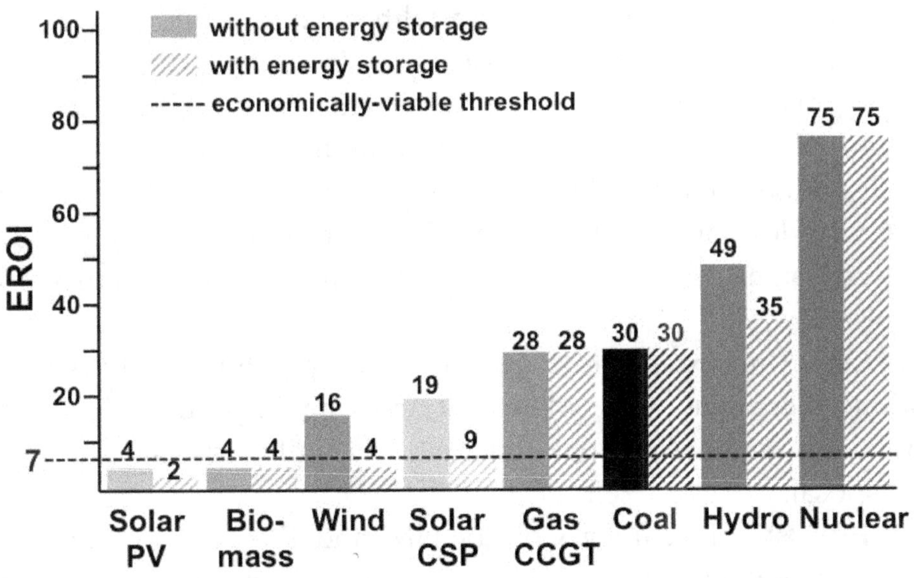

ENVIRONMENTAL SURCHARGE: Politically correct for a slush fund tax. In Gallup NM we pay a four percent tax on our utilities bill for "environmental endeavors". Hopefully environmental endeavors means "finding ways to reduce our utility bills", but I'm not holding my breath.

EROI: Energy Return On Investment is the amount of energy that has to be expended in order to produce a certain amount of energy and is a key determinant of the price of energy. In the table below, economic threshold equals seven.

EWD: Excess winter deaths occur from the inability to heat homes due to the excessive cost of solar and wind energy (fuel/energy poverty).

EXTERNALITIES: Costs or benefits to society that are not included in the market price of an item, forming the basis for the idea of "true cost". The hidden negative externalities (unintended consequences), including environmental, of green projects proves to come at a high cost to society.

EXTREME CLIMATE ANOMALIES: The 1940-1942 El Nino event created exceptionally low and high temperatures globally. There is only one decade that truly stands out over the past 100 years for extreme climate though. In the US, the 1930s had nearly as much extreme weather as all the other decades combined.

FOSSIL FUELS MORALITY: Since the late 19th century, marking the beginning of the fossil fuels energy age, there is a powerful historical link between increased fossil-fuel use and rising living standards, a doubling of life expectancy, decreased infant and child mortality, and so forth, as well as drastic drops in climate-related misfortunes, including deaths from droughts and storms, with no cessation of those benefits through 2015.

FRACKING: Hydraulic fracturing, a drilling technique for natural gas used since the 1940s. Modern technology allows the prospect of US energy independence with low oil and gas prices. Fracking is the trigger for our reduced CO2 emissions. Lack of it is responsible for renewable Europe's increase in emissions.

FRACKING SAFETY: After extensive studies, the highly politicized EPA was forced to admit there was no evidence of fracking impacting drinking water. Minor and rare earthquake activity is only associated with wastewater disposal.

FUEL/ENERGY POVERTY: McKinley County NM and the Navajo Nation's greatest environmental health hazard. Fuel poverty is the state of being unable to afford heating one's home adequately. Almost unknown in

Europe in 2006 the World Health Organization claims renewable energy costs in Europe now take tens of thousands of excess winter deaths (EWD) annually. The solution is affordable energy from fossil fuels, thus the silence of green activists.

GENETICALLY MODIFIED FOOD: Superstitious opposition to GM foods by environmentalists has caused starvation in the Third World. Genetically modified crops have probably saved a billion lives and are the strongest defense against hunger.

GERMANY'S COAL RENAISSANCE: Failed green energy programs in Germany have resulted in subsidy cuts resulting in skyrocketing electricity bills and the inevitable return to coal power as they have now built several new coal powered plants. None of this is what environmentalists promise voters when they plug the virtues of a low-carbon future. Germany's coal renaissance is a cautionary tale in what happens when you try to substitute green dreams for economic realities.

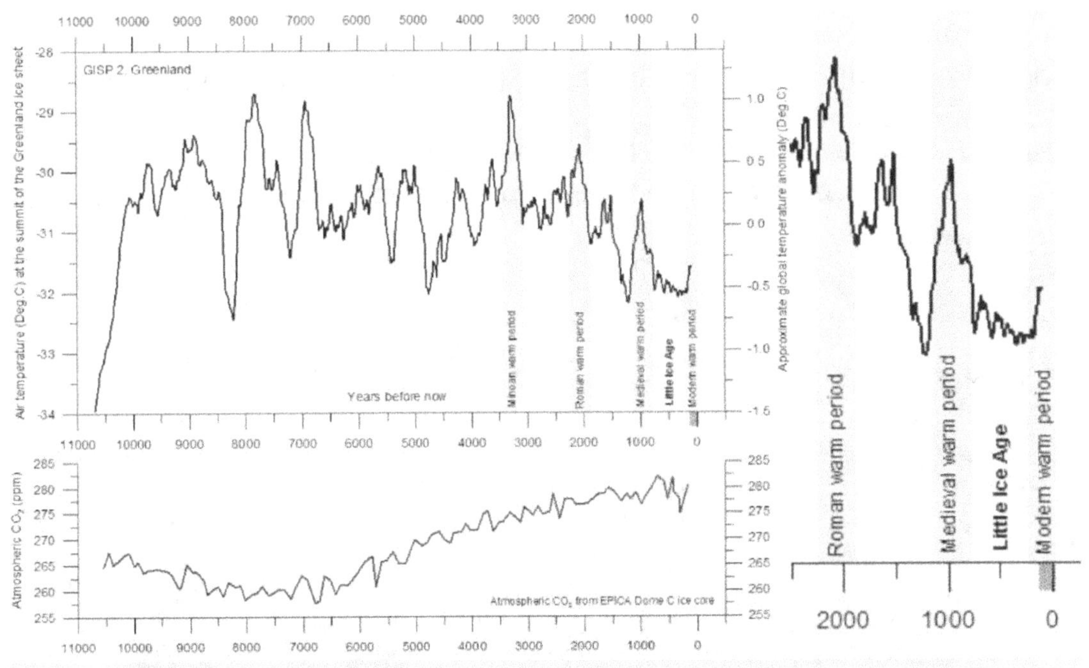

GREENLAND ICE SHEET PROJECT TWO (GISP2)

Climate Change Research Center, University of New Hampshire

GISP2: The Greenland Ice Sheet Project 2 from 1988 to 1993 was an example of old school science in contrast to the lazy science gymnastics of computer models. Ice core samples measuring temperature and CO2 levels over

10,000 years opened a new era in paleo-environmental investigation while further confirming the Little Ice Age, Medieval Warming Period and Roman Warming Period.

GLOBAL GREENING: The "CO2 fertilizaton effect" is the fact that rising carbon dioxide levels are making plants grow better. Satellite data shows there has been roughly a 14 percent increase in the amount of green vegetation on the planet since 1982, especially in arid tropical areas. Reduced world malnourishment due to higher crop yields has also been measured.

GLOBAL MORTALITY RATES FROM CO2: Since we are still awaiting the trends in climate change predicted by 30 years of complex computer models the number of deaths from elevated atmospheric carbon dioxide remains at zero.

GLOBAL MORTALITY RATES FROM EXTREME WEATHER: Have steadily declined by a whopping 95 percent since the 1920s when carbon dioxide emissions were more than ten times less than today. That from the International Disaster Database. Alarmists claim 1940 to 1950 to be the threshold period for the initial impact of elevated CO2 on climate.

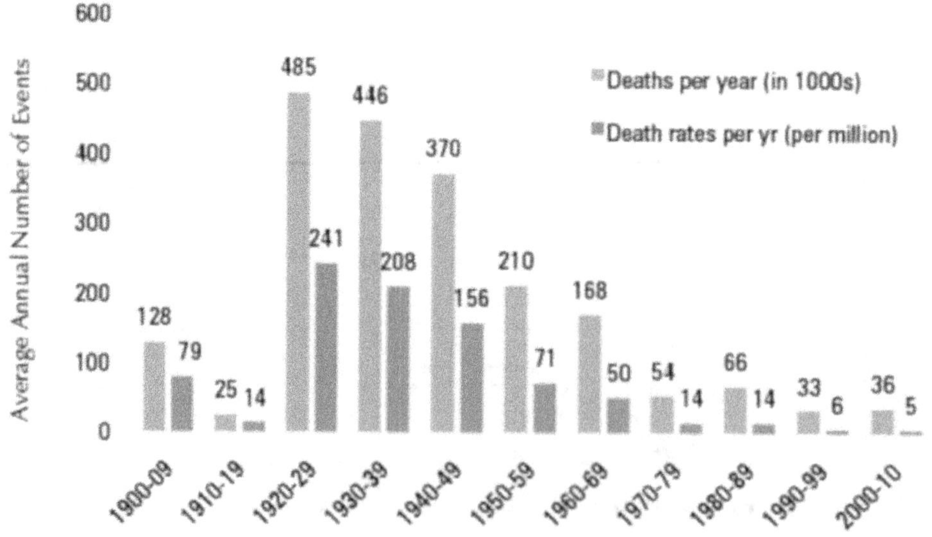

Figure 2: Global Death and Death Rates Due to Extreme Weather Events, 1900–2010
EM-DAT International Disaster Database

GLOBAL MORTALITY RATES FROM RENEWABLE ENERGY: The World Health Organization estimates the fuel poverty caused by skyrocketing wind and solar energy rates is responsible for tens of thousands of premature deaths annually in Europe alone. While the US has reduced CO2 emissions thanks to natural gas fracking, Europe has not and are even on the rise as they return to fossil fuels following the devastating economic disaster of their failed massive wind and solar projects.

GLOBAL WARMING CONSENSUS FALLACY: The widely cited figure of 97 percent of scientists supporting man-made global warming has always been a fraud. A review of the four main studies used to document the alleged consensus by the Canada based *Friends of Science* found that only one to three percent of respondents "explicitly stated agreement with the IPCC declarations on global warming" and that there was "no agreement with a catastrophic view".

GLOBAL WARMING PAUSE: After 300 years of warming since the Little Ice Age, NASA and NOAA satellite data reveals nearly 19 years without warming. Recently recovered NOAA radiosonde data (balloon) suggest the pause may go back as far as 1958. Computer model experts scratch their tin foil hats in bewilderment. The 2015-16 El Nino pattern was expected to end the pause.

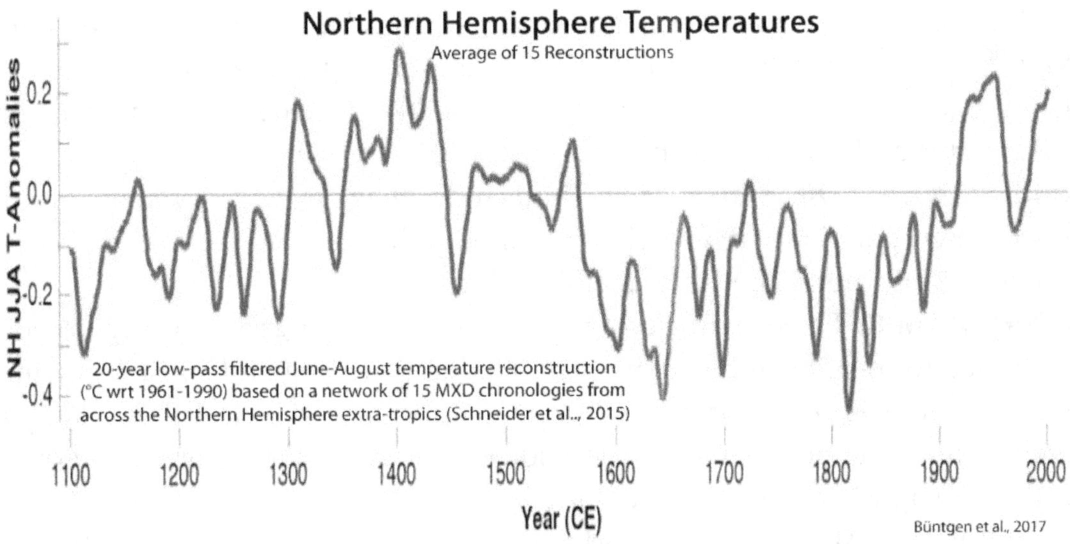

GREEN DENIAL SYNDROME: GDS is a form of psychological pathology of those who deny the existence of Antarctic ice levels, polar bear populations, computer model failures, global warming pause, hurricane pause, Little Ice Age, Medieval Warming Period, and the renewable energy footprint. Those who deny empirical scientific, economic, and historical data while claiming to have a special knowledge are known as charlatans, con artists, frauds and quacks.

GREEN ELECTRICITY: Also known as "renewable" or "sustainable" electricity has driven power rates so high in Europe and Queensland, Australia, that hundreds of thousands have had their electricity shut off due to skyrocketing costs making it the leading cause of rising energy poverty and resultant excess winter and summer deaths.

GREENHOUSE EFFECT THEORY: In 2009 physicists Gerlich and Tschueschner referenced over 200 scientific publications and addressed the merits of commonly held greenhouse "conjectures". By critiquing 14 different "fictitious" manifestations of the greenhouse effect theory as they had appeared over the course of the previous several decades, G & T determined that various definitions of the greenhouse effect were incompatible with the laws of physics. Thus, yet another climate change theory bit the dust.

GREEN JOB CANNIBALISM: Spending billions of dollars to destroy two jobs for every one created while dramatically raising the costs of energy along the way, as witnessed in Europe for over a decade. Spain's massive solar and wind projects promised thousands of so-called green jobs yet only killed productive industries, resulting in the unemployment rate rocketing from eight percent in 2007 to 26 percent in 2013 forcing a moratorium on solar farms and drastic cuts in subsidies.

GREEN LIFE IN THE STONE AGE: Thousands of years ago cavemen drank pure water, got plenty of exercise, breathed pollution free air, and ate a free range organic diet. They were dead by 35.

GREEN POWER: Three centuries ago, the world ran on green power. Wood was used for heating and cooking; charcoal for smelting and smithing; wind or water power for pumps, mills, and ships; and whale oil for lamps. People and soldiers walked or rode horses, and millions of horses and oxen pulled ploughs, wagons, coaches, and artillery.

GREEN REVOLUTION: Norman Borlaug's plant breeding in the 1940s turned out a profusion of new plant varieties that start earlier, grow faster, resist pests, tolerate drought stress, and preserve more of the harvest. The key to food abundance has been science. Plant breeding, chemical fertilizers, sophisticated pest control, artificial insemination for animals, and a whole host of high-yield food production technologies have been developed since then.

HEAT & COLD CLIMATE MORTALITY: A 2015 worldwide study by Antonio Gasparrini determined that for each global death caused by heat, 17 people died from cold.

HIGH-YIELD FARMING: If crop yields had remained at levels typical of the 1950s, farmers would have had to plow down an additional 10 million square miles of wildlife habitat to raise enough food for the current world food supply. High-yield farming is responsible for preserving a great deal of the world's biodiversity, while traditional low-yield is responsible for the highest rates of soil erosion. – **Dennis Avery**, 1995

HORMESIS: The science of "everything in moderation", hormesis is **a** biological phenomenon whereby a beneficial effect such as improved health results from exposure to low doses of an agent that is otherwise toxic or lethal when given at higher doses. Low cancer rates in regions of high background radiation is a prime example of hormetic effect.

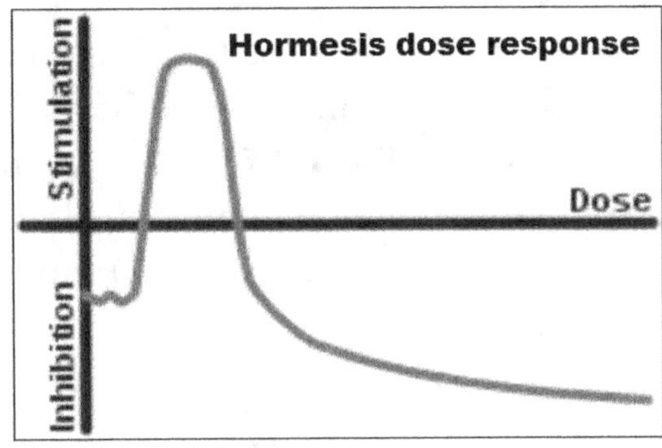

This may account for the exceptionally low cancer rates in McKinley County NM and Navajo Nation.

HORSE MANURE: The greatest environmental health hazard throughout the 19th century. Airborne pulverized manure and flies, far worse pollutants than automobile exhaust, carried several deadly pathogens along with the stench. Dead horse disposal also created tremendous environmental concerns. Coal burning electrical generating plants proved to be a far cleaner alternative.

HURRICANE PAUSE: Hurricane activity is Al Gore's signature indicator for extreme climate. The NOAA and National Hurricane Center report the US was at an all-time record (records back to 1851) for no major hurricanes (category three or above) for an eleven year span ending in 2016. The previous longest pause was eight years between 1860-1869.

ICE CALVING: Icebergs are created by the breaking (calving) of large chunks of ice from the edge of a glacier. Contrary to alarmists who would attribute this effect to global warming, it is actually the opposite - a cause of glacier expansion. Receding glaciers simply melt.

INTERNAL COMBUSTION ENGINE: One of the most important contributors to environmental quality and health in both city and farm, eliminating most horse manure, reducing farming acreage and eliminating vast amounts of methane from animal flatulence – a gas with far more greenhouse potency than carbon dioxide.

INTERGOVERNMENTAL PANEL ON CLIMATE CHANGE: Men in tin foil hats whom I refer to as the Inter-Planetary Climate Control. The IPCC is a "scientific" body under the auspices of the United Nations established in 1988 to promote the theory of man-made global warming by way of $billions of bureaucratic funding, enabling big government statists to expand power and control over mankind.

IVANPAH SOLAR FACILITY: The poster child and monument to failed "clean-energy" policies. The $2.2 billion solar farm lemon in the California Mojave Desert opened in 2014 and has been a disaster in every way imaginable.

KILOWATT HOUR kWh: The method for measuring energy subsidies is dollars per kWh, or megawatt hour, of power produced. US solar/wind subsidies are more than 100 times higher than fossil fuels and even higher in Europe.

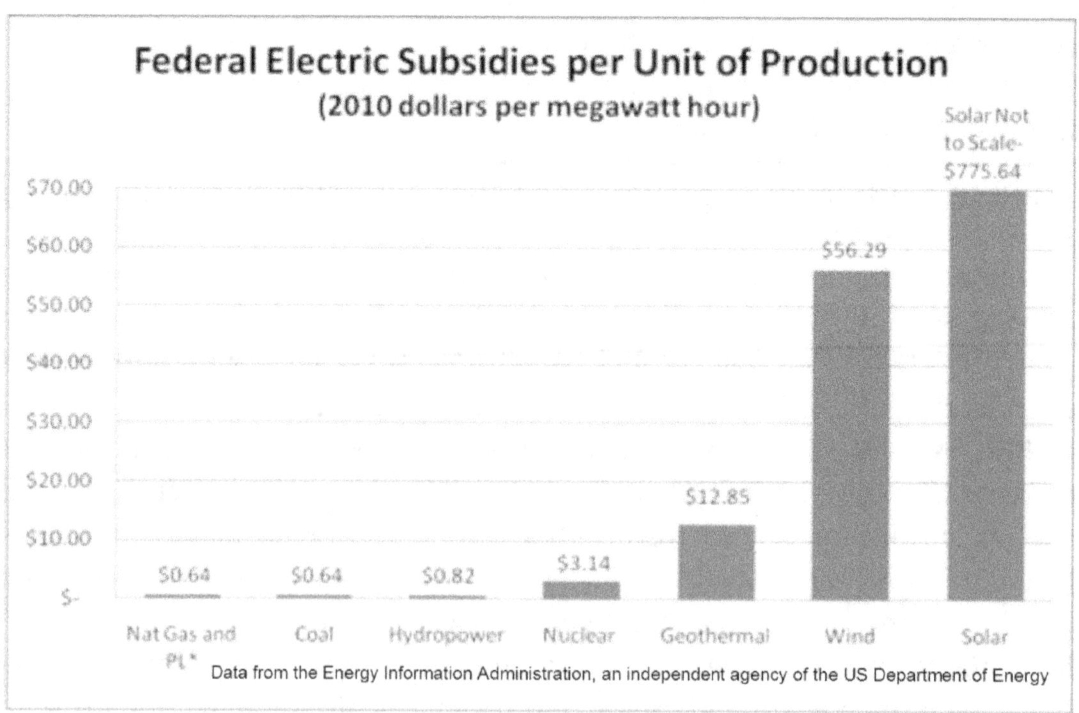

LAND STEWARDSHIP: Natural cycles of wildfires are one thing however mismanagement of federally owned forests and rangelands has created environmental devastation and economic hardships. Property rights make the environment an asset rather than a liability by giving owners an incentive for stewardship.

LGBT STUDIES: Analysis of data from over 200 studies regarding gender identity and sexual orientation by Drs. Mayer and McHugh established, among many other things, that the idea that people are "born that way" is not substantiated by scientific evidence, that sexual orientation in adolescents is fluid, and that non-heterosexuals are at a highly elevated risk for adverse health and mental health outcomes, even in locales with a comparatively tolerant climate to homosexuality, such as Sweden.

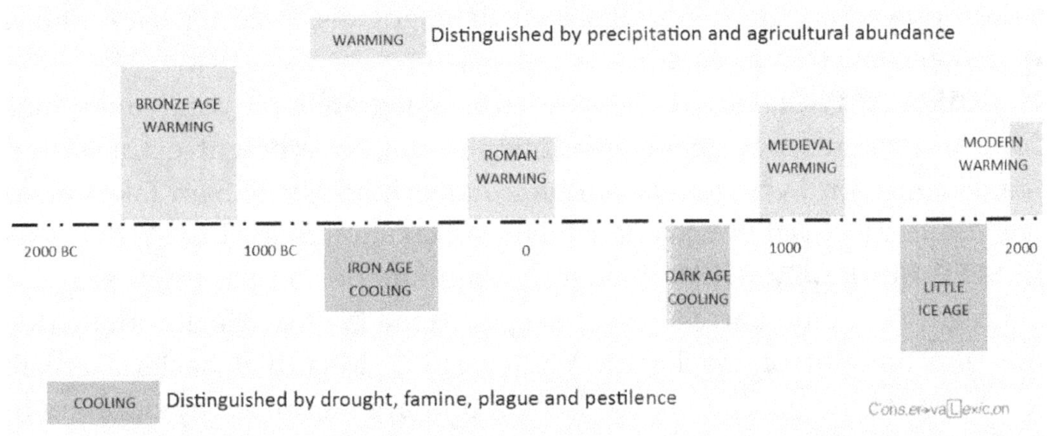

LITTLE ICE AGE: A 300 years global cooling anomaly circa 1500-1700 marked by agricultural and fishing decline, famine, plague and pestilence. It had the highest sea ice cover of the last 10,000 years, and flirted with excursions into year-round sea ice. Its mere existence is the most damning evidence disputing man-made climate change.

LIQUIFIED NATURAL GAS LNG: The fastest growing major energy market is LNG. It takes up 1/600th the volume of gaseous natural gas, and is odorless, colorless, non-toxic, and non-corrosive. The US did not begin LNG exports until February, 2016. With the fracking revolution, and coal-based countries turning to cleaner natural gas expect LNG to be the energy of the future.

MEDIEVAL & ROMAN WARM PERIODS: Numerous scientific studies reveal several centuries with global temperatures higher than our current "above average" temps. Warm periods are marked by agricultural booms and elevated biomass.

NATURAL GAS: An abundant affordable fossil fuel allowing the US to reduce its carbon dioxide emissions as well as electricity and heating bills. Considering the extensive hidden footprint of wind and solar energy, natural gas and nuclear are indeed the cleanest energy sources. Natural gas is ideal for fuel impoverished regions such as McKinley County NM yet it is vilified by privileged green activists thru media propaganda campaigns.

NUCLEAR ENERGY: The goal in 1953 was to provide abundant electrical energy to the power-starved areas of the world. Since then nuclear power has proven to be the safest of all energy sources, atmospherically clean and backed up with ever improving technology. Sadly, scaremongering put nuclear power at the mercy of green demagogues, holding back nuclear expansion some thirty years.

OIL COMPANY PROFITS: At the gas tank, integrated oil companies make about seven cents per gallon. Meanwhile, the government extracts more than 48 cents, on average, per gallon. That's right, Uncle Sam takes nearly seven times more out of drivers' wallets via taxation than "Big Oil."

OIL SEEP BIODEGRADATION: Staggering amounts of oil naturally seep into the ocean. A million barrels a year seep into the Gulf of Mexico alone (four times the amount of the Exxon Valdez spill). Microbial bacteria are the foundation of the marine life food chain and are nature's way of removing oil, whether natural or spilled.

ORGANIC FERTILIZER: *Warning*! Graphic content. "Organic fertilizers are fertilizers derived from animal matter, human excreta, or vegetable matter (e.g. compost, manure). Naturally occurring organic fertilizers include animal waste from meat processing, peat, manure, slurry and guano. In contrast, the majority of fertilizers used in commercial farming are extracted from minerals (e.g. phosphate rock) or produced industrially (e.g. ammonia)." – **Wikipedia**

PETROLEUM AGE: In 1901 a Texas oil well erupted which triggered a transformation of the US from a rural, agrarian country into an urban, industrialized nation. Petroleum continues to be the lifeblood of our technological civilization, and those technological advances have made it possible to access almost unlimited more oil resources. The environmental impacts of accessing and processing petroleum are virtually negligible in comparison to the benefits provided.

POLAR VORTEX: A large pocket of very cold air which sits over the polar region during the winter season. It was "proof" of global cooling and impending ice age in the 1970s.

POST ABORTION STRESS SYNDROME: PASS is psychological stress which effects about half of women with early abortions and two of three with late abortions according to the American Psychological Association's criteria for Post-Traumatic Stress Disorder (PTSD) symptoms. Mood disorders are common, but substance abuse proves to be the strongest link when it comes to post-abortion problems for women – three to four times more likely.

POTABLE WATER: Scarcity of clean water was once one of our greatest environmental health hazards. Water is abundant, however water that is safe to drink is a scarce and precious resource in the Third World. It was the age of fossil fuels that allowed access to potable water in the technologically advanced world.

PSEUDOSCIENCE: Junk science. Faulty or fraudulent scientific data and analysis used to advance special interests and hidden agendas. This includes beliefs, theories, or practices that have been or are considered scientific, but have no basis in scientific fact. This could mean they were disproved scientifically, can't be tested or lack evidence to support them.

PV BRUSH-OFF BLUES: Salesmen may whisper sweet promises in your ear however reliability, installation and safety issues abound with PV solar panels often putting forth less than half what promised (50 years rather than 25 to cover costs) and lifespans of only 15 to 20 years triggering performance anxiety. By that time, the fly-by-night operation is long gone with not even a Dear John letter. Solar regret is a terrible thing….. Pssst, I got a can't miss deal on some cheap PV cells – made in China.

RARE EARTH ELEMENTS: "Technology metals". They are the elements that have become irreplaceable to our world of technology, owing to their unique magnetic, phosphorescent, and catalytic properties. They make up a set of seventeen chemical elements in the periodic table, and are necessary for production of batteries, wind turbines and solar panels, along with other toxic elements such as cadmium, lithium, cobalt, lead, nickel, and sulfuric acid. The mining, processing, manufacturing, and disposal is extremely harmful to the environment, particularly in China, the dominant producer, where precautions are bypassed in favor of cost savings. As climate mortality continues to decline, mortality associated with technology metals, electric vehicle batteries, and renewable energy is on a rapid increase.

RENEWABLE ENERGY: A meaningless term with no established standards. Wind and solar don't deliver concentrated energy (the "diluteness problem") and require massive amounts of energy and non-renewable materials (many of them rare and toxic) to produce a unit of energy. The erratic intermittency of the wind and sun allows them to only be used as a costly backup to fossil fuels since there are no batteries large enough to store the energy.

RENEWABLE ENERGY COSTS, EUROPE: Since the European Union wind and solar energy revolution took off in 2005 with their carbon market scheme, residential electricity rates increased by an average of 63 percent by 2014. In the same time period the US experienced a 17 percent increase. The EU countries intervening the most in their energy markets – Germany, Spain and the UK – have seen their electricity costs increase the fastest.

RENEWABLE ENERGY COSTS, US: Despite the downward pressure on electricity prices by natural gas availability, the recent forced use of wind and solar energy by new EPA government regulations has led to the largest US electricity price increase in six years in 2014. This is in step with President Obama's green energy goal he set in 2008 that "electricity rates would necessarily skyrocket".

RENEWABLE ENERGY FOOTPRINT: The economic devastation, fuel poverty, indoor air pollution, cancer villages, habitat destruction, millions of annual wildlife deaths, rural and coastal blight all associated with solar and wind energy. The brunt of this massive footprint is borne by the world poor, weak and less fortunate.

RENEWABLE MANDATES COST: Many states such as California and Oregon are experiencing the harsh reality of soaring electricity rates due to the implementation of RPS mandates requiring certain percentages of energy produced by renewable sources. Electricity rates are 38 percent higher in the 29 states with mandates. The obvious consequence is a departure of industries with resultant loss of jobs and economy. Regions without mandates benefit which is why New Mexico had a bill to revise our RPS. Ohio, West Virginia, Texas, Colorado, North Carolina and Kansas have taken recent action to curtail or eliminate their wind and solar mandates. Even Arizona has considered repealing their RPS mandates.

RENEWABLE PORTFOLIO STANDARDS RPS: PC for "energy taxes". RPS is a government boondoggle benefiting corporate cronies at the expense of the fuel impoverished. RPS requires increased production from renewable energy sources which distort the energy market and ultimately make electricity more expensive and less reliable for energy producers and consumers. RPS taxes create or prop-up a false market for renewable energy companies that cannot compete on their own. Like almost all green projects RPS is a regressive tax impacting the poor.

SCIENCE, BUREAUCRATIC: When government controls scientific method, bad things happen. It is the role of scientists to challenge any hypothesis. They do this by using the scientific method of disproving the hypothesis (falsifiability). Scientists must be skeptics otherwise they are not practicing science. When bureaucratic scientists only work to prove a hypothesis, they are not practicing science, they are advancing a political agenda. The modern bureaucratic process of science is now not even trying to search for the truth, it's instead hunting for an impact factor, for attention, for headlines, and inevitably, for funding.

SCIENCE, EMPIRICAL: Scientific method requires that the scientist test a theory based on observed or predicted facts. Skepticism rather than faith is required. A simple definition of science is the ability to predict. If your prediction is wrong your science is wrong. How good is the climate "science" produced by bureaucratic computer models? The answer is, a complete failure. When computer model predictions fail, the theory fails.

SCIENTIFIC BIAS: It is unavoidable that scientists' culture, world view and even religion, impact the way they interpret data. The belief that all human influence on the environment is bad, is not scientific, but religious, and is held by most researchers in the Earth sciences.

SCIENTIFIC FASCISM: Coined in response to climate science scandals revealing data manipulation and scientific fraud by scientists concerning global warming theory. It is a

SCIENTIFIC CONSENSUS: The notion that scientists can't be bought or intimidated.

coordinated effort by a group of scientists to enforce a certain point of view upon others; to prevent the acceptance of points of view contrary to those beliefs; to prevent the publication of papers by other scientists with whom they disagree; to delay or stymie the release of data to other scientists who could check their work in accordance with the steps of the scientific method.

SCIENTIFIC METHOD: 1. Make an Observation – "What is happening?" 2. Define the Question – "Why is this happening?" 3. Form a Hypothesis – "I think this happens because. . ." 4. Perform Experiments – "Let's test my hypothesis. . ." 5. Analyze the Data – "Was my hypothesis right?" 6. Conclusion – "Experiments show my hypothesis was. . ." 7. Peer Review – "I will validate my method and results among my research community".

SEA LEVEL STUDIES: Disputing claims that climate change is causing increased sea level rise, several studies over the past decade have revealed that sea level rise and fall is cyclical and with no acceleration over the past 6,000 years in response to increased temperature or CO2 levels. A new study in 2016 by the Dutch Deltares Research Institute shows the Earth is actually gaining more land than it is losing.

SEX DIFFERENCE STUDIES: The brains of men and women are wired differently. "Males have better motor and spatial abilities, whereas females have superior memory and social cognition skills." – **University of Pennsylvania**. Add on the prodigious hormonal and anatomical differences and, unlike minute racial differences, sex differences cover a broad spectrum of the somatic, emotional and intellectual.

SMOG: Smog is air polluted with particulates and noxious gases – but there are no particulates or noxious components in carbon dioxide. Therefore, CO2 plays no part in creating smog.

SOLAR FARM POLLUTION: The behemoth Ivanpah Solar Power Facility in the Mojave Desert opened in 2014. The amount of natural gas required to operate the solar farm would have produced enough electricity to meet the annual needs of 17,000 California homes. So now for all those $billions spent on crony corporate interests, for all that destroyed pristine desert-scape, dead birds, displaced tortoises and more – the darn thing emits more CO2 than an ordinary power plant would've anyway, twice as much as the threshold required to pay carbon taxes. And not only that, it costs four times as much per kilowatt hour produced than a natural gas power plant. Ivanpah makes Solyndra look like petty larceny.

SOLAR FORCING aka solar irradiance: This may sound far-fetched to some, however there is a large body of evidence suggesting that changes in Earth's surface temperature are primarily driven by variations in solar activity. Examples include the Medieval Warm Period, Little Ice Age and early Twentieth Century (1910-1940) Warm Period… The Sun affecting our climate? Naah!

SOLAR and FRACKING WATER USAGE: You may have heard of California's annual 70 million gallons of water usage for fracking however you likely haven't heard of the typical annual water usage of just one solar farm, 500 to 700 million gallons.

SOLAR IMPOTENCE: Despite over twenty massive solar farms constructed over the past decade the total US energy production for solar is less than one half of one percent. They are quite impressive as an elitist community status symbol though.

SOLAR POWER INCENTIVES: Solar tax credits and subsidies are regressive, placing a greater burden on the poor and misinformed while reducing the tax burden of the rich.

SUSTAINABILITY: The basic idea is "indefinitely repeatable" however sustainability has become a euphemism for a fundamentalist faith marking out a new and larger ideological territory in which limiting economic, political, and intellectual liberty is the price that must be paid now to ensure the welfare of future generations. The cavemen certainly had tremendous difficulties obtaining sustainable resources however nowadays to say we've only scratched the surface is to greatly understate how little of this planet's potential we've unlocked. Scientific research has proven that we have enough of a combination of fossil fuels and nuclear power to last thousands of years. The amount of raw matter and energy on this planet is so vast that it is silly to speculate about running out of it.

UNSUSTAINABLE: Liberalism, Progressivism, Medicare, Obamacare, Social Security, the federal debt and renewable "sustainable" energy. That's right, wind and solar energy are so heavily subsidized they cannot survive subsidy cuts as European countries have learned the hard way as they are forced to scrap wind and solar projects in favor of fossil fuels. So when you hear "sustainable" tossed around, you can bet it's most likely referring to something "unsustainable".

URANIUM WORKER STUDIES: The Navajo Nation banned uranium mining on its land in 2005 despite modern methods of mining which are the safest in the world. Studies by world-renowned expert Dr. John Boice of the International Epidemiology Institute examined public health records for thousands of uranium workers from 1955 to 1990 and populations living near uranium mines in Texas, Colorado and New Mexico. Only underground miners showed increased rates of cancer. There were no differences in cancer rates between uranium mill workers exposed to uranium dust and mill products, and populations living in non-mining areas. Only miners exposed during the 40s and 50s had high rates with a large decline in the 60s leading to a low incidence in the 70s and beyond as mining conditions improved.

In modern uranium mining the average annual radon exposure of uranium miners has fallen to levels which are similar to concentrations inhaled in many homes.

WAR ON CANCER: Like the War on Drugs, a colossal failure. We're no closer to finding a cure today than we were back in 1971. If an investor was getting such a lousy return on their investment, they would have pulled the plug long ago. The dirty little secret is people don't die of cancer – they die of complications caused by radiation, chemotherapy or surgery. Three of five doctors would refuse chemotherapy. The obvious conclusion is that we should be investing time and money into preventing cancer, not into trying to find a cure. – **Stephen Skyvington**

WIND FARMS: …"they kill birds and bats, hurt the environment, cause sleeplessness and sickness in humans, drive up fuel prices, enrich rent-seeking crony capitalist scumbags, blight views, cause people to die in fuel poverty, harm property values, destabilize the grid, and inflate the cost of living – all while signally failing at the one thing they're supposed to be good at, via supplying us with the clean, abundant, eco-friendly energy which is going to save us all from 'global warming'."- **James Delingpole**

WOOD BURNING STOVES: The greatest cause of both outdoor and indoor air pollution. When energy costs rise due to absence of fossil fuel energy, renewable wood sources are utilized for heating and cooking.

ConservaLexicon

APPENDIX

Ten Commandments

1. You shall have no other gods before Me.
2. You shall not make idols.
3. You shall not take the name of the LORD your God in vain.
4. Remember the Sabbath day, to keep it holy.
5. Honor your father and your mother.
6. You shall not murder.
7. You shall not commit adultery.
8. You shall not steal.
9. You shall not bear false witness against your neighbor.
10. You shall not covet.

Bill of Rights

1. Freedom of Religion, Speech, and the Press
2. The Right to Bear Arms
3. The Housing of Soldiers
4. Protection from Unreasonable Searches and Seizures
5. Protection of Rights to Life, Liberty, and Property
6. Rights of Accused Persons in Criminal Cases
7. Rights in Civil Cases
8. Excessive Bails, Fines, and Punishments Forbidden
9. Other Rights Kept by the People
10. Undelegated Powers Kept by the States and the People

Republican Party Principles

1. Constitutionally Limited Government – to avoid restrictions on liberty
2. Localized Government – including the Federalist system of states rights
3. Fiscal Responsibility – limited debt, taxation and spending
4. Free Market Capitalism – economic freedom
5. Individual Freedom with Personal Responsibility
6. Aggressive National Defense – with foreign intervention
7. God and Country – moral responsibility to respect others rights to life and pursuit of happiness while resisting global legislation which threatens the integrity of our borders or Constitution

Eight Levels of Control That Must Be Obtained Before Creating a Social State – a corollary of the *Communist Rules for Revolution*

1. Healthcare – Control healthcare and you control the people.
2. Poverty – Increase the poverty level as high as possible; poor people are easier to control and will not fight back if you are providing everything for them to live.
3. Debt – Increase the debt to an unsustainable level. That way you are able to increase taxes, and this will produce more poverty.
4. Gun control – Remove the people's ability to defend themselves from the government. That way you are able to create a police state.
5. Welfare – Take control of every aspect of their lives (food, housing and income).
6. Education – Take control of what people read and listen to; take control of what children learn in school.

7. Religion – Remove the belief in God from the government and schools.
8. Class warfare – Divide the people into the wealthy and the poor. This will cause more discontent and it will be easier to take from (tax) the wealthy with the support of the poor.

MANIPULATIVE SCHEMES OF THE PROGRESSIVE STATE PLANTATION

1. Redistribution of wealth (duress, intimidation, coercion)
2. Collectivist priority of the group over the individual (slaves to the state)
3. Central economic planning (health care, education, energy etc.)
4. A classless society with income equality (class envy, racial division, gender warfare)
5. Confiscation of property (EPA, IRS, BLM)
6. Hyper-regulation of industry (crony corporatism in place of free market capitalism)
7. Politically correct multiculturalism (Cultural Marxism)

DEMOCRAT PARTY POLITICALLY INCORRECT PRINCIPLES

1. Establishment of a classless society thru expansive central government control of the economy by rule of "experts"
2. Contempt for individualism with the conformity of collective action and collective thought required for the sake of the common good
3. A "living" and evolving Constitution
4. Morality defined as "whatever advances the cause". The ends justify the means
5. Political populism tactics of Saul Alinsky

John T Flynn's Eight Marks of Fascist Policy

1. The government is totalitarian because it acknowledges to restraint on its powers.
2. Government is a de facto dictatorship based on the leadership principle.
3. Government administers a capitalist system with an immense bureaucracy.
4. Producers are organized into cartels in the way of syndicalism.
5. Economic planning is based on the principle of autarchy.
6. Government sustains economic life thru spending and borrowing.
7. Militarism is a mainstay of government spending.
8. Military spending has imperialist aims.

Alinsky's Rules for Radicals

1. Power is not only what you have, but what the enemy thinks you have.
2. Never go outside the expertise of your people.
3. Whenever possible, go outside the expertise of the enemy.
4. Make the enemy live up to its own book of rules.
5. Ridicule is man's most potent weapon.
6. A good tactic is one your people enjoy.
7. A tactic that drags on too long becomes a drag.
8. Keep the pressure on. Never let up.
9. The threat is usually more terrifying than the thing itself.
10. If you push a negative hard enough, it will push through and become a positive.
11. The price of a successful attack is a constructive alternative.
12. Pick the target, freeze it, personalize it, and polarize it.

LIBERTARIAN PARTY CORE PRINCIPLES

1. Maximum Freedoms
2. Minimum Government
3. Fiscal and Personal Responsibility
4. Free Market Capitalism
5. Less Regulation, More Innovation
6. Protection of Property Rights
7. Securing Liberty Defensively
8. Non-aggression
9. Free Expression
10. Live and Let Live

ELEVEN REAGAN PRINCIPLES

1. Freedom
2. Faith
3. Family
4. Sanctity and Dignity of Human Life
5. American Exceptionalism
6. The Founders' Wisdom and Vision
7. Lower Taxes
8. Limited Government
9. Peace Through Strength
10. Anti-Communism
11. Belief in the Individual

ELIZABETH WARREN'S ELEVEN COMMANDMENTS OF PROGRESSIVE STATISM (POPULIST FASCISM)

1. We believe that Wall Street needs stronger rules and tougher enforcement, and we're willing to fight for it.
2. We believe in science, and that means that we have a responsibility to protect this Earth.

3. We believe that the internet shouldn't be rigged to benefit big corporations, and that means real net neutrality.
4. We believe that no one should work full-time and still live in poverty, and that means raising the minimum wage.
5. We believe that fast-food workers deserve a livable wage, and that means that when they take to the picket line, we are proud to fight along side them.
6. We believe that students are entitled to get an education without being crushed by debt.
7. We believe that after a lifetime of work, people are entitled to retire with dignity, and that means protecting Social Security, Medicare and pensions.
8. We believe – I can't believe I have so say this in 2014 – we believe in equal pay for equal work.
9. We believe that equal means equal, and that's true in marriage, it's true in the workplace, it's true in all of America.
10. We believe that immigration has made this country strong and vibrant, and that means reform.
11. And we believe that corporations are not people, that women have a right to their bodies. We will overturn *Hobby Lobby* and we will fight for it.

JOHN HAWKINS' 7 REASONS I'M A CONSERVATIVE, NOT A LIBERAL
1. I'm a pragmatist.
2. I believe every human being has great potential.
3. I lack faith in government.
4. I'm a Christian.
5. I'm a student of human nature.
6. I'm a student of history.
7. I believe in the collective wisdom of the people who came before me.

KATE BACHELDER'S TOP TEN LIBERAL SUPERSTITIONS OF 2014
1. Spending more money improves education.
2. Government spending stimulates the economy.
3. Republican candidates always having a big spending advantage over Democrats.
4. Raising the minimum wage helps the poor.
5. Global warming is causing increasingly violent weather.
6. Genetically modified food is dangerous.
7. Voter ID laws suppress voter turnout.
8. Obamacare is gaining popularity.
9. The Keystone XL pipeline would increase oil spills.
10. Women are paid 77 cents on the dollar compared with men (the mother of all superstitions).

SCHALLER'S POLITICALLY INCORRECT CONSERVAPOSTULATES
1. Government is the root of all corruption.
2. Productivity is a primary contributor to mental health.
3. Fatherless children are the greatest threat to societal health.
4. Intentions have little value; consequences are what matter.
5. Liberalism is a neurotic escape from reality to satisfy a need for control.
6. Green and clean means inefficient, expensive and toxic.
7. The private sector does it twice as good at half the cost and half the time.
8. Orientation is not the problem; promiscuity is the problem.
9. Marriage is not about freedom, right to love or equality; it's about the security of a child's birthright to their biological mother and father.
10. Slavery is dependency – not just physical bondage. The consequence of progressivism is dependency.

ACKNOWLEDGMENTS

I am appreciative of several authors who have inspired me over the past 20 years, particularly Thomas Sowell. Others include Al Capp, Ayn Rand, Steve Milloy, John Stossel, Bernard Goldberg, Jonah Goldberg, Pat Buchanan and Mona Charen.

My father Clem, brother Jeff, Ross Perot and Rush Limbaugh were catalysts for my transformation from Sierra Club Marxist to Tea Party Libertarian.

I am ever grateful for my wife Louise and family.

ABOUT THE AUTHOR

Joe Schaller lives in Gallup, New Mexico with his wife Louise and is a freelance writer. He grew up in Pullman, Washington, home of Washington State University. As a hippie counterculture drop-out he returned to college in 1973 and graduated from Eastern Washington State College in 1977, prior to the age of politically correct indoctrination, with a Bachelor of Science in Nursing. He became a commissioned officer with the Public Health Service stationed at the Gallup Indian Medical Center beginning eight years of health care professions including orthopedics, psychiatric, home health care, materials management and air ambulance. Joe married in 1985 and obtained a private sector job as a turquoise dealer with a local jewelers supply lasting 26 years. Schaller was an active backpacker and Sierra Club socialist in the 1980s before rejecting liberalism in the 1990s. He has closely followed the environmental movement since the 1970s. As a hobby, he became an expert in basketball quantitative analytics with his NBA Total Performance Ratings, doing a sixteen year stretch with Rivals.com. Joe has utilized his array of lifetime experiences and dogged research to write as a citizen watchdog and conservative columnist for several Gallup newspaper publications.

THE DAWN
OF MAN

APES INSPECT THE MONOLITH AND ACQUIRE THE SPARK OF INTELLIGENCE FOR SURVIVAL

2017

IT'S BACK. AS PROGRESSIVES EXAMINE THE MONOLITH, A VEIL IS LIFTED FROM THEIR EYES, AND A WHOLE NEW WONDROUS WORLD IS REVEALED AS THEY ATTAIN TRUE ENLIGHTENMENT.

THE LIBERAL BUBBLE HAS BEEN BURST.

INDEX

www.ingramcontent.com/pod-product-compliance
Lightning Source LLC
Chambersburg PA
CBHW081227250726
48654CB00012B/1249